BY THE WATERS OF BABYLON

BY THE WATERS OF BABYLON

MORI ARIMASA

TRANSLATED BY J. THOMAS RIMER
WITH AN ESSAY BY MICHIKO YUSA

CORNELL EAST ASIA SERIES
an imprint of

CORNELL UNIVERSITY PRESS
Ithaca and London

This book was originally published in Japanese by Chikuma Shobō Inc. of Tokyo Japan with editorial offices at 2-5-3 Kuramae Taitō-ku, Tokyo Japan

Number 224 in the Cornell East Asia Series

First published 2025 by Cornell University Press
Printed in the United States of America

Library of Congress Cataloging-in-Publication Data

Names: Mori, Arimasa, 1911–1976, author. | Rimer, J. Thomas, translator. | Yusa, Michiko, writer of supplementary textual content.
Title: By the waters of Babylon / Mori Arimasa ; translated by J. Thomas Rimer ; with an essay by Michiko Yusa.
Other titles: Babiron no nagare no hotori ni te. English
Description: Ithaca : Cornell East Asia Series, an imprint of Cornell University Press, 2025. | Series: Cornell East Asia series ; 224 | Originally published in Japanese under title: Babiron no nagare no hotori ni te. | Includes bibliographical references.
Identifiers: LCCN 2024023470 (print) | LCCN 2024023471 (ebook) | ISBN 9781501780073 (hardcover) | ISBN 9781501780080 (paperback) | ISBN 9781501780097 (pdf) | ISBN 9781501780103 (epub)
Subjects: LCSH: Mori, Arimasa, 1911–1976—Travel—France. | Japanese—France—Biography. | France—Description and travel. | France—Intellectual life. | Europe—Civilization.
Classification: LCC DC29 M6713 2025 (print) | LCC DC29 (ebook) | DDC 944.08/004956092 [B]—dc23/eng/20241024
LC record available at https://lccn.loc.gov/2024023470
LC ebook record available at https://lccn.loc.gov/2024023471

This translation is dedicated to the memory of my late father-in-law, Paul Mus, who walked down many of the same streets as Mori Arimasa on his way to his own office at the Collège de France.

Contents

PREFACE

In the cultural and intellectual history of modern Japan, Mori Arimasa (1911–76) remains a significant presence, as a scholar, writer, translator, and philosopher. And perhaps even more, for the general Japanese reading public, he is still admired as the example of a special kind of hero. Mori was the rare Japanese intellectual with the courage to leave the security of the familiar mental constructs of his own society in order to seek out the contours of the deeper realities of a foreign culture.

Many Japanese people, of course, travel abroad, but as a young man, Mori became convinced that to truly know another culture must require the kind of immersion only made possible by living and working in that culture. He therefore made a highly unusual decision: He gave up his prestigious teaching post in Japan to order to go and live in Paris, where he remained for several decades. This challenge to himself, and his personal responses to his life in France, provide the subject matter for the first of his memoirs, *By the Waters of Babylon*, published in Tokyo in 1957 and long established as a classic account of how disparate cultures can entangle themselves in the thoughts and feelings of a single individual. This present translation is the first of his many writings to be made available in English.

Mori was the grandson of Mori Arinori (1847–89), the famous statesman active in the opening up of Japan during the Meiji period (1868–1911) and Japan's first minister of education. Mori began his studies of French culture and history in Tokyo during World War II at the University of Tokyo. His interests came to focus on European philosophy, and soon after the war, he was appointed at his university as a professor. His knowledge of France and Europe was already profound.

After Mori's arrival in Paris, his highly personal accounts of his experiences there made his writings serve as a major conduit through which his generation in Japan learned about European culture in general, and the civilization of France in particular. During these two decades,

Mori's published observations, which fall in a different category than do his more formal writings on philosophy, continued to find a wide audience.

Mori's personal response to French culture helped his many readers come to terms with what they perceived to be a crucial need to rejoin the larger world after the debacle of the war. This was the generation that found itself looking both backward, to see how and why Japan failed to understand the reality of the West before the war years, and forward, in order to attempt to ascertain what strategies Japan might now adopt in order to seek out more positive relations with the West in the future.

Mori's particular fascination with France was by no means unusual. Many Japanese intellectuals, writers, and artists, once first exposed to European culture in the latter part of the nineteenth century, found that France and French culture maintained the greatest appeal to them, more than of any other European country. By and large, this fascination still remains strong today, and Mori's writings in the early postwar period helped cement the ongoing nature of those enduring cultural and spiritual connections.

Nor, of course, is such a fascination with France confined to Japan. A long line of Russian, German, and British writers have long had similar responses, and Americans have their own enthusiasts as well, from Henry James and Edith Wharton to Gertrude Stein, Ernest Hemingway, and James Baldwin, among many others.

Mori did not always find his chosen path to be one of ease. He indicates quite clearly that he felt considerable trepidation about his commitment to his project at the beginning of his stay, and occasionally during later periods as well. Many passages in *Babylon* reveal a kind of gentle anguish, and indeed, there is often an implicit sense of personal exile behind his responses to much of what he sees and hears in Paris and elsewhere.

In following Mori on his intellectual and spiritual path, the careful reader eventually comes to a deeper understanding of the central issue that underlies so many of the author's individual observations: the crucial difference between an intellectual understanding of a foreign culture and the far more difficult effort needed to actually absorb the realities of that culture. For Mori, it is the experience itself that authenticates.

Mori is an immensely learned and enthusiastic guide to French and European high culture. His knowledge of and deep interest in the literature, history, philosophy, architecture, sculpture, and the other visual arts of France and Europe is extensive, and he is happy to share his intimate personal insights with his readers, who therefore find themselves pulled into his inner journey along with him.

Even though *Babylon* was written almost seventy years ago, the contemporary reader will find very little that seems dated or no longer relevant. This is surely because Mori unerringly seeks out the most profound layers of French and European cultures, in order to explicate to himself just how those differences define themselves when compared to the culture of Japan that he has now left behind. It may be not so surprising then that, for Mori, the deepest strata in the larger history of the French experience lie entwined with the Christian, and specifically Catholic experience, along with the psychology and the world view that develops from it. This is what separates France from Japan, and this is what remains endlessly fascinating to an outsider like Mori, for whom this reality must remain ever slightly out of reach. He shows a striking frankness in so openly acknowledging this gulf.

As I mentioned previously, for Mori's many original Japanese readers, *Babylon* provided a call to experience something of the realities and challenges of a greater world beyond their own experience, in that period just after the isolation of World War II. I believe that this appeal remains true for readers today, including those who read the book in English. For indeed, in every generation, any individual seeking to confront the nature of another culture must still continue to make the same journey toward understanding. Mori can still define that challenge and provide some wise and enlightened guidance as to how to proceed as well.

For readers wishing to know more about Mori and his contributions, there are two essays that follow the text itself. The first, by Professor Michiko Yusa, provides valuable insights into Mori as a philosopher and thinker, and the second, by myself, chronicles the social and literary background within which Mori thought and worked.

ACKNOWLEDGMENTS

I believe that it is important to remind readers that the English-language translation presented here can only represent my particular version of Mori Arimasa's elusive, erudite, and often poetic text. Another translator might well give a different nuance or emphasis to sentence after sentence in this often ambiguous and sometimes abstract flow of words. It is my hope that, if nothing else, this translation, whatever its shortcomings, can serve as an enthusiastic introduction to a fascinating and valuable Japanese writer and intellectual, one about whom we should certainly enjoy knowing more.

Mori's text is peppered with the names of European writers, artists, and thinkers, some well-known in the English-speaking world, some not. I have not burdened the text with footnotes, choosing rather to insert a word or two of identification for the more obscure figures directly into the translation itself. All the works of art discussed by Mori can quickly be found and viewed on the internet.

In particular I wish to acknowledge the crucial help I had in obtaining the rights to publish this translation. I had help from several colleagues, John Gillespie, Hiroaki Sato, and most of all, Hiroshi Kagawa, chief executive officer of IBC Publishing Company in Tokyo, for their stalwart efforts on my behalf, along with Miyagi Kana and the other helpful staff of Chikuma Shobō.

In preparing the manuscript, I want to give a special thanks to my editor Alexis Shimon for her unflagging support and encouragement, to India Miraglia, my acquisitions assistant, and to my copy editor, Brad Allard.

In preparing this translation I have had help and kindness from any number of colleagues and friends. Among them:

Professor Michiko Yusa, who as a colleague and friend, has provided so such sustained help and encouragement.

Professor Laurent Rauber, with whom I have enjoyed a stimulating long-distance email exchange about Mori. As I indicated in my essay, his dissertation and subsequent observations have provided me with much that has helped me in preparing this translation.

Toshiko Marra, who helped identify some rather obscure figures in French historical and artistic circles.

Manami Kawamura, who kindly explained to me the Japanese musical terms used by Mori when he describes the music of Bach.

Hiroaki Sato, who has permitted my use of his eloquent translation of a poem from the *Kojiki*.

Ms. Yurie Muramatsu, who helped me identify a number of names and terms.

Help of various kinds from Samuel Yamashita, Linda Ellison, and my son Mark Rimer.

This book was published with the help of a William F. Sibley Memorial Subvention Award for Japanese Translation from the University of Chicago Center for East Asian Studies Committee on Japanese Studies.

BY THE WATERS OF BABYLON

By the Waters of Babylon

Paris, October 8, 1953

When considering the totality of a human life, and the way in which it is conducted, is not its true nature already apparent, fully revealed, in one's childhood days? When I reflect on the present and look back on my youthful years, I am convinced that this must be so. From various circumstances, which I believe to be true, there can exist within us, and at the same time, both a sadness and a limitless sense of consolation. What do you yourself make of this? When we think of the European spirit, we always revert back to the Greek myths and those incidents in the Old Testament when temple priestesses or prophets could predict happiness or a path of tragedy for the future. You understand this point well, I know. In youth, everything seems already present in potential, later to be fully manifested. Is this not always a possibility? And why did this fact seem to bring a sense of comfort to those who first assembled the texts of those ancient chronicles? Fate can alter social positions, even the various dictates of society itself. And there exists as well those inevitable cares, concerns for family, affection, friendship, and all such vicissitudes that bring about our troubles, along with so many other reasons that surely can undermine our destinies. Such things, either in secret or openly, will soon enough be made manifest. Indeed, this must be so. And it is at just such moments that we realize that we human beings must acknowledge the fact that we must die. And it is at just such a time that we no longer fear our mortality.

So many young people have died in recent years because of the disasters that have befallen us [during the Pacific War]. I have read those letters you have collected into a book, and I found myself very moved by them, as you know, since I have also written about them. What impressed me so strongly in reading your little collection was the fact that the souls of those who were soon to die were permeated by the presence of Nature, a Nature stripped bare. The downpour of rain on a black creek; on an icy moonlit night, the cry of a flock of birds flying high in the sky; under the light of a scorching sun a single heron, standing on a muddy sandbar in an enormous river; a vast plain spreading out under a huge sky pregnant with storm. Such are the impressions from those letters that still remain so fresh for me. Here then is all that remains of the paths trodden by these young souls.

Nevertheless, their real selves cannot be found here. This understanding has allowed me to articulate one crucial circumstance of these lives: there is no joy here, and no sadness. And if there is no shouting, then there is no groaning. Rather, and simply beyond any form of verbal expression, these two qualities, *désolation* and *consolation,* separate as they may seem, now appear here as one single reality. So now, at this moment, I possess no feeling of mourning over the death of these young persons. I observe this reality, experience it; yet all I know is that, from here to the limitless beyond, however I examine my responses, and divided as they are in so many ways, I can grasp only that they simply flow and move along in quietude.

There should be nothing surprising in this fact. Indeed, this response is altogether reasonable. Simply said, there are so many events that can disturb the quietly overflowing, sparkling waves of our lives and so bring to the fore the fickleness of our human existence. Ah, if capriciousness was not such a fundamental part of human life. . . .

In all of this, there is one point that startles me concerning what I have just written. Do we human beings meld into the larger life of the universe, or does a human life merely return to emptiness? Such a concept for me is in fact very different from those teachings proposed by Buddhism, the mystic philosophers, and so forth. Rather, I refer to something more straightforward, simpler. As the German philosopher Leibnitz set forth in his theory of the monad, those boundless waves that spread ever outward and exist in the soul of every human being, those deep correspondences that lie within each individual entity, all serve to constitute the whole; perhaps it could be said that it is precisely this whole that constitutes the human soul.

But let me stop this argumentative chatter. After all, one human being is just a plain human being, nothing more, nothing less—that's the most essential thing.

Looking out from my window with its gauzy tulle curtains I see a corner of the sky, which, although blue until yesterday, is now filled with clouds tinged in gray, above the roof of the blackened stone apartment buildings across the stone pavements. In Paris, the fall is really the beginning of winter. At a slight distance I can sometimes hear an echo of the noise of the automobiles and trucks passing by on the Rue Gay-Lussac. In this small hotel, there is no sound. As I write, I sit in front of my desk, piled up with books and papers. I devote myself to this work, at least consciously, without any sense of the fallacy of my undertaking, yet knowing all the while that, within the limits of all our human frivolity, whatever we may do, whatever we may write, no matter what great work we may achieve, however splendid we may appear to be, everything that remains of us is no more than a fiction. A person who achieves such things remains no more than a spring in which the water has dried up; and from such a spot, no sparking waves of light arise, nor is there is any blending with other waves of light; there is no radiance which emerges. In the end, can one be sure of the ability to crush such frivolity within oneself? I do not know. I see proof to the contrary in every day that passes. Still, I must push my way forward.

As I reflect on things, I realize that I really began my travels some thirty years ago. My father died when I was thirteen, and he was buried in a graveyard in the western suburbs of Tokyo. It was a cloudy, cold day in February. On the gravestone was carved "Tomb of the M family," and the urn filled with ashes was to be placed inside a stone chamber. Then, as now, the trees had lost their lush foliage. A week later, I returned to the cemetery again, alone. Now, there was no sign of another human being, nor did I even hear the song of a bird. As I looked at the ground where the tomb lay, I realized that one day my own ashes would surely be placed there as well. Therefore, until that day came that I knew for certain that I was to return here, I knew I must begin walking, begin finding my way. And I have been moving forward for all those thirty years since. As I look back, I see that my study of French literature, and the fact that I have come to live and remain in a foreign country, indeed all this long distance I have traversed, all of this began at that gravesite.

And the fact that I myself am on the way to returning there—all these events are touched and blended in that same hue.

I began my travels with many burdens. And it is true that I do not know when this voyage may come to an end. But I do know that, since my youngest days, it is through a consciousness of my own personal fate manifested in me that I could sense within myself so many contradictions and to know as well that, until the day of my death, they will doubtless never be resolved.

Menton, October 9

On the night express from Paris to the south of France. Riding in my third- class carriage were some shady-looking characters: a man about fifty or so, with very rough clothing, along with three of his "lieutenants," in their twenties. With me, that made five altogether. Glancing at the "boss," he appeared to me rather like an Englishman, but his spoken French was altogether up to snuff. He chatted aimlessly with his companions.

If you are going to the Cote d'Azur in the south of France, then as far as buying a seat on the train is concerned, third class is perfectly satisfactory, and one suit of clothes will suffice very nicely for the trip. If you stay in Nice, the best choice is a cheap hotel near the Rue de France; you can go to somewhere like the salon of the Carleton, or the Carleton in Cannes, or the Miramar, or any other first-class hotel, to take tea or have a drink. So, for 120 francs you can hear good music and observe lots of people you pass by with whom you might chat; indeed, you can even pursue some conversation with attractive women, for all I know. They say that this is perfectly possible. You, who know the south of France so well, are certainly familiar with such an atmosphere. Since I have no interest in any conversations of that sort, I would offer only a perfunctory response before starting to read a book that I bought at a bookstore at Saint Germain, near the Musée de Cluny, a translation into French from an English-language text by Dr. D. T. Suzuki on Zen, *The Zen Doctrine of No Mind*. The translation was by Hubert Benôit and the book was published by Cercle du Livre, a bookstore on the Ave Raspaille.

Recently I've been going to visit Guy C at his apartment, and we've been talking late into the night. Guy talked quite a bit about this book, and because I'd been asked to contribute an essay for a magazine put out by a publisher in Iéna, I felt myself somehow encouraged to go ahead and buy a copy. When I began to look over the text, I ran across a passage rather similar to what I wrote to you on the 8th. So, I found myself pulled into the text and went on reading.

Suzuki writes that when one sees one's own true nature and genuinely comes to comprehend it, then, as all creation somehow dissolves into nothingness, this fundamental essence will manifest itself from within that nature, as though reflected in a burnished mirror.

As I wrote in my letter of the 8th, what I find significant is not this so-called enlightenment or satori. Rather, when a human being empties preconditions, or becomes "empty minded," and Nature becomes visible through one's transparent self, it is then that a certain feeling, in which "desolation" and "consolation" blend into one can emerge; and that feeling, that sensation becomes perceived precisely because it represents something, however ordinary, that is felt to be truly precious. And this sensation precedes any more grandiose conceptions found in philosophy or religion. It emerges in the midst of those attitudes found in our day-to-day experiences. This sensation is not something that might be viewed simply as merely some form of resignation, or despair. Nor is it the sense that any path taken in love or work will inevitably only arrive at a dead end. It is, rather, that this sensation represents the reality of the human condition that frames our existence. For even in the throes of a powerful love, even when one's life work is going splendidly, any authentic human being knows that those feelings I have described must inevitably follow along as well.

Why is it, do you think, that so many people from all over the world are drawn to Paris? In the Quartier Latin, which you enjoy so much, so many seem to walk happily together—Caucasians, Africans, Asians, Arabs, all seemingly satisfied to be there. And none of these people seems to be anxious to return to their own countries. Or, at least, it appears that they do not wish to. I have discussed such matters earnestly and at length with my handsome friend, who is a doctor from Iran, while listening to a record of Spanish music in his small apartment in the Quartier. He had been a doctor in a clinic at Val de Grace, but much as he wanted to remain in Paris, he found it was difficult for a foreigner to find appropriate work in the city, he told me, so he has decided to return home next year to work in a clinic in Azerbaijan near the Caspian Sea. The coffee he gave me was thick and delicious.

Surely this is why so many from so many countries are attracted to this city because, as I suggested earlier, that sense of sadness and of consolation can somehow surely crystallize here.

Under one corner of the gray sky visible between the roofs of the apartment houses I can see from my window, I can observe the colorful flowerbeds, red, yellow, and purple, in the Luxembourg gardens and the Parc Monceau, the old man selling newspapers, and the adorable-looking little girls, carrying their inflated rubber balloons. There is something charming about all this, yet there are more profound human feelings at work here as well. I tried to write something about this sensation I felt once before in my diary. Let me copy that passage here for you.

> June 20 . . . all the way from the Avenue of the Grande Armée, that ridiculously wide boulevard, and going through to the east, in the other direction to the Maillot Gate, the boundless white clouds of early summer spread themselves out in the sky, and at the plaza itself, the warm morning wind has been blowing. Above this suburban plaza, there is somehow an association in my mind with a desolate dry riverbed, where some reeds, beginning to wither, grow sparsely, as though on some vast, whitened plain, where the sun has already risen high in the sky, so that rays of light, following the breaks in the clouds, fill the body to over-flowing with a sense of "summer." The closely packed branches of the chestnut trees that overhang the walking paths in the Bois de Boulogne, their green leaves soft and bright, appear like seaweed in the flowing water, swaying in the gentle breeze. In this extravagant weather, some endlessly sad music flowed from a little hut where some gypsies lived, which made this moment seem somehow lonely. And there was not a person in sight.
>
> Yesterday evening, I visited with my friend in his cheap lodgings in the Rue Saint Séverin. We talked all night of various urgent matters, so that I became exhausted. My head felt heavy and numb until I found myself somewhat more awake from the coffee I drank. My body felt somehow vacant, empty, as I stepped across the wide asphalt pavement, following along the safety strip in the road as though I were pounding nails into it one by one. I seemed to move as though I were floating in midair. Only my new shoes seemed content as they moved forward on the hard pavement. A number of elegant cars sped along the as yet still sparsely populated street. So many ideas seem to be revolving around in my head, as if all by themselves. And one thought kept repeating itself: "I must order my ideas and actions based only on my own sense of reality. And I must make a promise not to go back on this decision." These words somehow seemed of great consequence to me.

On the wide sidewalk at the corner of the left side of the Boulevard Pereire stood a couple, both apparently middle-aged, in the midst of a conversation. The man, who was half bald, wore a gray suit, cut in good taste, and his necktie, with slanting blue stripes on a dark red background, was smartly tied on his white shirt. He was not concentrating his gaze on the woman. Rather, he was apparently thinking about something else; he seemed to have created a sense of amiableness merely on the surface. Yet the woman who pulled herself close to him seemed to hover on his every word. Her clothes were somehow out of style, and she looked too warm in her coat, with a design of spotted black quite out of season. Looking up at the sky, she seemed as if brooding over her words as she spoke. "As for Jean, he can't seem to make things." These words seemed to slip right past him. They did not appear to be lovers. The metal pillars of the lamps along the road, painted green, seemed to stand coldly beside the two of them. Off in the distance, at the corner of the Boulevard Pereire and the Boulevard de la Grande Armée, the figure of a waiter in white seemed to float into view on the level terrace. And in front, on the doors of the cars coming down the road from the Luxembourg, I could see reflected the sight of a new bus, the #28, which had stopped and began disgorging its passengers.

The apartment of P, on the Boulevard Pereire. He had already gone out. His wife told me that he was doubtless planning to meet me at five o'clock at the L Bookstore at the Rue de l'Université. "Damnation! Wherever I go, it's the same thing," I muttered to myself as I came down the staircase. It was still only 10:30 in the morning. I didn't feel at all like going back to my hotel for my breakfast, as it was so late. So now I had some six and a half hours to wait, meaningless hours piling up, and I felt the pain of it. "I must be able to do something useful with this time. . . ." I thought involuntarily to myself. Going outside, I found that the sun had already risen high in the sky. The pavement glistened from the oil it had absorbed, and I realized full well how bright it was, as the summer sunlight reflected downwards. Walking along the hard pavement, I remembered the café I had seen far across the plaza at the corner of the Grande Armée and Boulevard Pereire. I went inside and plunked myself down in a rattan chair. I couldn't manage to drink anything more than a glass of Perrier. I noticed three Algerians, in their blue uniforms, leaning on the iron railings around all three sides of the Métro station just in front of me, chattering away in a heavily accented French. Many such men find themselves coming to Paris, but how do they find a way to keep themselves alive? I absolutely can't imagine. And this is not just the case for these Algerians but for many among the population of France as well. Watching them, their leaning figures seemed at ease, yet somehow they gave off an air of sadness. Their bodies were sunken and thin, their skin, heavily wrinkled by the sun, their sharp eyes, which tended to be black. What were they looking at? I could not be sure. Those bodies would never return to the place where they came from; their flowers would never bloom, and no cry would come forth when they might wither and die. Each individual is born into a human life, grows up, and lives in the midst of desire, pleasure, and disillusionment. And eventually, one uses up one's own life, dwindles, and passes away. The reality of this great biological truth, common to all humanity, could be seen in the starkest fashion right here before my eyes. So, looking at these Algerians teaches me much. These men do not seem to support within themselves any system of ideas. It almost seems to me almost as though they may possess no souls. They themselves resemble the burning sun that rains down on them on the steep cliffs of Iberia and Africa, even Corsica, rising from the blue of the Mediterranean, where fragrant shrubs, juniper and myrtle, grow. These men adore dancing, women, and the rhythm of music. They love their food from the Middle East, shish kebab, rice pilaf, and strong rosé wine. They wear white shirts, without starch. Observing them, it seems as though some sort of pure nostalgia, a nostalgia of sensation, comes welling up out of them. This emotion is hidden within them and does not rise to the surface, yet they search out the extremities of a certain kind of fleeting, instinctual longing felt by those who find their destiny in love. Yet that love they feel, however strong that sensation may be, lasts only for a short time, intense and brief, and then it fades. Such is how their love appears. The silhouettes of these men, with the blinding white surface of the Place Maillol behind them, as they lean on the railing, appear quiet, still. They are men who seem only to respond to sensation, nervous strain, and their core reflexes. For them, love, joy, and grief alike are all products of their reflexes, functions related to no more than their love of dancing, women, music, food, and liquor. Risk for them does not involve any function of thought, only the movements of their instincts distilled from a consciousness of their own existence. In such a transparency, when such people love, their expectations must consist only of anticipation without self-consciousness. As for those men leaning on the railing, what do they wait for, what are they thinking about? When it comes to the matter of love, what they pursue, at the least, is the truth of the flesh, with nothing else lurking behind but the reality of their own desires. Someone or other said that love is the uniting together of two persons, but this thought surely only reflects the woman's point of view.

The morning breeze from the Porte Maillol seemed to blow through the very core of their existence. . . .

Yet my departure for my own voyage must now begin on my own terms.

These will set the trajectory I must follow.

I have become more than half-chilled sitting in this café. I suddenly remembered to drink my café-crème (although I had planned to drink a glass of Perrier, I apparently ordered the coffee instead). I felt a gentle breeze blowing from the woods I could see at my right. Something within me relaxed. My sense of malaise was gone, and I suddenly felt a sense of exhilaration. What might this be a sign of, I wonder? Did this sensation derive from something genuine? Or from a falsehood?

I've quoted myself at great length here because I wanted to illustrate one of those fruitless episodes that reflect my reactions and emotions based on my own experiences living here in Paris. And each takes on the tints of an emotional coloring, a quietude, which derives from a shift toward silence. There is no way to put this feeling into words. I am sure that you can understand. The blackened stone walls of this apartment, washed in the movements of time, the chestnut trees deep in the Luxembourg, the venerable sight of the silhouette of Notre Dame from the Place St. Michael—the appearance from time to time of such scenes around Paris, it must be said, parallels episodes in my own states of interior being.

The trains in France move swiftly. I have already passed Dijon. Then comes Lyon, Valence, Orange, and Avignon. As the sky brightens at dawn, the train going north from Marseille passes us on the right. Since it seems that we are beginning to follow our route to the Cote d'Azur, I can see, far off in the distance to the right, the church of Notre Dame de la Garde, the guardian of Marseille, standing high on the cliffs, as though floating upward into the sky, half-lost in the morning mists. The sight of this made me virtually weep. And then, the sea at Bandol. A deep blue, so deep, yet so yielding. Last summer, I descended all alone from the Nice-bound bus on the beach at Bandol. It was just at the shoreline. You know the spot. In my confusion, I had gotten the dates mixed up by a day or two, so that the letter I sent did not reach you, and we never met.

On this occasion, the beach was curiously quiet. Once in a while, a man in shorts or a girl in a bikini would come and go from a café. It was as though the whole beach was one where nudity had permitted all the men to be stained brown. The atmosphere remained strangely silent. After fifteen minutes or so, I boarded the bus again, and passing through village after village arrived in Nice. It was about that time when a certain incident in Marseille occurred as well.

About three years ago, at the end of September, I went into a bar in the old port section of Marseille. I was talking to a friend of mine there. I had just come to France from Japan, and I spoke about wanting to simply return home. I was frightened to go on to Paris, a task I found somehow too difficult to bear. I had a feeling that I would simply not be able to manage. The man I was talking with had studied art history for five years while in France. Listening to what I said, he replied that he took me quite seriously. Yet in fact, I didn't have the funds to go back to Japan, so, with a heavy heart, I traveled on here to Paris. Perhaps at that moment I really should not have done so. Nevertheless, here I finally was in Paris. And now that I had arrived, I knew that the fear I felt had by now penetrated into the very core of my being. But what was the nature of that emotion that I had felt in Marseille? Thinking back over the matter now, I realize that I had some sort of premonition that I was facing some insupportable obstacle. And indeed, I had a clear sense of this difficulty even before I left Japan. And when my ship, the *Marseille*, moved through the Suez Canal, leaving behind the Indian Ocean and coming into the Mediterranean, I had resigned myself to that fact. Three days later I landed in Marseille. Now I found myself in circumstances that I could no longer evade. When I try now to analyze my unease a bit, I realize that I felt in Paris that I had encountered something quite dense, something rigid. I sensed that Paris had no interest in knowing of me, and that I had nothing of necessity to contribute. Doubtless there were many things I could learn by coming to Paris. Yet, in my case, was this something that truly applied to me? Just what was it that one could learn by coming here? Surely it was not a question of any lack of intelligence on my part. Endless worry about such things seem to blow about, flutter up. If you think you are coming to Paris to learn for your own sake, then you could have mastered everything you need to know in Japan. . . .

When the train left Marseille and began to follow along the Cote d'Azur, I saw the steeple of Notre Dame de la Garde towering off in the distance, and the sight virtually brought tears to my eyes. For I did believe that this had been a signpost on my journey. You surely understand the significance of what I mean. Three years ago, I climbed that steeple with Tanaka Kidaiko. It was about three o'clock on a Sunday afternoon, and the sound of Gregorian chant for vespers rising from a small chapel on the top of the hill seemed to fill the air, soaring over us in waves. A number of ship models, donated by sailors in honor of the Virgin Mary, hung from the ceiling. The congregation overflowed the space available in the church. I was very moved by the sight. The blue skies of southern France were spread out above, and there was a strong wind blowing roughly from the top of the rocky hills. Below my eyes, I could see the harbor of Marseille, the blue waves, the long breakwaters, and the roofs of a myriad of houses, suggesting the count-less activities of their inhabitants. From here, even the large ship on which I came from the Far East, the Marseille, all two hundred tons of her, appeared as a spot no larger than a cube of sugar. The interior of the church, with its heavy stone walls, built on those rocky cliffs, amidst of this vast outpouring of nature, the wind, the light, the rocks, and the sea, suggested still another world altogether. Several hundred people were kneeling, and many were singing a piece of sacred music. The smell of incense rose up, spreading into every corner. The light from the candles, in this windowless space, shed a soft and glimmering light. The sight was truly a manifestation of the phrase "Our God, who provides a place of refuge." *Tantum ergo, ave regina caerorum*—I learned these Gregorian chants twenty years or more before, in the chapel of a French school in the Kudan area of Tokyo. I could still recite them here. But it is not enough to merely witness their external form.

At the time of my departure from Kobe, my old and revered teacher wrote to me from Yokohama. In the letter he made an urgent request. "Do not fail to give my regards to the Virgin of La Garde." I myself am not a Catholic; still, I felt a great surge of joy, having come all the way from the Far East with the responsibility of delivering this spiri-tual message. And this sensation was not merely based on some artis-tic impulse, but something more deeply personal. Indeed, in terms of artistic achievement, there is little of note in Marseille, other than the Romanesque church of St. Victor on the other side of the harbor. But at this moment I was not concerning myself with such matters. Rather, what moved me can be closely connected to the kind of pure, masculine intimacy expressed in a painting such as Roualt's *Intimités Chrétiennes*. To use the vocabulary familiar from Christianity, it would doubtless be "misericord." Could it not be said that this term bears some rela-tion to the phrase I used a while ago, "desolation and consolation," the manifestation of a deeply religious sensation felt by a soul caught up in the blending together of the two? In fact, I know of no words that can express the totality of such sentiments. Indeed, perhaps there can be no such a word.

As you know, I have since seen any number of famous churches: in Paris Notre Dame and Saint Denis, then Chartres, Rheims, Amiens, Beauvais, Bayeux, with its sturdy, soaring towers, the complex beauties of Rouen, the delicate lace-like structures of Coutances, the cathedral of Saint Gudula in Brussels, Albi, with its strong, fierce character, the tranquil and graceful cathedral at Fréjus, Carcassonne, Moissac, Le Mans, the huge, ghostly Spanish cathedrals of Burgos, Toledo, and the naïve and countrified cathedrals, overflowing with charm, in the Romanesque style of Segovia and Avila. I have seen countless others as well. And of course, my own reactions to each were different.

The various cathedrals of Europe, which in their beginnings absorbed the Byzantine manner, then followed a path of changing styles, each expressing in their naïve ways the spirit of the times in which they were created, so that the result of all these shifts, from Romanesque to Gothic, then Gothic to Renaissance, reveals a beautiful curve of continuous inspiration. In the attractive cloister of Saint-Trophime in Arles, where the space is divided into sections, you can see at a glance if you look in the corners just how the Romanesque style has blended with the Gothic, manifesting the change in spirit that this shift represents. But the impression that the church in Marseille provides is far deeper, revealing how the basis of this development continued unceasingly, indicating how strong such connections have been with the faith of the common people.

Reflecting back on my own impressions, I find them divided into several streams, sometimes merging together in the dimness of my spiritual memory.

As a child in Tokyo, when I was a pensionnaire at the school in Kudan run by the French Catholic monks, I heard Gregorian chants sung in both the morning and the evening services in the tiny chapel. I found myself fascinated by the symbolic significance of the changes in the vestments worn by the priests, and I was impressed by the artless miniatures I found in the prayer book. These revealed a real humanity. The choir in their seats, led by the old monk from the harmonium, began with Gregorian chant, then continued on with music written by modern French masters, as these shifting harmonies gently floated over us. The flowers on the altar and the sacred statues seemed to serve as an expression of an inner world of the spirit, creating a separation from our exterior existence, so that we might come in contact with still another universe, that within the interior of our own souls.

At this time, I am not a believer in Catholicism. Nevertheless, I would like to speak to the reality of this spiritual path, one that can articulate a means to seek out a harmony between in the inner world of the spirit, still more beautiful than whatever the external world might offer, and one that can bear witness to a reality beyond the domain of that greater world, the one for which the church has been established. From its very beginnings, this reality has provided a path to pursue all thought, all art, into this inner world. And I believe that since the Middle Ages, the Catholic religion has provided a powerful, unifying factor for all of Europe in the development of the religious faith of the people. I believe you have read *L'homme revolté* (The Rebel) of Camus, haven't you? His ideas in his essay on art at the end of the book are easy to understand yet very profound. Let me discuss this at some later point. To do so now would make this letter too long, so I shall write again tomorrow.

The sense of freshness I feel here in Menton comes from the reflections coming from the bright color of the sea. This is the fourth time that I have visited here, and, at this moment as well, just as before, the sea appears pale green, with its muted hues running clear to the bottom. This sight gives me a sensation of something at once limpid and bracing. The color of the sea at Sète, where Paul Valéry's grave faces the water, gives somewhat the same impression, but there the color is tinged with gray. My hotel room, on the fourth floor, faces the ocean. Before my eyes, as I look out at the offing, the color of the sea gradually deepens as the sea spreads out before me; to my right I see the cape of Roquebrune; to my left, passing over the port of Menton, lies Italy, where a series of many-layered peninsulas thrust themselves out into the sea. I have only one window in my room, but the large double shutters open out onto a little balcony with an iron railing. From the sea the undulating waves come gently in, moving along one after another as they approach the cliffs, piling up at the breakwater beneath the road and throwing up spray as they hit the large rocks.

When I first came here two years ago, I found myself very moved by the sight of Italy, now present again before my very eyes. I felt a similar emotion when I went to Perpignan and saw the Spanish-style churches and cathedral. At that time, I was of the opinion that French culture, at least as reflected in the realm of ideas, represented a kind of synthesis of all European culture, while the cultures of the adjacent countries—Italy, Spain, Flanders, and so forth—possessed more vehement emotional colorings that spoke out in a more direct fashion. And I still believe this to be so.

I focused on this same issue in an article I wrote about André Gide for the journal *Tembō* (Outlook). When I went to Spain, Flanders, and Holland, this reality became ever more substantial to me, and now that I have been in Italy for several days, my reactions still remain the same. French culture in its universality has clearly assimilated elements from a variety of sensibilities in order to construct its own unique synthesis.

When I think of a "culture," I think first of Greece, followed by Rome, Byzantium, China's Tang civilization, then of the culture of the Gothic Middle Ages, and so forth, all of which have brought about a certain kind of universality in their conceptions of culture. In that context, France certainly brought forth her own unique civilization. Now, however, what strikes me most profoundly is that while I still acknowledge these observations, my attitude towards them has changed, or, to put the matter more directly, how much change have I come to find in myself? As I look out the window of my room at the movements of the sea here at Menton, I am startled at these differences, those interior movements in myself.

Three or four days ago, I took the train from. Marseille, dappled with sunlight, passing on the way first to Bandol, Toulon, then Fréjus, San Rafael, and eventually Antibes. During that whole time, I found myself reflecting on what the meaning and the significance of my experiences have meant for me since I first came to Marseille three years ago.

What I have come to realize is the fact that if my thinking had not evolved, I would never have become aware as to just how my own views have actually deepened. The accumulation of my various impressions in and of themselves, therefore, has slowly come to bring a change in the ways in which I relate to the world. On this particular day, these invisible changes in myself seem powerful indeed. On the level of my self-understanding, I no longer have the feeling that I must penetrate further into the complexities of France. For there is no end to such examinations, and indeed such knowledge grows stale as time goes by. So then, rather, the work I seek to accomplish must come through an interior examination. I must be conscious of the fact that the efforts I will undertake must be suitable for my explorations of more general concerns, and on a broader level, of the very nature of civilization itself. And this same self-consciousness also brings to me at the same time both a sense of despair and of encouragement over my future reflections on the road ahead. I now feel more at ease when I observe the

world outside myself, and I feel that I have developed sufficient composure to observe that world. I chose the word "despair" because in
every case up until now, each time I came across some obstacle that
lay outside myself, then, despite whatever ardor I may have felt, whatever efforts I may have undertaken, and however filled with good faith
I may have been when I began, I knew that there was still that obstacle
which remained. And I also knew that, however energetically I wished
to overcome it, I realized at the same time that it could not be done.
My sense of despair has come from just such painful experiences. And
those experiences have had had a powerful effect on me. This situation
in turn has led me to adopt the attitude that I must deepen my understanding of my adversary and so adjust my understanding to that reality. As I reflect, I realize that I have already known this for a long time.

This was certainly the conclusion I came to while studying Pascal
and Dostoevsky when I was still living in Tokyo. But what I did not
realize then was that, in order for such an understanding to become
truly internalized within me, it might well be necessary to come to such
a perception by going through any number of just such painful experiences. I knew that I must change. And I did not think that it would be
enough for me to simply grasp what I was facing in some cool, objective
fashion. Nor did I believe that I could master the situation merely on
the basis of my own volition, through my subjective ardor. Yet the self
can change. Such a thing is surely possible, is it not?

I mentioned above that my sense of the significance of my accumu-
lated experiences has changed, and that their meaning has now altered
for me. Still, this is not the same as saying that I myself have changed.
Civilization and the Self. It would seem that if I do not acknowledge the
realities of this culture here in Europe, then, no matter how hard I may
try, I will never be able to fully participate in this civilization. Yet in fact,
this connection also works the other way around. The attitude I have
taken concerning French culture confirms this. If I do not reflect on that
culture and ponder as well on the potential of even of those elements
that have been cast aside by that civilization, unless I take cognizance of
all of this, then I can never truly make contact with that culture. At the
time when I first arrived in Marseille, did I have any such premonition?
Was it for this reason that I feared going to Paris? Culture and civilization represent human life on a high level; this is not something that can
be merely observed as a spectacle from the outside or simply reduced
to one's own personal use. Rather, this relationship is closer to a love
affair. One makes the culture one's own, and at the same time one then

becomes a part of that culture. If such is not the case, the connections between the two become trivial. The connection between Rilke and Paris is an example of such a true relationship of love and affection.

Generally speaking, whether dealing with human beings, or indeed with all things in general, it is hard to imagine the sort of person who can exist without this kind of loving relationship. This is certainly the case with Rilke, as with Van Gogh, and Dostoevsky. Yes, true enough, their fates were filled with tragedy. In virtually all such cases, they ended their lives shrouded in loneliness. Yet each of them, at such a point in their lives, were able to see things clearly and precisely as they were, and they finished their lives in just such a state of acceptance. Desolation and Consolation were fused together, passing beyond any boundaries. Gauguin, escaping what was for him the desert of Paris, went off to Tahiti and its blinding sun, far from civilization. And yes, this "desert of Paris" was indeed that "desert of love" concerning which Mauriac wrote. What a tragedy indeed. Yet surmounting this, Gauguin was able to bring forth his own art. And the fate toward which he was drawn was remarkably similar to that of his friend Van Gogh.

I recently saw an exhibition of Van Gogh's work in Amsterdam, including several canvases of his late work, with their strikingly bizarre and tragic images. One is filled with images of blooming poppies that cover a whole field. There is nothing else in the painting. There is no human presence whatsoever. Yet how powerful is the deep sense of pain that these flowers produce. There is a soundless wind that blows over the blossoms. The sun shines gently down on them. The red color of the poppies seems to float upward, spreading sporadically over the canvas. It is as though the painter's sadness extends itself without limits, as though everything he has felt has here been rendered visible: the love within him, however deep, however pure, all the wounds he has suffered, and his strong sense of betrayal. In another of his paintings, a crowd of crows descends on a wheat field. The color of the blue-black sky is pregnant with the sense of the arriving wind, the wheat stalks now flattened by the strong blasts. Again, there is no human presence in the scene. In this painting there is not even space for suffering and human tragedy, only the loneliness of a desolate and stormy fate, surely the fate of the artist Van Gogh himself. In contrast, how different is the Asian sense of resignation, which somehow possesses a sense of sweetness, even tranquility. But here a soul, exhausted, and failing in a search for love, is represented only by the harshness of this darkening night. This image represents the artist's own self-consciousness of his fate.

How intimidating, this moment of his interior collapse, embodied as it is in the yellow of the field and the black of the crows.

You must know the *Letters of a Portuguese Nun* (which Rilke mentions in his *Notebooks of Malte Laurids Brigge*), which provides an account through a series of letters of the emotional collapse of a woman living in the seventeenth century who is abandoned by her lover. If I did not grasp the nature of the resignation of this woman, I could have no sense of what it means to me to be here in France. I understand all too well the vanity, the fecklessness, and the selfishness of the man who abandoned her. Yet I cannot blame him for this. Moreover, by saying that the future of this woman seems unclear to the reader is not to invite any criticism. Rather it is simply that these letters reveal a certain gentleness that overtakes her as she submits to the pain of her fate.

The sea at Menton, under the glitter of the afternoon sun, now makes the water sparkle all the more. Yet somehow this very brilliance holds within it a deep sadness. Standing on the steps at the old port, where the winds meander as they blow in from Italy, I enter the church of the Pénitents Blancs. There is not a soul inside. When I saw the same interior, two years before, just as now, there was no one there. But I am not the person I was two years ago.

Eventually the night began to fall. As the "season" has passed, the reflections of the glittering lights of the promenade, now empty of walkers, can be seen spreading out onto the surface of the sea. There was no moonlight in the offing, and over the darkness far away could be seen on the Italian shoreline a group of lights, like points of silver, all in a row, spreading out in clusters as they sparkle in the growing dark.

Menton, October 14

Black clouds, coloring the sky, are moved by the wind, floating from east to west. From Menton to Nice, all along the French Rivera, the countryside is drenched in a cold, white light. There are only three or four others on the bus I am now riding. From time to time, the autumn rain strikes the windowpanes. In the south of France, on those occasions when the sun is hidden away, everything quickly seems to become steeped in a kind of melancholy, the desolate color of light ash. Looking at the surface of the sea, as the bus moves along the top of the cliffs, not even one ship can be seen.

With the rough sea, the white tips of the waves spread out, like patterns of lace, as far as the eye can see. The complicated patterns of the sky, the sea, and the land never seem to change even as we move along, and one place is soon left behind for another. Yet despite this melancholy of gray, I am surprised to find that I am at peace with myself. Everything appears as it should be. Those clusters of yellow houses in Monte Carlo or Monaco today look somehow withered and submerged.

The streets of Nice are soaked from the rain. The gray sky has spread itself over the whole town. At the port of Lympia, with no one about, there are ships docked and ready to travel to Corsica. So quiet and peaceful, this old port. Is this the same place I came to two years before, then with a deep blue sky, a sparkling sea, those vivid red and yellow houses, the bustling groups of people, all that greenery, and the deep echoes of the ship's whistles? Where has all of this gone?

The apartment of my friends the Galeros, is as it was two years before. However, the interior of the apartment has been completely remodeled—now there is hot water, cold water, central heating, and a completely new bathroom. Mrs. Galero sold the place to a former government employee from Paris, and she has become his *femme de ménage*. The couple had lost their money, so she became a maid, and a millionaire now lives in their former home. Still, I find no trace of sadness in her face. Wearing a white apron, she pursued her chores in a cheerful fashion. Watching her, I came to think that this activity must be somehow altogether natural for her.

The town, and indeed all of nature itself, seemed to change its appearance when the sun was sparkling and when it became hidden. The years revolve, and humans change as well. Two years ago, I was drunk on the sparkle and the beauty of the south of France. I even crossed the sea to travel as far as Corsica. The next year I departed from the southern tip of Spain. I traveled on as far as Tangiers in Morocco. Yet within only the space of two years, my former passion has disappeared. Awakened as I now am from that passion, I now feel that I am nevertheless closer to the culture of the Mediterranean. For that sea, whether dark or soaked in light, is beautiful just as it is. The light, on a bright and sparking day, is now for me a kind virtual image, long departed, one that I can no longer retrieve. The theme of Man and Nature has been a crucial one since ancient times, but the relationship of any one individual to Nature surely depends on the basic human truths of life for them. And that relationship bears no connection to learning or to art, but rather to whatever is the fundamental truth for each individual person. Yet before one dismisses learning and art as mere hyperbole, how much searching must be undertaken, it is absolutely necessary to seek some knowledge oneself. Such is our consonance with Nature.

Monte Carlo was also quiet. The atelier of A, the artist, although it looks out on the ocean, was somehow rather dark. I saw several of his paintings there. Tranquil, with a fluidity and a touch of the Impressionist style, all these paintings, within their prevailing greenish tonality, reveal a flow of bright yellow, moving in an arc from the top left, becoming all the more powerful as it moves to the bottom right. The colors seem opulent, as though they were in ferment, yet, with their subtle shifts, they manage to arrive at a larger sense of harmony.

At the promenade at Menton, against the background of an evening sea, stands a thin man, dressed in white. The houses, with their red roofs all in a row, seem to be hanging as though from a girdle of light, fusing with the clump of yellow trees below. Looking at a number of A's paintings, I recognized still another admirable correspondence between Man and Nature. When the soul of an individual is in a dutiful correspondence with Nature, then he can give rise to a creation that no other person can imitate. We must pay honor to that fact. Then, insofar as this creation binds itself to Nature, it can rise to the heights and end in a true vision of the human soul. In this it mirrors the path of a human life. Thinking in these terms, it is clear that each soul possesses its own special and unique fate, and aligned to this fact, even in despairing circumstances, are so many limitless possibilities for spiritual depth. I am now able, even if vaguely, to grasp this fact.

The evening in Menton has been silent, other than for the clamorous sound of the waves. The hotel was deserted. The next morning, I was planning to cross the border into Italy. I was now to leave the south of France, an act which previously had given me sensations so powerful that they were almost painful; now, however, I felt surprisingly light and remarkably quiet.

Genoa, October 14

My bus left Menton at ten o'clock in the morning. We quickly crossed the border and followed along the coastline from Ventimiglia and San Remo to Alassio and Savona, and we arrived in Genoa about four o'clock. You doubtless remember what the cliffs look like in this area. I felt such a sense of pleasure and satisfaction as I looked at the Mediterranean through the window of the bus. How I love the Mediterranean. In this area of the beach, where the water has hurtled down its banks all the way from the Alps, those great cliffs jut out like the teeth of a saw. Since day before yesterday, the wind has died down, and white clouds now float slowly about in an azure sky; on the surface of the sea, except for a few spots where there remains a bit of movement from the waves, the surface is as flat as a tatami mat, and the reflection of the brilliant light of the sun falls, as always, on these beautiful Mediterranean waters. Above and below the road where the buses pass, olive trees, pines, and an occasional poplar grow in a sparse fashion, and in a few spots, there are ripening persimmon trees. As on the French Rivera, the landscape is dotted with villas, with their red and yellow roofs. So, then, why is this atmosphere somehow different? Just by my articulating my responses, I am sure you will understand what I mean. The tranquility typical of France is no longer apparent here. At this moment, I feel no connection to this scene at all. And indeed, as for the circumstances that bring about such strong subjective feelings on my part, I must say that, beyond a certain point, I do not grasp the real reasons for them myself.

At the moment I am writing this letter to you from a room in a hotel not far from the port. The room is so small that the bed occupies half the space available. There is, of course, no hot water available. And there is no carpet. The door is fitted badly, so that I can look out through a crack. There is no desk. Nor any bed lamp. And since there is no central heating, this room must be terribly cold in the winter. But the towel at the washbasin is clean and the bedding is fresh. So that is enough for me.

The reason I came to Italy was to see the ocean, the skies, and the old cities; it is in the midst of these sensations that I hope to verify my former conceptions. On one hand, someone might well ask if indeed I hadn't come to see the great artistic masterpieces of the early Renaissance and later. I agree that this is certainly one element. But only one. Without doubt the arts in Italy certainly underwent remarkable developments, but what really nourishes the spirit here is the beauty of nature and of the towns themselves. Can you grasp what I am trying the express? Setting foot now in Italy, even before I have experienced anything in this country itself, I am moved virtually to tears when I think of the grandeur of French culture. I say this with no pretensions of any kind my part. Rather, it is because of the decisive significance France has had for me because of my own formation and my own work. What will be the meaning of all this for me? From now on it must be a matter of simply waiting to see. And how will this understanding be made manifest? I do not know.

Genoa itself is quite beautiful. The town itself, which, divided in two by the harbor, spreads out in a conical shape, and from afar come countless men and women who make their livelihoods here. In these dark and narrow alleys, through which a person can barely pass, there are lines of various shops all in a row, piled high with goods for sale. Red and yellow peppers, spaghetti, macaroni, rice, beans, tomatoes, fish, meat, various meat products, eggs, bread, clothing, cloth . . . And all the while, the crowds are pushing along in the face of all this merchandise. At this moment, however, despite the fact that it is early in the evening, there seem to be very few customers. And no one pays the least attention to me. There is little sense of animation. In some way, though, I find this quiet atmosphere very attractive. There are spots like this in Paris as well. And even more in Marseille. But here there seem to be important differences between them as well. Yet how surprising that, just as I am writing these words, an affection for this spot now begins to grow in me. I have no idea why this should be. Yet, by the same token, I somehow retain a desire to escape from here and to go on with my journey. Perhaps there is no significance to this feeling, but still . . .

I'm actually surprised at the nature of my unfocused impressions. To say "impressions" is inadequate. It seems a sad thing to me that I lack the strength to take hold of those impressions and find a way to truly grasp their import. This town holds something important for me. Something which can surely be found in my own responses. Yet I cannot find the means within myself to make these feelings apparent. I hold them within me, and surely they will ripen eventually; I must have the patience to wait until they correspond to something in my real self. And for this, it is all the more necessary to maintain self-denial, discipline, and enterprise.

Tired as I am from a day's travels, now that I've written this letter I feel the gloom has lifted and my mood can brighten. It's true that my physical state is not good. My spirits remain low; and will I continue on like this, year after year?

And what are you doing now, under those bright electric lights? I suppose our friend I is dancing in some cabaret. As for me, perhaps it is out of a despairing wish to return home that I came to Italy, for all I know. Perhaps I now have a capacity only for despair. Despair is a momentous thing. There are those who denounce despair, yet how many there are who remain prey to such emotions. Loneliness, despair, death—these are not merely threatening words, however tinged with pathos they may seem. They represent the very temperament of the human soul. If nothing else, if one does not move toward some understanding of these states of mind, there can be no opening toward a way forward. But by the same token, there is no guarantee that a way forward will be opened. Indeed, the number of times when things simply end in a state of darkness are all too many. Today, there has not been one moment when I have genuinely felt at ease with myself. To that extent, then, this has been a sad day for me. Still, such days are rare.

Looking at the port of Genoa from the inside of the bus, everything seems somehow filled with a sort of vacant light. Two years ago, when I first looked upon the coast of Italy, I was coming from Menton with such a breathless longing. Today, returning to Italy again, I experienced no such reverie.

Looking beneath my hotel window, streetcars are moving in the dark streets, and auto bikes chug along as well. On the passageway outside the hotel door, some girls are vaguely chattering about something or other. I myself, despite the desolation of my day, have no wish to be critical of anyone, and, whatever my negative feelings, I do manage to feel some sense of happiness as I climb into my bed.

Florence, October 17

On the fifteenth, in Pisa, I stood at the entrance to the plaza of the Campo Santo, where the cathedral is located. It was just at noon.

In the middle of a vast lawn rose the Leaning Tower, constructed of striking white marble, along with the Duomo and the Baptistery lined up, all in order, in a spacious fashion. The very first impression I had was of a kind of geometrical equilibrium. Yet I felt too a sense of great finesse. There are the great cities in Italy—Florence, Venice, Rome, Milan—designed in relation to the magnificent art they contain; yet those who live in Pisa, because of the high quality of their own environment, resist the idea that they are merely one of the smaller and less significant municipalities. The apse of the Duomo, in the form of a semicircle, serves as an elegant extension to the main structure; the buildings show a variety of styles, Byzantine, Moorish, Romanesque, and Gothic, all blended together in a beautiful organic fashion that can easily be observed, comprising one single large ensemble of architecture. The Baptistery possesses an intricate beauty. The tops of the columns are delicately carved, in Byzantine fashion, and the outer walls, in the style of the Romanesque, have been constructed in varying modes, with three levels surrounding the interior space. And the beautiful slant of the Leaning Tower.

I stood in the midst of this plaza, and I stared unstintingly at these three white buildings. This is a beauty removed from mere specifics, of a special presence. Such beauty bears no relation to any human subjectivity; this beauty has crystalized on its own. These buildings do not represent the human soul; they represent the wealth and ostentation of a great urban area. Yet setting such quibbles aside, of what exactly does constitute such beauty? Here I think I have hit on one of the key elements of Italian Renaissance art, and in one sense, of a more general European phenomenon. This powerful sense of space is common to so many places—the Place de la Concorde in Paris, as well as the Champs Élysées, Madrid's Puerta del Sol, or the line of the great hotels along the sea at Cannes. And all such places reveal in common both the grandeur and the finesse of a vital European spirit, as revealed in all this exterior beauty. Once, while listening to a recording of a symphony, you said, "This is Europe." Here today, I somehow had a similar feeling.

The sky has now become covered over with a layer of low-lying clouds. There is a trace of autumn rain. The inside of the cathedral is beautifully decorated with mosaics and wall paintings, and the stained-glass windows are certainly not inferior to those I have seen elsewhere. The effect is far more dazzling than in the churches of France, but the churches here seem nowhere as bright as those in Spain.

After looking at the inside of the Baptistery and walking around the apse of the Duomo, I came from behind towards the cloister at the Campo Santo, the "Holy Field." There was scarcely anyone in the area, only a young couple, sitting on the stone steps, apparently eating something or other.

The cloister was badly damaged during the war. Since then, some repairs have been made to the exterior, but the great wall frescoes of Gozzoli, Orcagna, and the others are in fragments.[1] Some have been restored and are on display in the Leaning Tower, but the Campo Santo itself with its rows of cool white Gothic columns has now become merely a large and empty space. As for the cloister itself (of course it is actually a graveyard), what of those pillars in the flamboyant style found in the corridors, or the delicate beauty of the arches? So beautifully polished, these columns show a true "beauty of form," one I can easily locate in the churches and cloisters of Spain, Flanders, and France as well. When I speak of this "beauty of form," I mean that the form, in and of itself, seems perfectly complete in its artistry. I think you can easily understand this notion. And this site is not the only such example. Such beauty is common to all Italian Renaissance art. Here, you might think to make some comparisons with the Spanish art of the same period. Yet although Spanish art may rest on the same emotional foundations, I feel an enormous difference with the art of Italy. In the case of Spain, the soul or the spirit becomes the basis for the sensuality depicted, one that pierces into the very center of these feelings. This is the beauty of the soul as materialized in terms of physical sensations. This is certainly true of the paintings of El Greco. I find the same qualities in Spanish music and dance. If I can posit the idea that the beauty of Italy lies, broadly speaking, in the beauty of elegant women in their fashionable social settings, then the concept of beauty in Spain is that of the feelings of emotion felt by one lover for another. The beauty of Spain is an interior one, closed in upon itself. In that regard, the mysticism based on religious feelings is indeed a kind of love for and of the self.

Do you happen to know the poems of the mystic poet St. John of the Cross? His are poems of surpassing and ardent love, filled with an almost inexpressible passion aimed towards God. The kind of beauty expressed in the rows of columns in the Campo Santo, however, is the beauty of light, of midday. The kind of dark and closed-in beauty of the poet's soul expressed in those poems does not exist here. Even the saints in Italy remain in the world. They feed the birds.

In the western gallery there is the statue of a woman. The statue is referred to as the *Inconsolata*, and I found myself touched both by the title and by the statue itself. It was doubtless placed here because the Campo del Santo is a graveyard; this woman has been left at an intersection with death, one that is virtually irrevocable. This moment brought forth in me a strong emotional reaction. And I would say that of course this unalterable moment exists not only for her but even more for the one for whom she mourns. Every human being is filled with a love of self and so fears the coming of just such a moment. The feel of death is only forced on one through the death of another. Yet the one who has died feels nothing.

I have been writing all this down in my letter to you. And I fear it has become a long one, a very long one. I believe I am putting all this down in order to give some solace to my own heart. You will surely understand what I mean to express.

Orcagna's large mural depicting hell and the Triumph of Death on the north side is now being restored and can be seen in an adjacent space in the Leaning Tower. I don't believe that any other painting depicts with this kind of primal horror such a vision of death and hell. Perhaps for that very reason as well, it provides a sense of pleasure. Still, despite this sensation, I have come to realize that having seen it, a certain sense of loss came over me soon afterwards. For if pleasure derives from a sense of a gratification of the flesh, then I am therefore forced to admit that if such pleasure does not ultimately derive from the Spirit, then bodily pleasures can have no meaning. Indeed, it was with such convictions that I came to France.

Now, standing at the Campo Santo in Pisa, I came to see quite clearly that, from the time I was a schoolboy until I became a teacher myself, all my worries over death, pleasure and love are here rendered visible before my very eyes. Of course, death will surely come to me at some point. And at that moment, I pray that, because I know that I have bonded together with other souls, I can feel a satisfaction even in my death. And so perhaps my seeking out in Renaissance Italian art this kind of clear, bright beauty and pleasure does provide a means for me to consistently undercut the fear of death and hell I feel. Dante's *Divine Comedy* is proof of this.

In the center of the Leaning Tower stands a statue in ivory of the *Virgin and Child*, a bit over a foot long, carved by Giovanni Pisano. The beauty of those flowing lines. The curvature of the body of the Virgin. The way in which the neck is thrust forward. There are a number of statues by Pisano in the Pisa National Museum, and they all show the same characteristics. Where did such a pose come from, and what is it meant to suggest? This posture can only represent a reflection of the élan residing in the very soul of the sculptor. What good fortune it was that the sculptor himself could crystallize that élan into a visual style.

I have been trudging along the quay (called the Lungarno) of the Arno river. The town of Pisa is so quiet that it seems asleep. Gray clouds were drooping low, and a slight drizzle fell on the surface of the Arno, which looked a muddy color, falling on the yellow buildings on both sides of the river, falling on the old stone steps of the road I was walking, falling without a sound. And this silent yellow, a town within a dream, seemed to continue on and on. *Why then did I come here, why am I walking along here?* I suddenly thought to myself. What is it that I am seeking?

I felt like talking, talking to someone. Alone, I suddenly found my situation unbearable. I felt as though my whole existence was in a painful ferment, and that I was fruitlessly attempting to seek out some escape. I felt that if I could only experience the existence of someone,

someone outside myself, I could quickly relax and truly find rest and sleep. But, still, I had to keep walking. My feet became sore, and the rain came down with increasing force. Someone on a bicycle came past me on the side. A dog looked over my way, wagging its tail just for a moment. I descended, turning toward the train station.

Florence, October 18

Ever since leaving France I have been in a state of fatigue, which has now become much worse, and today I am in low spirits from a bad headache. Yet it may be that precisely because of this that occasionally my impressions of a place such as Florence can remain all the deeper.

The room I have now looks a bit like the kind of parlor that might be attached to a dormitory in a Dominican monastery; my room is intended for one person, but there are two beds here. There is a grand wardrobe and a desk with a thick slab of glass on top. There are also two small tables and two chairs, and a bed lamp at the head of the bed. The corners of the room are tiled, and I am equipped with a washbasin. The bathroom is close by and very convenient. The windows are of glass and open right down to the floor, toward the east, and I have an iron balcony. A large apartment building is being constructed just opposite, and as I am on the second floor, the view is obstructed. I can hear the Italians, who chatter incessantly, from the lobby. And sometimes I hear a piano, badly played.

How should I begin to write to you of my impressions of Florence? The town itself is simply beautiful. The cathedral, Santa Maria del Fiore, is near the train station, and is one of the most attractive of all the cathedrals I have seen. There is no decoration of any kind on the exterior. Just naked architecture. But the line, and the sense of equilibrium, are remarkable. There are very few churches that produce such a sense of balance and stability. The square apse of the church thrusts out obliquely into the square near the station. The front of the church has large gothic windows, set with beautiful stained glass. In the evening, when the inside is lit, those walking by can see the beauty of the stained glass. My hotel is to the east, about a half a kilometer from the opposite side of the church, in a corner of Independence Plaza. I can go to the cathedral from there; or, alternatively, I can go by the basilica of San Marco to the east, then go through the main shopping area to the south.

It was during the evening when I first walked about in Florence. The streets were crowded with people. I expected that the streets would be brightly lit with decorated windows, but in fact I found only dark alleys, often with few pedestrians. In front of the bars, people were standing, drinking coffee or beer, and nibbling on sandwiches or some such.

Winding through any number of these tiny alleys, I suddenly came out in front of the lighted Duomo. The church is constructed of green and white marble sections evenly piled one on top of another, divided into three sections, with three gable-like structures crowning the entrance; high above on either side of the center there are rose windows set deep in the façade. Near the top there is a row of statues of the prophets and kings of ancient Israel. The tall square bell tower designed by Giotto is on the right, and the symmetry of the whole is quite beautiful. The minute I looked at the ensemble, I thought I could feel the kind of joy that a citizen of Florence might feel. The cupola of the cathedral rose dimly with the dark sky behind.

Every day and every evening I come to observe the Duomo, the tower, and the cupola. The Duomo rises up in the clear blue Tuscan sky, and in my mind the building seems to blend with the grey of the Paris skies. Walking about in the vicinity, my spirits somehow feel cast down. Up until now, as I traveled to various places in France, or made trips to Spain, Holland, and Belgium, I have always found myself to be cheerful, in a positive frame of mind, and happy in my desire to absorb new experiences. Now things are different. Does the truly superb beauty of these works of the Italian Renaissance weigh down on me? Or, more simply, is it the bad state of my bodily health that influences me? Both reasons might well be true. But I think that the real reason lies still elsewhere. It is because my feelings and emotions are now turned inward, deep into myself. And I cannot master these emotions and make something of them. Indeed, what could I make of them? I feel that it's not a simple question for me. Is it that I hope to see my own spirit come to ripeness, maturity? Still, that spirit, that heart of mine, cannot reach such a stage only by itself. I feel this very keenly. Yet those things that exist outside myself, be they works of art or oeuvres of literature, however magnificent, seem not to satisfy me.

Looking at works of art or reading great works of literature are solitary activities. One must place oneself in a state of isolation. Up until now, at least, this has been my strong impression. Nevertheless, at the same time, I have felt, and just as strongly, the fact that any such great work cannot satisfy if it is only grasped in isolation, and that, while taking cognizance of what has been learned in isolation, one must realize that other beings as well are watching over the same work, and that in fact these other sets of eyes are needed as well. When such is not the case, a sense of isolation can entrap the self and force its degradation.

Rilke sought this understanding when he wrote of the progression from woman to angel, then angel to God. Humankind can render attractive what is exterior in them and so cleverly attempt to maintain a façade in as impressive a fashion as possible. And with consistency from beginning to end. Yet, at the same time, in one's inner heart, how is it possible to hide from oneself that sense of desolation, and of loneliness? And how is it that one is able to misrepresent even to oneself those inner feelings of desolation, of loneliness, that sense of nothingness? How then can I ever explain the deeper significance of that trajectory of my feelings of happy surprise, so full of complex responses, when I come in contact with these great works of art here in Florence? I must grasp the meaning of those tracks in my soul, with fidelity and with integrity, so that I can actualize for myself the progress of my own inner being. In the past, when there may be any false probity involved, or when I depended merely on gathering together factors of external logic, I never did take cognizance of how these responses hindered my own growth, and how painful this situation actually was for me. If indeed it is my fate to walk such a lonely road, then how can I be spared this fierce sense of desolation? Yet on the contrary, if I can manage to push away, without any loss of integrity, this sense of desolation, then perhaps I can hope that this loneliness will somehow be assuaged. Loneliness has no value in and of itself; yet depending on the nature of one's own destiny, there are times when it can become a precious thing.

There are few examples of any sort of loneliness generated from particular circumstances that are not without any significance. True loneliness does simply come into being from the mere sensation of loneliness itself. Here I am thinking of the lonely fate of such men as Dante or Savonarola.

There are quite a number of silent and beautiful religious complexes in Florence. In particular, I am particularly struck by the beauty of San Marco and Santa Croce. At San Marco, the convent is filled with wall paintings by Fra Angelico. I have seen his *Christ on the Cross* in the Louvre, as well as his *The Coronation of the Virgin*. Yet the sight of his many paintings in Florence, here in this quiet spot, leaves a profound impression. He was truly an artist of gentle heart, redolent with deep emotional and religious feelings. He was a painter who was also a monk, dedicated to the Spirit. Therefore, the art he created was truly authentic, and his large-scale wall paintings were conceived on the basis of deep religious beliefs. Of course, there is no direct connection between art and any convictions concerning art and morality. Angelico's paintings are not beautiful because of his religious beliefs but because they are superb works of art. However, these works are so moving precisely because he was able to give such a sincere artistic expression to his own faith.

Among the many paintings of his that I find particularly moving is one located in the left-hand hall of the second floor of the convent, *Christ and Mary Magdalene in the Garden,* which chronicles a chance meeting of the two. With the light of the dawn in the setting of a nearly tropical Palestine, a fresh breeze is blowing. Inside a kind of fence, made from what looks like bamboo or sugar cane, a number of tropical trees are growing, and there are blooming flowers of various colors. Behind this fence, lies a grove of green trees. On the left-hand side can be seen a small hermitage, carved out of the rock. Mary Magdalene kneels in front of the entrance. Her arms are extended to Christ, as if in supplication. Her dark hair dangles down her back, and her body is draped in a flowing robe, which has a purplish hue. She looks toward Christ, and her gaze is concentrated on his figure. She appears to be waiting for something. She looks as though she would be ready to rise at one word from the Savior. The appearance of the figure of Christ who stands in front of her is splendid. His left hand is slightly extended in her direction, and He appears to be looking towards her. His right leg, however, is positioned in such a way that He appears to be stepping away from her. His bare feet step silently on the flowers and grasses growing there. At this moment, He speaks only one phrase to her—the famous *noli me tangere* ("Touch me not!" [John 20:17]). There is a brief moment of an intense emotion, perhaps revealing the love of Christ for her, or her love for Christ. The whole image is infused with a sense of freshness brought by that morning breeze. Here a moment of a perfect fusion of trust, respect, and love has been created. What I hope to describe here does not concern matters of faith or morality. A scene like this one, which captures the noblest level of human emotion, shows no ordinary human beings, but those created by the artist's brush, formed in such a way as to urge on our responses, our witness to the emotions that overflow here.

And what astonishes the viewer as well is the fact that the figure of Christ is that of a real man, and Mary Magdalene is represented as a real woman. In the Bible, she is portrayed as a woman of Samaria. But this woman, at this moment, does not strongly manifest any feminine qualities. In the end, I am startled at this superb work of art, which shows the rise of a Renaissance spirit of paganism within the Renaissance art of Florence.

In what realm can a man and a woman create their most profound connection? This not a matter of any mere abstract logic, but one of experience. In the case of this particular work of art, despite the fact that the object of concern is the figure of Christ, an altogether special being, we see emotions ranging from respect and trust to love. There is a deep connection between these emotions with the ideas of St. Augustine, who lived in Milan in the fifth century, who wrote that human sin is based on carnal desire. I find his words to be of the greatest interest.

Sexual desire is surely the basis for human love, and this fact has a number of implications. For if such were not the case, that is to say, if no direct sexual relationship were involved, then would it not be difficult to escape a sense that some final step may well be missing, and that a destructive element could just at such a time be introduced into such a love? I do not believe that there are many men or women who give no heed to carnality. I say this because sexual relations truly reveal the nature of a love between two persons.

In short, what I mean to suggest is that while there may well be any number of forms in which various attitudes toward human relations can be posited in terms of the human spirit, there can be no room for margin in the interpretation of a direct sexual relationship. These are absolutely plain. Such intimate relationships are manifested in one clear fashion and are unequivocal. They may represent a pledge of love, yet they can also serve as a means to undercut such a pledge as well. They can represent a harmony between the sexes, or they can reveal the subjection of one sex by the other. Of course, I am explaining this in very simple terms, but there are certainly cases when harmony can take the form of conquest, or subjection as a form of harmony. The essence depends on the true nature of the relationship. And therefore, the foundation of that relationship must depend on issues of attitude. In the end, if indeed there can exist a complete level of trust without the guarantee of any fleshly relationship, then surely this work of Fra Angelico illustrates this "spirit," this state of being. And if this "spirit" does in fact exist, then it can only be manifested in precisely those conditions.

Fra Angelico himself lived in this belief and so in this context created this work of art. There are no traces whatsoever of any decadence in this work. And in the sway of this beautiful luminescence he witnessed the universal power of God's love. Standing before *Christ and Mary Magdalene*, I found myself deeply moved. Yet, at the same time, I realized all too painfully that such a world of harmony does not belong to me. I examine myself, and with an uneasy glance. I think of Rilke's poem "Falling Stars," in which the poet dreams of the stars coming toward him. At such a moment, I can feel at ease with myself. And whatever the path of that star may be, I will remain at peace. And I know that I will rise and move toward it. Whatever path I follow. And it may well be that dark storm clouds can momentarily rob me of the sight of that star. And that I may fall into a state of confusion. But I do know that this star will come and seek me out. And that I will rise toward it. There can be no other path for me.

In a corner of via Ghibellina, full of pedestrians and old buildings packed in together, lies the Casa Buonarroti, the house of Michangelo. Inside this gloomy building it is impossible to see much unless the lights are turned on. A very kindly old gentleman who speaks French showed me about the place. It is a calm, a splendid spot. As the old man chattered on, I found myself quite carried away in my state of excitement.

Michelangelo! It is here in Florence that I now have my first glimpse of Michelangelo! In the Louvre, none of his works are on display to the public, nor was I able to visit Bruges while in Belgium, and since I have not yet been to London, this is truly my first encounter with his work. Michelangelo is a whole universe. In him can be found Greece, the Renaissance, and the modern. When I first saw his *Saint Matthew*, near the entrance to the Galleria dell'Accademia, I thought that I was encountering a work of Rodin, and I was startled to think that this was in fact a work of the Italian Renaissance master. The figures in his project for the *River Gods*—how vigorous they are compared to similar river figures created by Maillol and Rodin. Visiting the room in the Casa Buonarroti, where Michelangelo's drawings are on display, one immediately understands that, as with Leonardo da Vinci, the artist begins with a visual analysis, one that reveals a penetration arising from his ardent grasp of every area of the design. His small relief carving, *Madonna of the Stairs*, said to have been created when the artist was seventeen, overflows with a grace and stillness redolent of Greek art. And the complexity of the folds in the robe in which the Virgin is draped! Then, too, there is his extraordinary statue of David. The energy from the huge, earth-shattering figure bursts forth, overwhelming the space in the Galleria dell'Accademia. The posture of this standing figure is altogether suggestive of Greek sculpture. The slightly leaning posture preserves perfectly its balance on three points of gravity. But the quiet of this figure is the silence in that instant before a storm begins to break. His head turns resolutely toward his enemy, and the pupils of his eyes seek out any negligence on the part of his enemy Goliath. In his right hand he clutches a stone, and the leather strap attached to it hangs down so that he can grasp it with his left hand. The muscles of his limbs are gently stretched, waiting for the instant when they will be tightened. The tension he feels in the depth of his being can be sensed from the wrinkles around the base of his eyebrows brought about through his intense concentration; before long, he will be ready to spring forth with his entire body. This quiet anticipation of such a fierce moment is one expression of David's peerless masculinity. This stance is not something taken from Grecian art, but from the Old Testament, or from more modern times. Nor is his appearance redolent of the sort of pride a Roman warrior might show. Rather, David is revealing his desire to overthrow the enemy of his God and his nation. This figure overflows with a sense of the determination possessed by a spotless and pure young man. But what of the beauty of his body itself? Donatello's *David* certainly has a serviceable physique and fully reveals a pure and energetic spirit as well. The appearance of Michelangelo's *David*, however, shows an altogether masculine beauty, unlike the somewhat feminized beauty of the figure portrayed by Benevento Cellini. There is no slack in the line from his back to his hip, and indeed that taut line itself shows great beauty. The statue as a whole shows the triumph of the spirit as opposed to the body. This one perfect male figure dominates all. In this regard, this work of art possesses a universal character.

Now, what about his *Palestrina Pietà* nearby? This statue calls to mind the great masterpiece of the French sculptor Bourdelle. The Blessed Mother is supporting the heavy body of Christ, from which all life has been drained away. The corpse portrayed here is truly dead. Mary wears a kind of headscarf, and she stares directly into the face of Christ. But this body is not merely a lifeless lump of ordinary matter. It is dead flesh. There is no way that any return to life could be possible. And it is nothing short of astonishing that these deep human feelings can be captured through the art of sculpture. Whatever Mary's feelings may be, they are not directly expressed. She supports this heavy body and inclines her head toward Christ, her profound emotions captured through the totality of her bodily stance.

Then, too, there are the four nude figures of Morning, Day, Evening, and Night in the Medici Chapel, which taken together illustrate the Renaissance ideals of human beauty.

"Morning." The figure is preparing to arise. The curtain of night has not yet completely left her, and her ample flesh, as yet without strength, remains languid. Still, her breasts are strong and full. Her left arm is bent, and her heavy thigh is preparing to allow her to rise.

"Evening." The male figure thrusts out his left hand, and his head hangs down as he looks below. His right foot dangles loosely down, and his left foot is placed above, with the end of a piece of cloth lying over the left leg. His body is brawny, from his chest to his stomach. The upper body is bent in a concave manner, while the limbs hang down in a convex fashion, bringing about a strong and sturdy line, and with a powerful rhythm. The man has finished all his exertions for the day, and with his body at ease, he appears to be deep in thought.

"Night." The woman's left leg is raised, while the elbow of her right arm rests on her thigh; her fingers support her head as she sleeps. Her body appears somewhat twisted, and her nighttime posture seems calm. Her fulsome shoulders determine the movement of her head, and her splendid breasts, and her limbs in particular, are magnificently rendered. There is a small bag of some sort placed under her raised leg, which helps to emphasize a certain sense of sexual desire apparent in her heavy thighs and hips. She is thinking of nothing; she is asleep. Yet the complex way in which her body is twisted speaks with great eloquence of an overflowing of energy.

"Day." The male figure's legs are crossed and his body is twisted; his head is turned and he is looking out with intensity at something. The muscles of his whole body are clearly articulated. His eyes are not those of a person who is reflecting inwardly. They are the eyes of one who is staring, and with intensity. These are the eyes of day.

The first two of these figures flank the tomb of Lorenzo de Medici, and the latter two that of Giuliano de Medici. What is particularly striking about all four of these figures is that they appear to be unaware of the beauty and splendor of their own bodies. It is as though this physicality can be taken for granted as they sleep, awake, pursue their thoughts, or look at something beyond themselves. There is something truly wholesome in this. By the same token, these sculptures in and of themselves glorify the beauty of these bodies. They have no other purpose. It is simply that the pure beauty of this flesh is there to see. There is no spiritual aspect to these figures, one way or the other. Their value lies in their revealing both beauty and strength. There are no regrets visible here.

In the Michelangelo Room of the National Museum of Bargello in Florence is the famous sculpture of *Leda and the Swan* by Bartolommeo

Ammannati, but since the label indicates that this work is "after Michelangeo," the original was apparently by him. In the Casa Buonarroti, there is a preparatory study for a section of her head. Ammannati's sculpture suggests an overt eroticism: the top half of her body is drained of energy, and this beautiful woman is lying down, looking at the swan she presses between her strong legs, and she appears to suck the swan's beak with her own lips. Yet, despite this spectacle, the woman shows no emotion; only the line from her hips to her limbs suggests any heightened sensibilities. In Michelangelo's case, he has consistently, and in a magnificent fashion, found a way to fuse all these elements together.

Then too, he made quite a number of powerful portrait and full-length sculptures, among them statues of St. Petronius and St. Proclus in the Basilica of San Domenico in Bologna, the portrait statues of Lorenzo and Giuliano de Medici, and the statue of Moses in San Pietro in Vincoli in Rome, as well as sculptural renderings of Leah and Rachel. As for his paintings, I have only seen reproductions of his *Holy Family* in the Uffizi, and so I cannot comment on this work. But in terms of the group of sculptures that I have seen, it is clear the artist contained a whole universe within himself. His human portraits, on a huge scale of emotions, range from the highly spiritual to the carnal; and at the same time, he captures not only the attitudes of the Florentines of his day but creates a sense of time and space that is altogether "European," like a musical scale extending ever outwards. Michelangelo is a great artist who has expressed a special kind of complex music. In this regard, he is the antithesis of Fra Angelico.

Yet sadly enough, when I stand before these artistic masterpieces, I feel a kind of split or disruption within myself. Facing the Pietà, or the Four Seasons, or the statue of Leda, I am filled to the brim with impressions, yet I do not feel any direct connection to the subjects, or any essential line from those subjects to my own internal being. I certainly do sense in Michelangelo a consistent cohesion of dignity and a commanding presence.

And yet is it not true that, somehow, I do sense the reality of certain divisions within myself? And so, because this, when will an understanding of this be born within me? This I have no way to predict. I simply proceed along until I reach that destination. There is still the distance I must close before I can attain my authentic humanity. And it is still a long one.

Florence, October 20

I can certainly say that the symptoms of this phenomenon, this sense of a rupture within myself, if it can be called that, was apparent to me long before I came to Paris. Indeed, one hope I entertained in coming to France was that I might somehow come to discover what lay within the depths of that rupture. I speak of such a hope. Undoubtedly this was, in the end, my sole desire. Religion, passion, scholarship, or to put it another way, morality, love, and work: whatever forms these desires may have taken, they have always torn me asunder. However earnestly I might respond to any or all of these possibilities, I could not make any decision as to which one I might fully dedicate myself. The most important thing I took from my observations of Fra Angelico and Michelangelo was a sense of their inner coherence. Perhaps these artists too felt some tension in their inner lives, but observing their work from the outside at least, there was no apparent sense of any such rupture. Yet for me, at this moment, I seem to be in a fearful state in which each one of my desires has crystallized in a separate fashion. And yet, since coming to Florence, I now feel, and with a terrible force, that these dispersed states of mind of mine, with all their power over me, are perhaps to be replaced with a true sense of a communal and healing resonance, so that I can begin to sense the possibility that I may come to find a means of escape. It is truly a frightening thing, it seems, that my volition can oscillate back and forth, resonating from these various poles. But, leaving this matter as it is for the moment, let me say more of Florence.

In the southeastern section of the city, facing the six-sided Piazza San Croce, is the Franciscan church of Santa Croce. You can find there the graves of so many of Italy's greatest writers—Dante, Machiavelli, Ficino, Galileo, and others. (Actually, Dante is there in name only; his actual grave is in Ravenna). The façade of the church is in Renaissance style, constructed from white and green blocks of marble, but the rest of the building is made of brownish brick. The profile of the building, seen from the interior garden, is truly beautiful.

One is profoundly struck here by the predilection of the Florentines for a sense of balance and symmetry. There are no words to adequately describe the beauty of the interior. The nave, constructed in the shape of an Egyptian cross (something like that of Notre Dame in Paris or Chartres) has a wooden roof, which gives a sense of great spaciousness. In France, I have only experienced such a similar sense of space when I saw the Cathedral at Perpignan and the basilica of St. Nazarius and

Celsus in Carcassonne. The nave is divided into three sections, and the columns dividing these areas show a rich and fulsome curvature quite unlike any others I have observed. The wooden roof gives a feeling of lightness, and its line, also revealing a generous curvature, appears very natural.

The main altar is flanked by side chapels, all four lined up in a straightforward fashion, each facing the entrance. It is here that I first saw the frescos of Giotto. Until now, I had only seen two of his works: the *St. Francis Receiving the Stigmata* in the Louvre, and then, in an exhibition held last summer in Paris at the Petit Palais of the art of the Middle Ages, when one of his works, *Saint Stephen*, was brought from Florence. The latter made a great impression on me. The image, lofty and disciplined, overflowed with true human sentiment. For me this was a portrait that expressed, and in a moving fashion a deep interior sense of order. Giotto's frescos at Santa Croce, on the other hand, found me transfixed, particularly the one that portrays the death of Saint Francis.

In the center of the fresco, St. Francis, in his habit, is lying down; by his bedside, behind him, stand five monks, and some five or more priests stand near his feet. Three of them hold aloft a banner inscribed with a large cross. In front, a man in a red robe, probably a priest, and two monks kneel; across from them, behind St. Francis, a group of five priests, expressing in various ways a sense of wonder and awe, stand or kneel. Behind them rise the walls of a monastery. There is no roof, and above that space, born by four angels, the soul of Francis is seen rising to heaven. The surrounding walls are constructed in a geometric fashion, so that the space is tightly enclosed; the monks on the right and left stand straight and provide support on both sides, and in between them, the monks who surround the bed appear in various postures. They wear robes of varying colors—white, gray, black, red, and green. St. Francis seems to have a kind of golden halo about his head. The walls are rose-colored, the sky is a deep blue, in the middle of which can be seen the rounded bodies of the four angels in gold and white, creating a profound harmony. Indeed, the light and airy atmosphere make the entire work appear as though it has been covered with a veil of thin silk. Here Giotto has rendered a sense of solemnity and prayer—intensive grief, alarm, as well as hope and a sense of quiet peace hold sway. Some six hundred years or more of time have left an ineffable shadow on this image, one that suggests an inexpressible sense of an overflowing dignity and grace.

I lingered, alone, in the side chapels, looking intensely at the frescos. The faint evening light came through the stained-glass windows, falling soundlessly on those peaceful walls. A quiet death. Both for those who left and those who remained. The kind of peaceful death that can only come when, through submission to a sense of strictness and discipline, the conscience can be at rest. One of the priests is raising both hands, expressing a sense of wonder. Another points to heaven. Still another by the bedside reads from a prayer book. Heidegger insisted that each person is alone and must die their own death, a form of absolute loneliness, and of a very masculine sort. Such was the artist's idea of death. In our own times, we surely all feel this way. For us, death is the absolute end. There is no return. But here, in a moment of death as depicted by Giotto, we see souls bound together. These men truly become as one through death. And this is because they are protected on their road by that same strictness and discipline that they observe among themselves. The image of this new kind of human being, brought about by the Christian faith, pursues the viewer in this many hued, sharply clear image that Giotto has provided us. For me, at this moment, how far away this vision seems. And yet this same peace radiates from so many of these other works here as well.

There was no sign of anyone in the interior courtyard of the church. Looking out across the green shrubbery, the dark silhouette of Santa Croce rose in the midst of the darkening sky, and in the dying light that still remained in the deep blue sky over Florence, the imprint of the church stood out sharply. For me, at that moment, the works of Giotto I had just been studying seemed now all the fresher and more vigorous. Some six hundred years have passed since these harmonious works were created. And many more years will come to pass for them as well. But these works of art, in their quietude and harmony, will always remain to attest to that particular road which men have long followed.

Walking down a path leading from the apse, I entered the museum attached to the church. Until now, I had been alone. Now, after I managed to buy a ticket from an employee whom I could not even see, I entered the museum. The three rooms were bustling with visitors. There were a number of striking sculptures of Donatello on display there. Others were outdoors, and I found them marked by time and weather.

Moses is putting his hand to his cheek and appeared to be cogitating deeply, with a stern expression. Jeremiah reveals in his solemn face a sense of doom and woe. Habakkuk, washed over by wind and weather, reveals wrinkles in his wan appearance and seemed to be haranguing a crowd of people. All of the rain that has slid down and over these statues over the centuries has only served to make these works of Donatello all the more beautiful, more splendidly full of life. Just in the same way that the face of a person who has stored up rich experiences throughout his life becomes ever more attractive. A similar beauty can be found in a peeling fresco or a faded tapestry, for indeed these artistic works too continue to fill with life as time passes and their beauty grows. I would really like to allow you to grasp the splendid quality of these works. These four statues of these religious figures, located in one corner, have also been left to the bleaching of wind and weather. The label reads "IGNOTUS," for the name of the sculptor is unknown. These works can in no way be considered as inferior to those of Donatello. The names of the statues themselves have been forgotten, and only good fortune has left for us these works by this unknown stonemason. I wonder if I can make you fully understand just how splendid these sculptures are?

What remains real to us in the work of this unknown artist, so visible in his beautiful works, is the fact that he has truly revealed his own soul in them, and by so doing, vindicated the path that he had chosen to take; this quality alone remains to us, as his epoch fades away in the twilight of the past. No one today can provide the identity of this artist. His joy, his sadness, his loves, his hates, all of these have been lost to us forever. But the universality of his vision, which all can understand, has been left for us and shines on through these later generations. He can make no appeal should we question his work, nor can anyone now plead his case. Nor can anyone disturb him. Nor can he emerge from the past to disturb his present viewers. And indeed, how unlucky or not is it that we cannot discover his name? Such confusions will assuredly continue on. In such cases, when the phrase "work of art" is used in labeling some object, it inevitably means that the artist himself has vanished, don't you agree?

So it was that I lingered here, as the afternoon sun played gently over this quiet spot. I hoped that somehow I might simply find an excuse not to walk away. Suddenly, as I looked up, my eye caught sight of the *Cantoria* [Singing Gallery] of Luca della Robia. In this sculpture, a number of children, their mouths open, are raising their voices in song. On the upper section, lovely women are playing various musical instruments. Some of the children appear to be dancing about. This sculpture is truly silent music. It is as though I could strain my ears in order to hear in this quiet their melodies, the chords they create.

Indeed, remembering what Christ once said, I now came to understand that "even the very stones can cry out." It was because of just such a conviction that I did not want to disturb this voiceless choir filling this bright room and so moved outside.

Florence, October 22

(The dating of my letters is a bit off, so this part follows that of October 20).

Yesterday evening, I went to visit the church of Santa Maria Novella. It was about 6:30 in the evening, and the sun had by now completely set, so that the light around the station was dim, and the whole surrounding area was now darkened. On the main road to the left of the station there were crowds of people returning from work. Hawkers were selling newspapers. On this side, the café terraces were filled with people seated, drinking their *cinzanos* and other beverages, while they read their papers. On the other side of this congested plaza, at some distance from the left-hand corner, stands the church of Santa Maria Novella. The outlines of this beautifully symmetrical building rose up distinctly in the night sky, and the light shining through the broad windows of stained glass rising up in the middle of the apse, which is laid out using a plan in the shape of a Greek cross, makes them look very beautiful indeed. Thinking to myself that something might be going on inside, I crossed the busy plaza and entered the church.

Once inside, I was immediately struck by the colorful interior. In the apse are various frescos by Ghirlandaio—the *Birth of John the Baptist*, scenes from the life of the Virgin Mary, and St. Dominic—that are of surpassing beauty. Painted in pale colors, these images seem to float up from floor to ceiling. The light from behind the stained-glass windows reflects with a glow. On the deep blue ceiling, the images of St. Thomas Aquinas and others have been painted in a majestic fashion, while countless lights shimmer like flowers above the elaborately crafted altar. The apse, filled as well with light, glows brightly like a sort of furnace, and high up from the center, rises the dark shape of the cross created by Giovanni Bologna. In the major areas of the church, however, the light was dim, and a lone priest was delivering a sermon to those in attendance.

The main area was packed full. Since I don't speak Italian, I had no idea what the priest might have been saying. Occasionally he used a phrase in Latin, *ora et labora* [pray and work] the only words

I understood. He was doubtless addressing a crowd of lay persons who were on their way home from work and wanted to hear him speak. The priest was a Dominican, who wore a white robe, over which he had slipped a black stole. He moved himself in a dramatic fashion, making use of various gestures, as he spoke to his audience in what seemed an earnest manner. The listeners were turned in his direction and were listening carefully, occasionally nodding their heads in assent, and sometimes laughing. There were beautiful young women in attendance, and some old ladies too. There were heavy-set gentlemen, who seemed to be persons of importance, and some scruffy and thin men as well. All sorts of people were listening, and with care—students, laborers. I thought to myself how remarkable that for eight hundred years or more, priests dressed in this fashion have been giving their sermons, and always with the same general physical appearance. Yet these days, I must confess that I feel no response at all to this sort of religion. These people were listening meekly to his words; the priest was apparently speaking out with confidence, making use of the authority of the church. Looking inside myself, I thought over the various dark aspects I find in my own soul as I imagined to myself just how I might interpret what he must be saying. All the while, I continued to observe, and with something of a contrite heart, this group of believers seemingly content in their simple, ordinary faith. Still, I have no urge to become a Catholic myself.

Eventually the sermon was finished. Suddenly, from a spot high up in the church, the pipe organ sounded out with heavy, sonorous tones. Looking up, I saw the lights suddenly come on; at the seat for the organist, I could just manage to observe the musician, visible from his shoulders up, as he was playing. It was not a piece that I knew. I am very fond of the sound of an organ when it is played at full force. I suddenly remembered how, so many years ago, I had first been entranced by the works of Bach. At that time, when I was so deeply troubled, the only real pleasure I had in life was to play the organ. Using my fingers and my feet, I could bring forth into life with a cascade of notes some beautiful melody as it flowed on by. Music does not stand still, like a painting or a piece of sculpture. In an instant it slips past, and away.

In particular, I had always loved one particular pipe organ of British make. The instrument was an old one, and the response of its action was a bit slow, but it truly gave forth the sound it was meant to create. On rainy days, and windy ones as well, I would go by the chapel surrounded by greenery in the Yamanote district of Tokyo, with my music score under my arm. And as my fingers and feet brought note after note to life, the music began to flow, the sounds sometimes in harmony, sometimes in opposition. When playing Bach I felt in the depths of my own heart the profundity of the composer's own most powerful feelings, ones which now arose here again in me. As with the music of César Franck, when as that froth of soft sound was gathered all together, a jewel-like melody would be sounded out. The fugues of Jacques-Nicolas Lemmens reveal the musical character of a real musician, pure and solid, and they created in my very being the same effect that a fine teacher might stimulate. The fugues of Mendelsohn so filled with silken brilliance and sparkle when moving forward and played with full volume on a large organ. I studied with diligence the famous textbook on playing the organ written by Lemmens, recommended to me by one of my teachers, a method based on the medieval Gregorian system of scales and melodies. Some of these Western musical pieces were new to me, yet despite their antique elements I was still able to absorb them through my own emotional responses. And I was able to deepen my appreciation of this music because of my exposure to the missal used by the French Catholic fathers in the chapel at my school, as well as through recordings I obtained of the Sistine Chapel Choir.

Suddenly the sound of a pipe organ resounded here inside the church, calling back so powerfully many of my own reflections and memories. My own playing, and all those difficult circumstances of that time momentarily forgotten, I found myself drawn back into some dream of the past. But this was only for an instant. In the next second, as the choir began to sing, I was abruptly brought back from that chapel in Tokyo's Yamanote, green in the smoky rain, to the church of Santa Maria Novella in Florence.

I understood that the communion service was now beginning. Four priests, wearing white silk robes embroidered with gold, knelt before the altar, having removed their Dominican hoods that usually covered their heads. The interior of the church was filled with a flow of music from the organ and the choir, and the altar seemed to glow ever more brightly. This, and the gentle beauty of the frescoes. All seemed to harmonize with the music and the sound of the choir. Here was proof that every aspect of the experience did seem to emerge from the same Spirit.

Ravenna, October 24

I haven't written for a couple of days, so I will fold in my various impressions into this one letter.

The sky over the Adriatic was filled with rain and mist, and the scenery, as I peered through the train window, seemed increasingly lost in the haze, as everything ahead, sea and sky alike, now seemed melded into a single band of gray. The fields were well plowed and lined with rows of cypress trees. This connecting autorail I took scampered quickly along from Bologna to Ravenna in little more than an hour.

The dusk slowly began to deepen, and the lights were turned on inside the passenger cars. As I vaguely observed the darkening scenery outside, my reveries of my time in Bologna continued on. There, the church of San Domenico, all built of brick, the dome, apse, chapels, and its barren outside walls alike, soaked in rain, revealed a kind of complex formal beauty. Just now, I had seen the kneeling angel and the statue of *Saint Proculus* of Michelangelo. The statue is located behind the tomb of a Dominican saint and was difficult to see, as the viewer is separated by a kind of barrier. The angel holds out a candlestick, while St. Proculus holds in both hands the model of a church. These are both small sculptures, less than a foot in height. Yet, my eyes now opened to the work of Michelangelo I had seen in Florence and Sienna, I could not overlook these small statues, having seen so many works of a similar nature by other artists. There is such tranquility in the angel, kneeling with one foot on the ground, the other knee supporting the candlestick. A perfect demonstration of the possibilities of equilibrium and proportion in a work of sculpture. The round face, surrounded by a mass of hair. The edges of the wings are sharply delineated, and the long robe, with its fulsome curves, has no strong silhouette but is amply filled with pleats. The splendid beauty of the candlestick itself. All these elements place the focus on that candlestick, which is in perfect harmony with the stone from which it was carved, and reveals as well the docility and purity of this jewel-like angelic figure. The statue of St. Proculus appears to be moving forward; he wears a hat typical of a Dominican priest and holds his miniature church in both hands. His appearance, the position of his hands, his posture, and his robe, all suggest a heroic figure wholly dedicated to his spiritual path, which the viewer can understand at one glance. The complex swirls of the edges of his robe, like his emotions, seem controlled, in consonance with the taut face of this old man.

In the interior of the church, now mostly deserted, there were only two old men saying their prayers. In the choir seats in the apse behind the altar, some twenty priests of the Dominican order were chanting the noon service. The priests in their hats all rose as a group while continuing their worship, then sat down again. I witnessed a similar sight when I observed the black-robed priests at prayer yesterday during my visit to Assisi, when I witnessed a service at the Basilica of San Francis, with its beautiful frescoes by Giotto and Cimabue. Now, as the voices drifted through the nave of San Domenico, just as at the Basilica, the sound seemed equally youthful and clear.

It was some two years or more ago when you and I went to Notre Dame in Paris on All Saints Day to hear a mass being sung. We observed the young priests while the offering was being taken, and I remember saying "I feel sorry for them." And, if I remember properly, did you not experience the same feeling? At that time, I believed that to abandon oneself to the priesthood was to sacrifice too many human pleasures, too much personal growth. Even now, I still do not deny the honesty of my reaction, but my point of view has shifted a bit. And that is because I have come to realize that any particular young person, before he has been worn down by the various vicissitudes of life, might well not be wrong to dedicate himself to all of humanity. For at the end of one's life, looking back, it is surely those youthful years that seem the best; what comes afterwards can never rank as highly. Is that not so? Therefore, if a person burns with a passion to dedicate himself, then should he not obligate himself to humanity and so make use of his youth? Perhaps then he can be able to sustain that level of commitment that he first felt as a young person. I really do believe this must be so.

I recently had an intense conversation with an older man, soon to turn seventy. "Seventy! It's like a dream I've been through. These days, all I seem to do is to look back with such fondness on my younger days. It's often said that the time of our youth is fleeting, but I feel differently. And what follows simply disappears, and quickly." I believe that this old man spoke from his feelings of truth.

As for the passions of my youth, they were scholarship, music, and the pleasure of having kind and charming friends with whom I could converse, and in whom I could place my trust. Such friends included both men and women. The first time that I realized that I developed a passion for scholarship was in my third year of middle school, as I recall. I had the idea of becoming a historian. And I have now finally understood why this was so. It is because in my textbook of Western history, the illustrations of the pyramids in Egypt and Assyrian reliefs spoke so strongly to my consciousness. Of course, at that time I possessed no understanding of this; I simply felt that I found history fascinating.

Afterward, my interests shifted to French literature, and in particular, French philosophy. And I have now actually come to France, so that this youthful dream has continued on until today, although as yet I have accomplished virtually nothing of my own. It was in the late 1930s that I began to experience some doubts about pursuing such studies, and so I felt a certain distaste in proceeding. I thought to change my occupation altogether; fortunately, I surmounted those feelings and so I am who I am today. At that time, however, I thought of applying to medical school with the idea of becoming a country doctor; now of course, I am happy that this did not come about. At that time, I was still a bachelor. There were also some delicate emotional issues involved, but there is no need to go into that here. In any case, I have certainly understood since then that the "work" that we choose to do bears a close connection to our own intimate human sensitivities. Indeed, when we speak of work, for whom is that effort intended? There are those who reply that it is for the sake of the work itself, and others who say that it is for the sake of the one who performs the work. Neither constitutes the ultimate reason. True work is carried out with love and respect for others, who happily receive the fruits of that work with admiration. All other reasons are false. Because of the love and respect for God felt by those living in the Middle Ages, they gave their whole lives for the creation of these great works of art that I am now observing.

Yet what of the existence of that which becomes the subject of such work? What must it be? The question now shifts to one that concerns the quality of that work. This question troubles me. I mull over this issue again and again.

After seeing those examples of the art of Michelangelo at San Domenico in Bologna, I walked in the drizzling rain to find the basilica of St. Petronius. The exterior of the building has no decoration whatsoever, and the same is true, by and large, of the interior as well. We are made aware of the very bones of the architectural frame itself. Built of red brick, this is quite a severe example of a large church in the Gothic style. There is little to compare with the élan of those great arches that span the interior space.

Recently I find myself thinking again and again about the works of Michelangelo. "They constitute a language." I suddenly came to this realization. And what a splendid language it is. Beginning with his early work, the *Virgin and the Child*, the angel in Bologna, the *David* in Florence, the *Palestrina Pietà*, the *Madonna of Bruges*, and everything else I have seen, all reveal this unique language, and one that surely transcends any mere verbal expression. This is a language of the soul. It was from this moment that I came to begin to understand the true nature of sculpture. This one word contains within it so much: richness, breadth, depth. The powerful feelings engendered in each period, Grecian, Gothic, Renaissance, modern: all are made manifest within this one simple term. Whatever one may say about the power of faith in the medieval concepts of Christ and Mary, the *Rondanini Pietà* of Michelangelo soars above all other such representations. When it comes to the matter of grasping the meaning of sculpture, there is no way that such sensations can be translated into merely verbal terms. A truly successful comprehension must derive from one's direct emotional impressions. In the case of Michelangelo's *David*, once the viewer has been made to apprehend the folds in the youthful skin of this figure, with its astonishing representation of youthful happiness, one can understand the nature of these emotions. In this embrace of joy, the statue represents a poem of a youthful spirit ready to risk everything. Then again, in Michelangelo's *Victory*, the wily warrior has been defeated and lies at the feet of the triumphant young warrior who, seemingly unconcerned, clear from both his expression and his gestures, represents such a powerful image of the idea of victory in and of itself.

Among the artist's many masterpieces is the sculpture of Bacchus and the satyr. The young god Bacchus holds a kind of goblet, and behind him, a young satyr is gobbling up the grapes. The rounded limbs of Bacchus, and his oval face, narrow forehead, and rotund eyes only serve to manifest his sense of joy. His well-proportioned nose, not too high, as well as his slightly opened lips, suggest a sense of limitless pleasure. From whatever spot on his skin, a touch brings a current of pleasure running like lightning over his whole body; all his faculties seem to work to that end. The young satyr not only eats the grapes but tugs at the cluster as though drunk with pleasure.

Ranging from the pure carnal desire of Bacchus to the elevated emotions of the *Rondanini Pietà*, the territory covered by Michelangelo's sculptures extends to embrace all aspects of humanity. As with Giotto and Fra Angelico, he does not examine every subject exclusively from a spiritual point of view. As far as he is concerned, the whole range of emotions—carnality, the desire for conquest, righteousness, the realm of sentiment, religious faith—all of these can be expressed directly, and to the fullest extent. He expresses the universality of the human as a complex chorus of music. Yet, is there not a single note of unity as well in all of these works? At this point, I do not have the capacity to render a judgment. But I can say that within the scope of what constitutes beauty, the artist reveals whatever depth and breadth can exist in the human realm. And I do not believe that there is enough time in my own brief existence to resolve this question for myself.

I first enjoyed to the full a glimpse of the rolling hills of Tuscany from the windows of the bus on my way to Siena. When I went to Assisi, I looked out from the terrace in front of the basilica of Santa Chiara to observe the end of the dying light over the fields of Umbria. On such occasions I feel the possibility of a deep connection between Man and Nature, a kind of delicate shading. In the midst of such a faint, dim, and tender linkage, humanity can truly sink itself into Nature. Now, look at the Isle de France. Not born in the midst of those brought up in such a place, can I, and others like me, truly imagine that we can fully come to grasp these realities found there? I doubt it. So, in the end, all we can do is to continue on as far as we can. There is nothing else to be done. I plan to walk on, ever further, until the time comes to face my own death.

The surfaces of Michelangelo's sculptures, which reveal such depth and delicacy, put me in mind of the mellow atmosphere of Tuscany, where the artist was born. In just the same way, the surfaces of the churches in Paris, Chartres, and Rheims remind me of the richness of Nature in the area in the Isle de France. However, one issue cannot be set aside. The art of Michelangelo, so universal, so humanistic in its nature, provides one absolute standard. Faced with his work, we must scrutinize with care every aspect of our own existence. This is truly a trying, even painful path to follow. In this instance, one must proceed with just such an examination, and all the while without shattering one's own ego. I feel that, in addition to my previous encounters with Bach and Dostoevsky must now be added this third object of contemplation.

Until now, I have seen virtually none of Michelangelo's paintings. I do not know how I will react when in the future I may see them in Rome. But on the basis of his sculptures, I am convinced that I will be profoundly moved. I must internalize these powerful impressions within myself and seek to further discipline my understanding as I go forward. For this realization alone, my trip to Italy has been of value. For surely it is one of the great joys of human existence that, pulling oneself along as best one can through the days, one can manage to experience such profound encounters of this sort. By the same token, this is a huge responsibility as well. Can I endure this kind of self-scrutiny, or not? At this moment, it seems that everything hinges on this.

The figure directly behind Michelangelo's Pietà in the Duomo Museum of Florence is that of Nicodemus, who helps support the figures of Mary and Christ. Until this moment, he had not been able to believe in Christ; now, the old man's face reveals his profound emotions. Although all the disciples fled when Christ was killed, he was in fact the one who looked after the remains and helped to spread sacred oil on the body. It is said that when creating this image of Nicodemus, Michelangelo carved the image of his own face on the statue. When I understood the meaning of this gesture, I believe that I truly came to understand the artist himself.

Now I am following along the coast of the Adriatic Sea. As for the beauty of the Tyrrhenian Sea opposite, this space somehow seems filled with a sense of desolation. Now it is the dead of night. There is absolutely no sound of any kind. I finish my letter under the dim light of the lamp.

My three-week trip to Italy has finished in the wind and the rain, and I am writing now from my Paris hotel room, which is on the fourth floor. Coming through the gauze curtain, the soft, faint light of early winter falls on the papers on my desk. Looking through the curtain, the buildings across the way stand out in clear outline against the hazy tinted sky. From where I sit, the Hotel de Nivers, where Rilke stayed, is hidden behind the left side of the window frame, so I cannot see the building itself. But I feel that his spirit is somehow close at hand.

While in Ravenna, the rain fell and stopped fitfully all day long. The town itself is without atmosphere of any kind. The train station itself is a crude affair, without even any chairs in the waiting room, a real country station. And the plaza that faces it is tasteless. A kind of entertainment truck used by gypsies is installed there, its flashy painted images soaked by the rain. A number of dirty, dilapidated carts with fading colors were lined up there waiting for passengers, but no one exiting from the train seemed to want to have a ride in them. Despite this lack of activity, there were many neon lights flashing on the small streets.

There were a number of men, dressed in Hawaiian shirts, so popular since the war, gathered together on the street corners or on the plaza and speaking in shrill voices about something or other. Most were middle-aged men, in shabby, unclean clothing. They sit in the cafés, but apparently they order nothing and merely sit and stare at the rain falling on the darkened plaza. Their decaying clothing was in muted tones. They looked exhausted. After a five-minute walk, this busy section of town was left behind.

My hotel room is empty of any furniture. There is no carpet covering the stone floor, which is cold and covered with dust. The only noise I could hear was the high squeak of my own shoes, a lonesome sound.

Braving the driving rain, I made my way to the Basilica of San Vitale. I saw the central worship space, which is an octagonal shape, surrounded by greenery, which thrusts up under a leaden sky. The somber red bricks of the walls, placed there some fifteen hundred years ago, can in no way be compared to the new bricks manufactured today. Inside, the space below the cupola is completely empty. The famous mosaics that remain can be found only in the side aisles.

When I think back now on my first impressions of San Vitale, I remember only those long figures with their large eyes on a gold background, figures that somehow gesture in an artless fashion, as well as the geometrical pillars and their bases. Yet at the same time, I did find a kind of severity, a sternness in those figures, somehow revealing a certain Asian quality in them. In one mosaic, Abel and Melchizedek are making some sort of offering to God at an altar.

And this is not all. There a feeling of joy in acceptance, and the sense of a real individuality that comes through from these bits of cold stone knitted together. The two great figures on Mount Horeb, Moses and Jeremiah, while portrayed as superhuman, still manage to express their own individuality, as well as their humanity. Although all of these figures seem created to serve as eternal symbols, and despite their arrangements in a kind of fixed system of representation, what is conveyed, through faint suggestions and nuances, is the existence of their own human and individual personalities. These images speak of deep emotions, which, without any diminishment of the individual, manage to convey a sense of overarching solemnity. There is a cohesion here, and of the highest order. Combined with this hard, cold stone is a delicate sense of the spiritual, rendered in a subtle fashion that is at first not easily visible.

The emperor Constantine, along with Maximianus, stand together, surrounded by their attendants. The empress Theodora stands with a group of women. These solemn figures are placed facing a large empty space near the main sanctuary. With a background of deep green, purple, these groups of figures, displayed in an orderly, almost geometrical fashion, represent a remarkable fusion of the formal beauty of Greek art with the spirituality of Christianity. The unmoving lines of solid stone are combined with an expression redolent of the interiority of Christian emotion.

The figures in the church of St. Apollinaris create an even more striking and splendid atmosphere. On the walls above the columned arches some twenty-odd virginal figures hold up the crowns of the martyrs as they face the Holy Mother. At the head of the group are the three kings who have come to Bethlehem, dressed in robes of various colors, who bend their knees as they present their gifts.

On the right-hand wall, there are some twenty male figures, martyrs, dressed in white robes, holding up their crowns as they face the figure of Christ. But these figures are not inanimate. Each one is different. Their faces, the look in their eyes, their clothing, the placement of their feet, all show differences in nuance. At the same time, there is also a great feeling of symmetry and balance, which somehow makes me think of the sense of order that can be seen in the columns of the Parthenon. Still, these figures do not suggest a *majesté première et silencieuse*. And if the concept of hierarchy does exist in this world, these figures certainly express that conviction in a unique fashion. Still, at the same time they are deeply human. There is a kind of grandeur here that European Christians can no longer summon to mind. I find the depth of my soul seized by the sense of adoration portrayed here. That world has doubtless been destroyed forever. At the least, the conception of the existence of such persons no longer exists. The eyes of the figures in these Byzantine mosaics seem filled with an élan, one that comes from a sense of souls humbling themselves before the sight of such majesty.

Within the grounds of St. Apollinaris is found the tomb of Galla Placida. In the midst of the dark and narrow burial chamber, within the heavy piled walls of stone, there are a number of mosaics, and among them, there is one that I found of particular charm. Two birds have perched on the edge of a water basin. One looks up, the other is drinking from the basin. The deep purple behind the basin reminds me the sea at Menton. The basin is filled almost to the brim with a lighter color of water. There is a striking red line running around the edge of the basin. The white pigeons, with their red claws and beaks, the brilliant blue of the background, along with some yellow and light green in the foreground, all blend together within what seems a grassy space. This tiny mosaic possesses a beauty beyond words.

When I see this particular mosaic, I think back through all those tangled years fifteen hundred years ago to the nameless sculptor who created this. When he put this image together, he must have gazed on it with rapture for a moment, then gone on to create still other, larger works. But, oh, the preciousness of that instant! And as for us, in our own lives, so filled with toil for some fifty, seventy years, is everything not worth it just for this very moment? Our impressions that remain from that instant are surely light, fleeting, and they will soon vanish altogether. Our toil, our life, even the names of those we know, will all vanish into the great darkness of eternity. And at times, even these works of art will disappear. Is there thus no meaning to be found in all of this? I take no stand on any such debate. But I can say that this instant of joy brings strength to our lives and allows us to bear our fatigue. And such instants, for those prone to speculate, can provide a pivotal point for those who would seek to renew themselves. Yet I have doubts. Is that all there is to it? Does such a moment really allow me to find a sense of peace in myself? I do comprehend this small track I created for myself in the midst of this vast universe of space, and with that knowledge, I realize the peace of mind I receive; all this leads me towards an encounter with a star. Where did this star come from, to what place will it disappear? How did it find its way to an encounter with my own tiny space? As for those who simply believe that everything has simply been there from the beginning, they are bound to remain dissatisfied. Such people can surely never know real loneliness, real joy, nor, above all, the deep truth found in a true sadness.

To the right of St. Apllonarius, as one follows along the corridor of the monastery wall, there is an enclosed garden, beautiful in its ruined state. Weeds grow and flourish, and the rose vines climb up as far as the roof, their leaves casting a bright green shadow below them. The columns of the corridor delicately support the wooden roof, and the capitals, crafted in the mesh-like Byzantine style, have great beauty as well. The walls, like the church, are built of red brick. There is a small chicken coop, where a number of white hens are clucking away. And there is a cat, crouching in the tall grass. The square of sky above, restricted by the four corners of the walls themselves, is the color of ash. A large tower, in the cylindrical Byzantine style, stands in the middle. An old woman sits by the edge of the wall, her postcards lined up to sell. There is no sign of anyone else. Utter silence.

How I loved this ruined garden. A space open only to the gray light, the color of ash, that filters down from the sky. Yet within this closed space, how much skill, knowledge, and discipline can be found. How many human souls, after evening prayer, must have stood in a corner of this ruined garden, with chastened hearts, looking up at this gray sky above the Adriatic Sea. And yet, those saddened hearts were not those of woodcutters in the wild or of farmers laboring in the fields. These were the hearts of those living in the city. Byzantium was all of one culture. And this culture gave birth in the Renaissance, to Michelangelo and Da Vinci, flowing on just as it had for a thousand years.

In the midst of a gloomy dusk, with the rain pouring down, I boarded the train for Paris.

As I looked out the train window at the beautiful morning sunlight on the Riviera, the ripples on the Tyrrhenian Sea seemed to spread out forever. I passed through Ventimiglia and entered France, then passed through Lyon, Dijon, and finally arrived in Paris.

I retain such powerful memories of Italy. As far as I am concerned, I cannot seem to find the strength to sum up those impressions properly, nor the will. Indeed, I do not seek to do so. These impressions have burrowed into my very soul and transformed me. Therefore, there is little I can do but wait until I can present a fresh countenance.

North of London, December 25

I am so glad that I can finally write again since the time I began those letters from Italy two months ago. For these two months I have been following along the path of my own interior life. Does this life now possess a great meaning for me? Or perhaps not? Objectively speaking, I cannot answer. Nor do I feel, at this moment, that it is necessary for me to make any judgments. But I do want to ascertain for certain the significance of those traces of whatever it is that has led me into the realm of my inner feelings. So I continue to write, with only the hope that I can at least try to explain myself to you.

At the beginning of my letters, I wrote something to the effect that the soul, as it moves from childhood through maturity, and then to old age, surely changes very little. That is perhaps an intuitive response on my part, or simply a common, everyday feeling, but in any case, I certainly cannot identify what in my own particular experience has led me to this conviction. It is true that, through the ages, many have expressed a belief in such a continuation of the soul through various stages, and some would even extend such convictions to future or past lives, stressing the unchanging nature of the soul. As for me, I have no idea as to whether the soul establishes itself before birth or after death, nor is it necessary that I harbor any such belief, one way or the other. Yet, I cannot agree with the conviction that each person has their own individual soul, which is "theirs" and is different from those of all others, a fact that so, in turn, provides for an existence that can give meaning to the spiritual, to learning, and to the arts. Rather, I can only go so far as to acknowledge a vague hunch that it does seem that indeed each of us has some sort of fixed self, one that is somehow different. And the fact that I have made such progress in my own thinking during these past two months is surely because I have come to realize that some of my convictions have, in fact, begun to shift. To put it another way, since I can posit my own self as my cornerstone, I now have lost the necessity to be fearful of other possibilities. Now I must deepen these convictions, and confirm this for myself.

Still, I continue to mull all this over. What is it that remains vital to me from the distant past in the subsequent flow of my own life? I ask this because it is not sufficient for me simply to say that that I have clearly identified the nature of whatever "fixed self" I might possess. If this were so, then anyone possessing a voice and words to speak could surely insist as well that this was also true for themselves. But I do not believe, objectively speaking, that some forced crystallization of any such explanations into one thought, or any single verbal expression, can truly be possible. Certainly, in my own case, I do not know if that can ever come about. For from the time when I was still a small boy, I always dreamed of moving forward to some far off and distant realm.

From the second-story window of the family house where I was born, which was located in the northern section of Tokyo, I could see, looking to the north, one distant oak tree that grew on the embankment where a water filtration plant was located. In the early evening, in the reddened sky, this lone tree bravely stood up, small and dark as it was. For me, this tree was a symbol of that distant realm that I sought. At that time, a group of crows would come to alight in the group of trees adjoining the tank.

One summer, at the time when I was entering middle school, I had the chance to visit the beach at Ōiso. By the time September came, a considerable number of the summer guests had already left, and the ocean had become inundated with jellyfish. Storms had become common, and there were many days when strong winds blew from the south. It was just at this period, when the seasons were shifting, that I found myself standing on the sandy beach, feeling the powerful wind and watching the whitecaps piling up, one on top of the other, the ripples following one after the other, as I continued to stare out at the wide and endless sky.

This is perhaps a digression, but it was just at this time that I first felt something like a sense of yearning for a certain girl, both a longing and a faint sense of desire. She must have been a girl of fourteen or fifteen, wearing a bathing suit with a yellow bathing cap. She came to swim every day. Her face was dusky, having been browned by the sun, and she was somewhat scrawny, her eyes were almond-shaped, so that she always seemed half-asleep, and her eyelids were covered with long lashes. Her nose was remarkably high for a Japanese, and quite admirable in shape, and her mouth was always closed. She seemed to exude a sense of coolness, even loneliness. She was always alone, not swimming with the others, and when she finished, she never looked around but went straight to the changing room, then left to go home. During the two months or more that I had been observing her, I don't believe I ever saw her once go along with a friend, nor did anyone ever accompany her.

Whenever this girl appeared by the sea, my attention would be entirely caught up in her. As I watched her swimming by herself, day after day, my father came to caution me. Even now, the image of her face appears as fresh as ever in my eyes. I can still see her so clearly, even the mole on her cheek. Doubtless I did come to understand that I had come to feel, in some hazy and distant way, a certain closeness to this solitary girl, who showed no concern for any friend, a dog, a cat, or even a small bird. For all I know, I developed, and to the fullest degree, a sense of an intimacy akin to love. Of course, this was a connection that had no connection, and it has been over twenty years since I have actually caught even a glimpse of her. And of course, I never knew her name. But I have come to understand that this is just as well. For I believe that this sense of affection was entirely subjective on my part, and that I had constructed this ideal object of my affections without the reality of any actual contact. And further, that this model of love I had constructed involved neither calculation nor solicitude on my part. Indeed, this model lay within me and was unrelated to the girl herself.

The misfortune that this incident brought to me affected my own sense of self-worth as well. Remembering this moment brings back to mind the person I was at that moment, who stared at her, and at the distant sea. For no matter how far I might follow along on this path, I could not seem to halt; and this intimate sense of attachment penetrated into the very center of my being, producing a profound sense of unease. In the midst of such an attachment I felt strangely stubborn and so remained strongly steadfast. Since then, I have seen a great deal of the natural world and have observed many persons. I have felt a closeness with all these encounters, and I have learned much; in fact, until the time I came to France I somehow had come to believe that I had a developed a suitable self-understanding as to the nature of the world, of friendship, and of the proper way to lead one's life, as well as of the form that my own life's work now should take. I take no pleasure in recounting the suffering I went through. Everything would be fine, I thought, if only I could make some progress from now on. Indeed, I came to France with a renewed sense of determination to achieve just this. Yet, here in Paris I feel a sense of fear that I cannot articulate, one that has remained deeply hidden below the level of my consciousness. On the ship, I would stare absent-mindedly at the waves that seemed to stretch on forever. Sitting on a deck chair on the deck at the stern of the ship, while staring at the foam of the wake left by our movements, I could not achieve any sense that I could manage to prevent me from returning to that state of mind again. I kept trying with all my might to suppress that concern. Yet at some point or other, these thoughts would return again, unbidden.

I was seized, first in the ports of Singapore and Colombo, then all the more in Djibouti, by the force of the powerful sun and the deep blue of the sea. This was not merely a realization on my part of some exoticism. Rather, I was taken with a new series of sensations; I felt that something had been destroyed in me and that I wanted now to move forward in a new direction, and with a kind of almost brutal desire that now seemed to manifest itself in me. In this hot and desolate spot, so close to the equator, I quarreled with T, insisting that I would like to live my life out there. As far as I was concerned, I stressed to him that for me to abandon my previous efforts could provide instead a kind of new happiness (and how many souls have perished because of such luckless words) where, under this relentless sun, one could feel the joy of testing one's most extreme desires and wishes to the limit, and then to die. This would be surely such a good path to follow. Perhaps indeed this would not be a source of joy but rather one of limitless sorrow, for all I knew, but at least it would surely represent some sort of clear victory over my present existence.

At this point I now realize that I am required to now look back at the path I have traveled during this past three years and four months. This road would take me first from Marseille to Paris, then to the various regions of France, Spain, Belgium, Holland, Italy, and now all the way here to London, where I am writing this letter to you in my modest hotel room. This coming spring, I would probably like to visit Switzerland and Italy, and then the Dalmatian Coast.

Then too, I have been devoting a great deal of attention to looking at sculpture, as there was very little opportunity for me to do when I was living in Japan. This has been a rich and meaningful experience for me. There have also been so many experiences for me, even in my daily living. My most vivid experience was during my trip to Italy this past fall. I believe that I will find a chance to write to you about all this at some later point, but let me explain to you now the conclusion I have taken from what I have encountered. My experience of the world has attained a circular character, and I have begun to grasp a sense of what might actually constitute the boundaries of human experience. And, at the same time, an astonishing thing has happened to me. After passing though this dense stratum of new experiences, now, when I go back to examine myself still again, I seem still to remain precisely the same person that I was destined to become beforehand.

Today is just the kind of dark and cold day one might expect at the beginning of December. In my room in the Quartier Latin, before starting to work, I smoked a *gitane* cigarette and thought things over in an aimless way. I could see the gray skies of Paris through the top of the gauze curtains.

When I contemplate the world of form, I have discovered that I cannot be at peace unless my thoughts are brought together and put in order. Because, under the tutelage of my professor [in Japan], when I studied with great care the writings of Descartes, one principle had become quite clear to me, one that still propels me, even now, to continue to visit the Bibliothèque Nationale. I had achieved this understanding while still living in Japan. The basic configurations of my thought, having since passed through so many layers of experience, have now manifested themselves again. Moving ahead so far into the unknown has been possible for me because I have been able to return to my past. Does the meaning of this merely indicate, then, that I have made no progress? Or, rather, does it suggest that these rich European experiences have made that manifestation of that "self" I now possess all the stronger? At the moment I cannot answer such questions. It will surely take a lengthy stretch of time before I can provide any proper response. But I do know that, within myself, I do feel the beginnings of a sense of some sort of circular return. So then, for better or worse, this is the person I am, and my moving forward into the unknown involves the matter of this return as well. And this "self," which has come back from the past, is not involved in any simple retreat to some older Japanese experience, but to my true self. And the substance of that self does not involve Japan. Rather, it has been developed from the sensations that have now become part of me, bound up as they are with my European experience. I do not believe that I can be certain I can make others understand what I mean by this. But whatever of myself I until now been able to position, and without contradictions, within the framework of Japanese society, be it in the realms of learning, art, or thought, now seems to me to extend outward. Indeed, if such were not the case, no further deepening for me could be possible.

Not to fit into the framework of Japanese society? For better or for worse, is that the sort of claim I might make about myself? A conceit on my part, perhaps. Still, I can certainly state that this conviction has now become a reality for me. I don't expect that this is a travail that others can fully grasp. This is something I must go through alone. But what about the suffering that will surely come to me concerning my life in Japan, the loss of my status, as well as the possibility that my friends will begin to drift away from me, start to criticize me, and eventually come to have no concern for me at all? All I can do is to endure this situation with a steady mind, continue to scrutinize myself, and pursue every effort that may be required. At the moment, I have only a dim sense of what lies outside myself. Because these interior problems are now paramount.

What do you make of my situation? And indeed, is it in fact even necessary for me to explain all of this to you? You are very important for me, not only in terms of our mutual interests in learning, art, and thought, but in still another domain, for I treasure your friendship. So, I must communicate with you concerning all these things. This is because you will listen to what I am saying, and without criticizing me. For I am indeed in a terrible predicament, spiritually speaking.

I suppose that a situation such as this one can doubtless only be made manifest through some expression in literary form. So, this letter can only be seen at best as a kind of meditation. But I do not wish to shirk the pain I feel. Indeed, I cannot. How often have I gone out into the beyond, far from myself, then come all the way back? It was three years ago that you pointed out to me Gide's use of the word *retour* [return] in that short fictional memoir of his, *Theseus*. For me, with the birth of the flesh, now comes the "return" of the spirit, and I imagine that such a pattern will continue to occur again many times in the future. Inside my psyche have been layered Bergson's idea of *durée*, as well as Proust's *intermittences du coeur*, and this "release" of Rimbaud and Gide has begun to make this concept feel comfortable to me. My own thoughts are shallow, and I detest my clumsy writing. And I dislike as well the slowness of the process that should lead to a purification, a catharsis, of my own spirit. Yet, however many decades it may take, I will truly work toward a confirmation of the real nature of what lies within me.

It has now been two days since the end of my trip. On my return, the low-lying clouds were dark over the harbor of Dieppe, where Normandy overlooks the English Channel, and big drops of water were falling. Standing on the rear deck of the ship in that rain, I looked vaguely at the landscape as the train returned along the cliffs toward the town. Across the canal from me, the houses all seemed a blackened and somber yellow.

Dozens of seagulls flew lazily about in the vicinity of the ship. They loosely flapped their wings as they moved themselves through the sky, carving so many complex lines in the air, far more than any that any swallow, dove, or pigeon might create. Existing as they do in that vast space that lies between the sky and the boundless sea, they cannot, as other birds do, control their motions from their coordinates of the Earth. Other birds merely use their own motions as a means of moving themselves about from one spot to another; for the seagulls, to fly, to soar, is to live. Seemingly without purpose, these birds sustain themselves between sky and water, as they set out on the orbits they have chosen for themselves. I feel jealous of them, yet without any particular reason.

Still, as my English boat came to the coast on its way to New Haven, I felt myself to be at peace. Because of the headwinds, the channel had become rougher and rougher. The high white cliffs of Normandy, which reminded me of the paintings of Corot and Courbet of the beach at Étretat, began to recede farther and farther from my vision. Black clouds were swirling swiftly through the sky. The rain beat sideways. Standing on the deck in this driving rain, I stood, with my feet planted as firmly as possible, and stared out at the cloudy straights off in the distance. I felt no excitement. Nor had I any expectations. Nor any sense of ennui. I wonder how to capture such a state of mind in words. . . .

When I came by ship from Japan to Marseille three years ago, when I crossed so many seas and oceans, and then again, two years ago, when I left Marseille for Corsica, or even last year, when I traveled to Morocco, my mental attitude had been quite the opposite of this. Yet is it really true that, on this present occasion I have no sense of excitement? Or, would it not be better to say that I am now feeling a different kind of excitement? But if this were so, then what has brought this change about? As I watched the steep cliffs of Normandy fade further away, I discovered that I had no inclination whatsoever to embellish my memories of the beauty of this moment. That would not have been the case before. Usually until now I would have wanted to have recorded the richness of these emotional responses.

I spent considerable time travelling on foot from the south of France to Corsica, then back to the Pyrenees, going quite a distance in order to witness the beauties of nature, works of art, and the various churches I found of interest. And I believed that these fresh impressions have truly enriched me. So, I therefore remained convinced that I would be delighted to continue to go about, visiting museums at random, in order to seek out still fresher sensations. Yet, in the end, I found that even at those moments I was able to recognize that there had been no real change in myself, and so, in turn, there had been no alteration in the substance of my impressions. As for these larger problems as to what my "self" may be, I have no need at the moment to touch on such details here.

However, what I would like to touch on here is an issue I have referred to before. It is not a question of my shifting from one interest to another; rather, it is a question of bringing real changes to myself. Yet my "self" remains always the same; it does not change. And so, if that "self" remains without alteration, then somehow I must find some means to bring about another kind of change, some deepening of what I already possess. Therefore, when I return to myself from afar, what seems somehow distant in my temperament can perhaps now come closer to me, and I will thus be able to draw closer to the real substance of "myself."

And I feel a responsibility to lift myself ever higher. This is not simply a matter of my feelings or my impressions. It is a question of the real task that is set before me. For each time when I come back to this question as to the true nature of my "self," I realize that I must go higher, go deeper. Such is the desire I truly feel. For at the moment when I sense that there is any gap I sense between my "self" and my sensations of the outside world, then I must truly experience this difference, and in all simplicity.

It was with my embracing this sense of "self" that I came to England and so arrived in London. At the time when I set foot on this country, so rich in history, I felt that I could not deny that in fact this was precisely the right time for me to be here.

The city seems organized to provide the best atmosphere only for those who work here. The buses and subways are not identified in a friendly manner, as in Paris. The signs are easily understood only by those who go back and forth to their employment while following the same trajectory every day. For those wishing to do some sightseeing, taxis become their only option. Then too, there are no cafés, as in Paris, where one can lounge in a chair and chatter away; instead, Londoners only manage to make do with the various sorts of cafeterias where one can eat quickly in a few minutes. For those living here, it seems, they possess only their home and their places of work in their lives. Such is the situation in which I find myself here in London. I am happy to be able to provide you with a few such details.

Let me write something about the schedule of my daily life, which I first began to follow in Paris. I set the alarm to wake up at five-thirty. I quickly wash and boil water for coffee, then drink it along with a piece of bread. Then, until eight-thirty, I toil away on my translation into French of works on Eastern medicine; as soon as I finish this, I go out and, at my usual café, I drink another café au lait for thirty francs. Then, at the corner of the Rue St. Jacques and Gay-Lussac, I take a bus from in front of the Luxembourg station, a 21, 27, or perhaps 81 and then get off at the Palais Royale, cross the Boulevard Richelieu, and then enter the Bibliothèque Nationale. There I work until six o'clock in the evening (my research on Descartes). I take my lunch at a small café nearby, getting by with a sandwich and a cup of coffee; sometimes I make my own lunch and sit somewhere to eat it. Unless I leave to listen to lectures at the Collège de France, the Sorbonne, or the Collège de Philosophie, I always remain at my desk, with my research.

When I finish my research at six o'clock, I board the bus again and get off at the Quartier Latin, where I eat at an inexpensive restaurant or simply cook for myself in my room. Then, from about ten o'clock to eleven, I use my time as I wish, preparing articles for various Japanese newspapers or magazines, writing letters, or reading books that interest me. Once a week, I go to the Panthéon Institute at the Sorbonne for my seminar on writing in French; then, two times a month, I go to the Rue Jacob to visit Madame M (a friend of Professor Wahl) to read through some of Heidegger's texts in German. All of these tasks are pursued from Monday to Friday, leaving me with two days that are completely free to make use of as I wish. I have been pushing myself to follow this system of organizing my time.

This sort of life, seemingly simple from the outside, has allowed me to master all the necessary discipline I require. I have followed this pattern since coming to France three years ago, and just about the time when this routine was finally established, I decided that this was the moment for me to visit London, an important occasion for me. I believed that I could transfer this same daily plan for my life in London; and through this way of living, I thought I might come to feel a deep affection and respect for London itself.

My train arrived at Victoria Station at five o'clock on Christmas Eve. My baggage deposited at the hotel, I went out for a walk, found something to eat, and then went to visit Trafalgar Square. The neon lights were glittering near the Charring Cross and Strand stations, and by the fountain in the middle of the square, now brightly lit, stood a large Christmas tree, under which some hundreds of people were gathered together, all singing familiar Christmas carols, surrounded by an enormous crowd who were listening. The Catholic Church in France has no such public presence as this, which made me reflect on just how deep the roots of Christianity are in this country.

Walking around the streets, I gained the firm impression that London, like Paris, was a city of the highest caliber among all those in Europe. All the buildings, constructed as they were of stone or brick, were strong and imposing, with their deep carved surfaces. In one shop, when I received some pence in change, the date on one coin was 1891, another 1918, and a third 1947—the first from the reign of Queen Victoria, the second of George V, and the third George VI; each coin held their respective portraits, and how admirable that the size and the materials of each coin were precisely the same. It made me realize afresh the power of British perseverance, their sense of tradition. By the same token, it must be remembered that unlike Spain, for example, which also possesses a profound sense of tradition, Britain is on the forefront of contemporary civilization.

My lodgings are in the northern part of the city. Number 39 in Leicester Square. This is a boarding house, which is called a *pension de famille* in France.

I take Bus 15 from Trafalgar Square for about twenty-five minutes, then the subway to Paddington Station or Bayswater Station, which takes seventeen or eighteen minutes, and then I need to walk only a short distance. This section of the town has no distinguishing characteristics of any kind. The main street is lined in a meaningless fashion with shops of no particular distinction, as is typical in the usual kind of suburban residential area. My room is on the sixth floor, which is divided into five apartments, but as this is the "off season," I have the whole floor to myself, so I feel most content. But it is annoying not to have central heating. I am writing this letter in the bracing cold.

December 27 (Sunday)

Three days have passed since I arrived in London. But at the moment, I have as yet no desire to write anything about the city. This is all the more so because you already know the city well.

For these three days, I have been walking the streets at random. Unlike Paris, there is no sense of any larger coherence here (although it is reasonable to suppose that Paris too has its own puzzlements as well). Rather than giving a sense of being simply spread out, London gives me a sense of being beautifully grounded in each particular spot. As I walk about on these stone streets, along which stand these imposing buildings of stone, all in a row, in this city of stone, my wandering thoughts always come back to my own problems. Quietly, as I ponder over these issues again and again, my impressions remain scattered and fragmentary.

I studied El Greco's *Agony in the Garden* at the National Gallery. Christ is kneeling at the top of a desolate mountain landscape. The whole space, seeming to swirl about, appears warped in some peculiar fashion, so that the center of the entire world now seems crystallized in the pain that the image reveals. Christ's robe is red, and he kneels on a blue cloth, while the angel that now descends to speak with him is robed in yellow; in this pale desert-like setting, these primary colors speak out with a surprising strength. The curvatures of the lines that form the composition as a whole reach the very limits of an expression of utmost nobility. Below the angel's feet, the disciples, seemingly unconcerned with Christ's agony, appear to be sound asleep. In the upper left, the moon shines forth with an eerie light, and in the lower right can be seen a group of soldiers talking together, holding spears, as they prepare to arrest Jesus. This whole universe seems darkened, and in the midst of all this malice and apathy, which breathes such hostility, Christ's agony, and his fervor, reach their greatest intensity. This image put me in mind of my trip to Spain a year and a half ago. This one painting brings back to me all of my own powerful experiences of that time. In this dark winter of London, I now think again of this southern land, so filled with the power of sunlight, and deep emotions well up in me.

In this, there was no question of any effort on my part. My sensations seemed to blaze forth, without hindrance. The clear sky was blue; indeed, it burned with blue, as the rocky mountains and the sand stretched together on and on, and in the midst of this space, I saw innumerable animals intended for use in the bullfights pursued by cowboys on their horses as they chased after them. The women were strikingly beautiful. They did not have the kind of delicate skin of the women in France, and these Spanish women, as they thronged together, seemed to reveal their emotions more directly. Prices were extremely low. In Seville, a pension with three meals cost only twenty pesetas (something like 270 or 280 francs).

On the way from Irun to Madrid, as the light of dawn began to appear, I looked with sleep-filled eyes out the train window and saw there, in the midst of those desolate and undulating sands, rose up the specter of the vast grey palace of the Escorial, which seemed to speak to me as though a dream from some other world. My drowsiness vanished altogether. Ah, the nights in Madrid! Do you happen to remember that at some point or other the Symphony Orchestra of Madrid visited Paris, and we heard them play Glinka's *Summer Night in Madrid*? That piece of music really seemed to capture the atmosphere of such a summer night. Now, deep in a grove of trees in El Retiro Park, in the midst of that city, under the dazzling arc lights, I heard an orchestra, seated in a box-like structure, playing rhythmical Spanish dance music, while women in their long white evening dresses danced with their partners, their tuxedos dazzling with their white fronts.

Under these brilliant lights, the surrounding trees seemed even greener than at midday, and through the spaces between them I could see a jet-black sky filled with twinkling stars. All these sensations were mixed with a slight sense of intoxication from the sweet liqueur I was drinking, as I contemplated the music, all the color, and my own consciousness of the opposite sex. In the midst of a moment such as this, why do human beings sense, even boast, of a certain kind of satisfaction that they feel? For however the fleeting sense of this pleasure may be, there is no denying that such a sense of satisfaction exists. Yet as for this satisfaction, and this pride, should the person involved be engaged in an effort that involves some higher spiritual purpose, they will paradoxically experience such sentiments all the more strongly. Then so, unlike those feckless others, they will feel all the more keenly the pleasure of what they are able to accomplish. Even for we others, even though the banquet may be finished, we still take boundless pride in what remains of those fleeting pleasures. This is because a human being is made up not only of spirit but of a body as well. And all of us, selfishly, are seized with the desire to enjoy both. And, as a human being, I cannot deny that this applies to me as well. Now it is certainly true that the demands of the flesh are more urgent than those of the spirit. They call out strongly to us. Yet truthfully, when a person is pushed to the extreme, is there not something that exists beyond that volition of the flesh that wills such pleasure? In fact, at such moments, of what does such pleasure consist? To eat something delicious, to see something, hear something beautiful, all of these are pleasurable. Yet is not the greatest pleasure when one flesh joins together with another who feels the same desire? This is no matter for speculation. It is simply the truth. In terms of this pleasure itself, one gives pleasure and the other receives it. And because any secondary pleasure is no longer direct, it becomes a pleasure of the spirit.

It is Jean-Paul Sartre who has dug deepest into these problems of the spirit. He sometimes is in error, however, when he makes every effort to stress the centrality of our connections to the physical as a means of attempting to enter the realm of the spiritual. What a grave error Christianity has created by making light of the body. And what suffering this fact has brought to humankind. If we say that for each of us, we have only one life, then that conviction relates to the life of the body alone. Logically speaking, this doubtless consists of childhood, adulthood, and old age. The body itself grows, matures, and withers when approaching old age and death. All of this happens only once. So true love can only occur once; it is unique. Happy is the person who has been able to pour everything into this emotion. I have written "unique," but for a person who has truly led an authentic life, more than one profound love surely constitutes a surplus, and therefore love itself would be destroyed. If an individual cannot manage somehow or other to once achieve such a distinctive relationship, however, their humanity will remain without meaning. If this unique connection can be achieved, however, even if other elements may be lacking, a full ripening of the individual is possible. And with this connection comes a widening of the whole human spirit as it now begins to extend itself outward. This wider love most often begins with those direct sensations that derive from a connection with the flesh. It is in this respect that the element of chance enters in. And this brings distress to the preponderance of human beings. I suppose I have gone too far in trying to explain this problem in such a simple fashion, so I will stop here.

I suppose that this unique kind of human love constitutes what may be classified as "passion." Certainly in Spain, their culture is filled to overflowing with a conscious sense of the pure power of these sorts of sensations. Surely those who inhabit that culture know the grandeur, and the fleetingness, of so many of such feelings. In that context, love and death cannot be separated. And there is no escaping the profound truth that cruelty represents at least a part of the truth that lies within the reality of passion, a truth that no one can deny or explain away. As for me, I would like to investigate this reality, even to its greatest depths.

There is a kind of nihilism here that may be overlooked by the Spaniards themselves. The best proof of this is the fact that their very souls seem completely absorbed in the world of sensation. To best understand this, look at the portraits of El Greco, and in particular, at his masterpiece at the Church of San Tomé in Toledo, *The Burial of the Count of Orgaz*. All of Spain itself seems to soar above, whirling around these subjective impressions. Greco, born in Crete, was an itinerant artist, who studied under Titian and Tintoretto in Venice, then found himself wandering about in southern France. Eventually he discovered his devotion to the natural features of Spain. No, rather it seems he regained a heightened sense of his own culture when he returned to himself while in Spain, just as the spirit of far-off Bohemia returned to Rilke while he was living in Paris. Both their two souls had acquired a universality, which, while remaining uniquely their own, still could participate fully in the culture of a larger world. So it is that the various individual aspects of the Spanish sensibility can be said to lie within this deeper, larger spirit.

Albert Camus grew up within the Algerian cultural tradition, yet the fact that he adored Spain as well provides another good example of this phenomenon. And the fact that he made a translation into French of Calderón's play *Devotion to the Cross* indicates the certainty that that these sensibilities to which he found himself attracted indeed do lie within the realm of that larger spirit. Yet, within that same tradition, there also exists a force that resists the usual course of love and can freshly lift and exalt those sensations to a spiritual level, so that a path can truly exist for the soul when, in a state of exaltation, it urgently seeks the benediction of God. In this regard, Calderón differs from the other great playwrights of the seventeenth century such as Shakespeare, Racine, Corneille, and others because, with his uncompromising purity of spirit, he was disinclined to follow their paths and so went his own way, and in doing so, finally took the universal spirit of defiance to the very highest degree.

For me, El Greco is the great master at expressing Spanish passion at its highest and most noble level. He is truly able to penetrate human emotions to the spirit that lies deep within them. And the fact that such paintings can be found in these galleries in this foggy London urges us to accept them as virtual dreams, seemingly without boundaries. There are so many masterful works gathered here in the National Gallery, among them such Dutch masters as Van Eyck, Rembrandt, and Vermeer, as well as superb examples of Italian Renaissance art by Da Vinci and Michelangelo. Still, as for the Dutch painters, my impressions based on what I saw in Holland and Belgium remain even stronger, and the works of Da Vinci I saw in the Louvre in Paris were even more accomplished than the examples of his art on display in London. As for Michelangelo, the sculptures I saw recently in Florence were altogether overwhelming, so I find I have no particular interest in writing about the works of his that I have seen here. By the same token, I do not mean that the works here in London are without interest, merely that my responses to Rembrandt, Van Eyck, and Vermeer in Amsterdam and the Hague, and to Michelangelo in Florence were far more profound. Only in the case of El Greco were my impressions here in London as strong or stronger than in Toledo or Madrid.

As concerns other painters about whom I might comment, there is a fine collection of Ingres here. I have thought of writing about this artist before, but I can't remember for sure if I did so, so I will refrain from any comments at this moment. But I should mention at least that one his major works, *The Apotheosis of Homer*, which can be seen in the Louvre, reveals a remarkable mastery of detail, and a sense of geometry, which allows this work to overflow with a deep sense of the spiritual. As with the work of Leonardo da Vinci, this work of Ingres truly reveals the heights of what art can achieve. The works of such painters are capable of overwhelming their viewers. All I can do is bow my head when I stand before them.

Aside from El Greco, I was freshly struck with the beauty of the frieze from the Parthenon at the British Museum and with the Turners at the Tate Gallery. Looking at both, I lost all sense of time.

Yesterday, with the sky dark from the gentle rain that fell, the day was uncomfortably warm. Christmas, Boxing Day, and Sunday followed one after the other, so that it was impossible to obtain money from the bank; I had only a few pence left in my pocket so that, feeling a bit gloomy, I simply trudged along the pavement from Leicester Square to Charing Cross, then going off toward Oxford Street.

Even though it was noontime, the skies of London were dark. All the various shops had their lights on, so that the neon signs glittered in their various colors. Although the atmosphere was more relaxed than in Paris, the shop windows were filled with luxurious goods. Huge crowds were walking about. People really do wear all sorts of clothing here. Overcoats, raincoats. And, even though it is the middle of the winter, many young people move briskly, oblivious to those around them. This is the virtue of a large city. In that regard, Paris too is quite the same.

On the streets there were the continual comings and goings of those two-story red buses, the old-fashioned square taxis, and ordinary automobiles. Still, the traffic is less confused here than in Paris. And as I only needed a sandwich at noon to appease my hunger, I spent all my time walking about.

In a brightly lit cafeteria, in the self-service section, there were throngs of customers standing by the counter or near the windows, drinking coffee or eating sandwiches. Compared to the relaxed atmosphere in the cafés in Paris, the atmosphere here seemed merely prosaic, business-like. From the crossing at Oxford Street where Tottenham Court Road begins, at the point where Great Russell Street curves off to the right, the sidewalk ends at the spot where a series of stern-looking dark brick office buildings rise sharply on both sides of the road. Suddenly, I felt completely exhausted.

Yet, given my response to the wonders to be seen at the British Museum, I was able to shed my fatigue. Usually I am weary of Roman sculpture, but here I saw a group of superb pieces. This arrangement is quite in contrast with those works seemingly placed at random, which I saw in the Louvre. The Greek pieces are of particular note. However, I don't wish to comment on them here. This is because they suggest a purity in the face of which I feel helpless. And this may be because I do not know what my perceptions of Greece may have been when that culture entered into the rhythms of my own consciousness.

When I saw the friezes of the tomb of Halicarnassus, or of Athena from the Parthenon in the British Museum, I found myself invariably attracted to them without reservation, yet without quite grasping the reason why. Recently, when in Paris, I have been in the process of studying the metaphysics of Aristotle. So then, if at some future moment I come to an understanding of this purity through something I will have read in Greek philosophy, then that understanding will allow me in turn to comprehend what I now observe directly in these works of art.

Looking at these friezes, I was reminded of something that Valéry apparently said to Gide, to the effect that at some point all of us lose the ability to comprehend the purity of the Greek spirit of beauty. For because of the times in which we live, we may well no longer be able to grasp either such a clarity of sensation or a purity of spirit. This observation reminded me of the fact that last fall I had watched an outdoor festival performance of a play of Euripides. I had found myself completely immersed in the bitter power that the play projected. Yet we now seem to have truly distanced ourselves from the innate nature of the human creature as portrayed there. I wonder if at some point I will ever be able to comprehend the Greeks. For I have powerful, contradictory feelings. This is because we must face the fact that it is we who have moved so far away from the purity of Greece. Yet, at the same time, even when such purity lies at the very limits of our comprehension, it can still and always serve as a coordinate in our own efforts to return to a purity in our own minds and spirits. The eternal return, fate—in what way can we come to comprehend the profound nature of those truths?

This coming spring, if possible, I would like to return to Italy and the Dalmatian coast—a compelling inner desire on my part. But I do not wish to go to Greece. At least not in the frame of mind in which I now find myself. At some point, I hope that there comes a time when I will be called to visit Greece while on my spiritual pilgrimage. But I truly do not know if this will come to pass. I would very much like to see Egypt and the Aegean Sea. This caution I feel about Greece surely stems from the fact that I cannot grasp this culture, which sums up so mightily the significance of the entire ancient world. When I look at Greek sculpture, I feel as though I were looking at some totally different species of human being.

And it must be said that this fear of Greece represents something similar to that sense of dread I felt concerning France before I left Japan.

It is Turner who taught me the existence of a poetic subjective spirit in English culture. Leaving aside the question as to whether or not Turner's work provides a foundation for the French Impressionists, it is from him that I learned how such a subjective spirit is able to relate to the outer world. It is a wonderful thing that the British, so utilitarian and empirical, could produce such poetry. Without any influences or personal compulsion on Turner's part, this spirit becomes manifest simply through his own palette. I have stood before dozens of his paintings, and I have found myself quite unable to stop observing, studying them. In every painting there rests a kernel of emotion that the artist locates somewhere in the midst of Nature. The entirety of each of his compositions, therefore, revolves in turn around this kernel, which serves as a sort of magnetic field, so that all the various elements he introduces are attracted like grains of sand to that center, creating a shifting of colors, resulting in a kind of crystallized fluidity. The use of such a kernel represents the essence of this artist's accomplishment. The French Impressionists, on the other hand, proceed in an opposite fashion, moving rather towards a more objective analytic style. In Paris, I recently saw an exhibition of the paintings of Eugène Boudin at the Museum of Modern Art, and it seems to me that there can be no appropriate connection between the styles of these two artists. Of course, I am only expressing my own views on the subject, so perhaps none of this makes much sense to you. I feel an easy familiarity with Turner's work. Yet at the same time, I feel that my own issues and shortcomings are inevitably connected to my own responses. In this regard, I have been studying Turner's works with care, looking at them over and over again, so that I believe I can achieve a way to think properly about them. As for William Blake, I had been looking forward with great anticipation to seeing a variety of his book illustrations, but when I saw the actual works themselves, I found myself somehow disillusioned with them.

I am sure that you know this area already, but I find the spaces around the Houses of Parliament and Westminster Abbey to be very beautiful. It is an error to make any comparison with, say, Notre Dame and Chartres, but these buildings do harmonize effectively with the city of London itself. The abbey is very fine.

I did not find St. Paul's of much interest. Westminster Cathedral itself, which is Catholic, has been constructed in an imitation of the Romanesque style, with mosaics inserted in the walls, which I cannot admire. In terms of beauty, I would choose rather Southwark Cathedral, across the Thames.

Walking up from the vicinity of the Tower Bridge, I noticed a blackened Gothic building of great beauty across from a road on the other side of London Bridge. I did not go inside the Tower of London, but merely sat in a nearby chair for a half hour or so, which I much enjoyed. And I wondered to myself how many, many people had suffered within those stone walls. As I reversed my steps and went back by the Bridge and St. Paul's, I came to realize how almost unbearably delighted I have become with this business-like and placid city. London, like Paris, I was beginning to feel, was a place to which I have become deeply attached.

Despite the fact that Christmas was upon me, I realize I have written virtually nothing about this holiday. Indeed, there is little that I actually wish to say. We were given a Christmas dinner at my lodging house, but there is little for me to note concerning that occasion, other than the amount of cheerful noise made by the young students. On Christmas day, I went to Westminster Abbey, and for the first time in many years, attended a Protestant service. Other than the beauty of the pipe organ and the chorus, however, I gained nothing special from the experience.

Paris, January 5, 1954 (Tuesday)

We are now in the first days of 1954. The dark, cold weather continues on. I wonder what may be the significance of those meanderings in the path that I will walk this year? And, yes, how difficult indeed it is for any soul to determine what should be the proper path to follow.

As I wrote to you recently, why is it that I have now determined to imagine going off again to some far-off place, simply to follow my craving for distance? And above and beyond this, I know I must find the means within myself, with my own sacrifices of blood and tears, to carve out for myself a proper "form" for this conviction, remain true to it, deepen it, perfect it.

I left London on the twenty-ninth of December, at nine in the morning. As I shut the door, there was as yet virtually no one walking about in this still quiet city, and the pale winter light was flowing along, just brightening the dark red brick houses in the neighborhood. The train going to New Haven speedily moved itself up and down through the pale green fields and gently rolling pastures. Occasionally, when encountering a patch of fog, in those spots where it was difficult to see ahead, the train would slacken its pace. Then, after two or three minutes, as the fog lifted, the pace of the train would return to its normal speed. From New Haven to Dieppe, the sun above the North Sea seemed to remain low in the sky, and the cold sea, pale in the subdued light, cast up a clear white spray surrounding the ship.

Leaning on the railing on the ship's bridge, while watching the reflection of the silvered sun on the dark waves, I observed the scene with scarcely a thought in my mind. Several seagulls made slow, great sweeps in the sky as they followed along after us. Sometimes the birds would dive like arrows toward the surface of the water, then in turn rise in the sky, languidly flapping their wings. As for me, I felt that up until now, there has been nothing that has forced me to seek out and identify any change in my own interior feelings, or to locate any sense within me that there has been a definitive alteration in me since my childhood and my youth. Neither in my own sense of joy, of sadness, of unease, nor even of hope. Thus, as daily changes occur to me now, and as a new sense of time comes into being within me, it is no longer a question of my seeking any particular hope, or any definite yearning. Rather, it has become the case that I must now carry out my duties with patience, and with a steady rhythm. And indeed, I greet this new situation with open arms. And not as any loss. Nor do I have the sense that I have somehow gone astray. In our unique, our only life, we possess but one youth, and for me that time has departed for good. What still remains for me now is my sense of myself, my work, and my consciousness of human attachment. I will surely seek no longer in every quarter a fresh sense of self, new work, or a new love. Just as one has only one youth, this new sense of patience and time can also not be repeated again. As for the feelings of my youth, I seem to have left their impossible burdens behind. What I needed to give up I have abandoned. What should no longer have remained within me has departed. The path I walk now covers an ever larger radius as I move forward. Now, I must analyze in depth what does remain within me, and I must examine the meaning and significance of each of those elements that I have now identified, meditate on them, and then move forward with care, so that they will again be able to crystallize within me. Such will be my task for many years to come. Within that fierce flowing current of my own past, which can never return, all those things which I abandoned, reflected upon, hesitated over, everything, all together, will now be completely washed away.

As for the city of London, shrouded as it is in gray fog, this place has come to represent a new symbol to me. In Paris, my youth has been swept away from me like the fallen leaves of the chestnut trees. Now, in this new time for me, what has replaced it seems somehow captured in this piling up of these sober stone London buildings. This enormous turning point in my daily life is something that I believe I must slowly learn to accommodate between now and the advent of summer this year.

When spring arrives, I plan to make a long trip from the east to the south. Before that, however, I plan to look back at the concept of the "Self" in order to see if I can actually grasp the essence of that term. Individuals go forth from themselves then retreat into themselves. Exactly as Pascal has written. And in addition to the Self, there are so many other things—Nature, for example, the beauty found in works of art, the theatre, and music. Then too, there are social relationships, there is love . . . and so many other likely possibilities.

When I was a child, an adult would take my hand, and under the darkening evening sky, we would walk and walk, far along the banks of the river where the Yodobashi Water Purification Plant is located. Or we would go to the Yoyogi area at the Meiji Shrine, at a time before the parade ground had been constructed. Or I would visit the homes of some of my relatives—my uncle's home in Aoyama Minami-cho, or to the home of my grandfather's mother's side in Sendagaya, or sometimes to my grandmother's home in Ichigaya, or to the home of her younger brother in the same area. Or, occasionally, to her family home in Shibuya. I paid no other visits outside of these. Still, despite the apparent superficiality of those encounters, I was surprised to find myself imbued with a sense of their spiritual aspect.

The environment in which I found myself was a very quiet one. I would go to visit these relatives in their homes, where with my cousins and other various relatives I would eat and play games and cards. In my maternal grandmother's house, I distinctly remember the meandering corridors, large gloomy rooms spread with white tatami mats, the faint smell of incense from the family Buddhist chapel, and the gravel spread before the entranceway, as well as the garden with its thicket of trees, with quite a number of small buildings lining the walkway from the entrance gate to the door of the house. I often remember my aunt kindly showing me various albums of photographs. There were quite a number of pictures of my various relatives, beginning with my uncles; all of the men are dressed in elaborate formal attire, while the women wore those long black Western dresses peculiar to the Meiji period. This memory even now gives rise to a peculiar metal state in me.

Before my grandfather joined the Ministry of Education, he served as minister for America and England (at that time, proper embassies had not yet been opened). My aunt and my father had become Christians, and all my uncles had received their primary and middle school educations in England. This old-fashioned sort of atmosphere (if forced to make a comparison, I might suggest that this kind of stagnant, quiet life, which even now may be found among the noble families of Austria or England, is quite different from the sort of lives lead by the nobility in Japan since the 1930s, about which you yourself do know a little something) added to the kind of "European" way of life which at that time was as yet unimagined by the general population in Japan—for better or for worse, I was brought up with such a sense of things. Was

I content being brought up in this way, or was I troubled? I do not know. In any case, it is true that I was imbued both with a sense of "frailty" inherent in this style of life, as well as developing a "European" sensitivity in my response to my surroundings. Let me see if I can dissect a bit both these ideas of "frailty" and of "sensitivity."

When I think about this "frailty," which I see as part of my own nature, I have wondered as to just what was and still remains the nature of this sensation that I seemed always to face, from the time I was fourteen until now. I found myself forced to recognize in myself a certain sense of humiliation coupled with a sense of limitless abundance. In this context, what is the meaning for me of the word "humiliation?" What could be my understanding of this term as applied to myself, when I am not sure, emotionally speaking, what the word itself might convey. When an emotion represents an inborn trait of a person brought up to believe in a certain set of ideas, then this person will come to have a kind of perverse pride in such beliefs, even if they do not know how to articulate them. This sense of humiliation is a response that a person possesses as a fundamental part of their basic personality. Yet why is it that I associate this sense of "humiliation" in myself with the atmosphere apparently connected to the old aristocracy? Given the fact that such people would not be able to continue their lives without their inherited resources, I sensed, in some half-conscious fashion, that their lives had no relationship with current realities. Such people show no productive capacity of their own, and since they do possess some consciousness of guilt over the fact that they have made no contributions to society, the result involves as well a certain sense of culpability.

Somewhere in the midst of the psychological state of these people, there is a sense of pride related to a nominal sense of their social superiority, as well as a curious mixture of both distain and admiration for those who would attempt to rob them of their former place in society. And in a corner of their hearts, they are convinced that, whatever efforts those usurpers may effectively contribute through their own efforts, and whatever newly established social status they may attain, these usurpers can never attain the status of the rank, say, of the first son of the family of the old nobility. Such are the deep roots laid down on the basis of that inflexible sense of security that still manages to depend on those old traditions. Therefore, concerning the actual strength of the newcomers, a peculiar psychology is created in which the old nobility seems unconcerned with the fact that they have become the ones with little influence and so have now become the weak ones. In truth, many of them are now dependent on those who, in prior times, may well have been no more than their retainers but have now moved into positions of power. In terms of that real power, the old nobility can only continue to exist thanks to the protection provided by this new social class.

Yet, actually speaking, those old retainers often still continue to kowtow to these former lords, now powerless, who may now possess scarcely no more than a cushion of their own to sit on. Thus, there has come to exist a peculiar kind of reversal, a perversion of the normal relationship between certain of those who are stronger and those who are weaker, in which the roles now seem reversed. And this peculiar pairing of these conceptions of strong and weak allows for the development of this mixture of pride and shame. In this context, the ordinary concepts as pride and shame have lost their moral significance and have become instead a kind of label for an epicurean style of life.

The end result of this shift is that those who truly possess the power remain the powerful, while those who feel themselves nominally superior can only become even weaker. Therefore, within those lives built on such untenable foundations, there often develops a complex set of mental attitudes that in turn spin out certain mental patterns, like castles in the air, assembled as in a mirage. The idea of a weakening of racial stock, in this peculiar psychology, has managed to seep into the very fiber of all of those concerned. Such concepts are not unrelated to ideas of the virtues inherent in the old nobility. Those who hold the real power see these patterns of this psychology as a somehow necessary step and so pay superficial homage to such attitudes, while those belonging to the old nobility seek to live out these attitudes as a part of the most profound elements that govern their lives. Those who do not grasp the terrible sadness in this situation faced by the nobility, even should they select such people as a subject to write about in literature, are never able to truly describe the truth of their situation.

Proust is able to characterize the life of such people with such brilliance because he has grasped such secrets so admirably. The psychology of Marquis de Sade's sadism, as well as Proust's masochistic homosexuality, are shown through the unsparing depiction of the psychology embedded in the men and women these writers have created as their characters. Here, the old social classes are depicted as enfeebled, and the new classes are shown as powerful. The complex psychology of strong ones is always made visible, shown in use, and made to appear quite natural in terms of their authority, while those who are weak are dominated by their dreams. Their identities are enveloped in the patterns of their own mentality, now internalized to such an extent that every aspect of their physical being seems penetrated by these attitudes. When I mentioned such kinds of weakness previously, it was just to such complex meanings that I was referring. Are you aware of the true meaning of the term "degenerate?" It is precisely what I have described above. Or, to put it still another way, within this mental world, such dreams are not of the flesh; yet for these tragic people, such apparitions have completely taken over the actual reality of their lives. The true nature of such people lies in the realm of poetry, of art. So if there are any persons of such abilities among them, then real literature, real art, can be created. And if a truly polished and refined artistic result cannot be achieved, one reason may be that the culture itself is not sufficiently overripe.

Indeed, such persons living in this culture often cannot succeed at any ordinary work, and even the loving relationships in which they are involved are often unlucky ones. Indeed, they are failures in the ordinary aspects of daily life. It can be said of the kind of "weak" people I am describing that their dreams have truly devoured their lives. On this point, I think particularly of El Greco, who travelled from Crete to Venice, then on to Toledo in Spain, where he came to feel that he could finally live at ease; or of Rilke, the author of *The Notebooks of Malte Lauride Brigge* and the *Duino Elegies*, who wandered over the whole of Europe, and, of course, of Proust himself.

Rilke went through great efforts to prove to himself that his ancestors came from noble stock, which at a glance may seem a foolish effort. But to him, it was nothing of the kind. Simply, what saved such people as these was that, in attempting to somehow force a crystallization of their own dreams, they were actually able to grasp the concept of real "work," and so found their ability to realize their wishes. This is what saved them, at least in terms of their daily lives. Yet for them, their "dreams" maintained an extremely close relationship to those same daily lives; indeed, such "dreams" helped to define the very basis of their being. Rilke in Paris and El Greco in Venice both awoke to the concept of their "work." When they followed this path, that effort doubtless pushed them towards the ideas of the craftsmen of the Middle Ages, and even as far as those of the workers in the temple sanctuaries in ancient times. At this point I need to write no further about this. I know you will arbitrarily say "degenerate," drawing on Gide or others of the upper classes; then too, I know your affinities for certain aspects of Spanish culture, and I certainly share your understanding and love of Baudelaire, Proust, and Genet.

There has been an interruption of several days since I last wrote. My days have now again been freshly organized, due to an endless pressure from work. In order to get sufficient money for my expenses, in the morning I do translating work and research at the library at the Sorbonne, then afterward I work on my various manuscripts until after midnight. For me, you see, this kind of activity gives meaning to my life. I would like to strictly maintain this rhythm of work and continue on, even for a very long time. In my own case, my youthful years are now a thing of the past, and indeed I have been waiting with a kind of joyous anticipation for the time when I can pursue just this way of life. And I am already well aware that my dream to leave behind some splendid piece of writing behind is no more. That too was a confusion of my youthful years. What is now crucial to me is to continue on as I am and conduct my life in just this present fashion, until the time I die. Truly, this is all I hope for. And should something remain of me after my death, it will only be like some fruit, ripened on the tree, which might happen to fall. Could it be some fine piece of work? That question no longer troubles me.

Geneva, December 16 (Tuesday)

My life seems filled at the moment with distractions and emergencies. Or rather, it is with a consciousness of the fact that I must face these issues that I have come to this quiet old city. As a traveler with a double purpose, there is little else I can say about the situation, even if I could manage to express in words my present state of mind. In my recent letter, I broached the question of "feelings," and at this moment, as I slowly meditate over such issues, there is a fierce rainstorm raging outside. So I will interrupt any such discussion. Let me try to explain instead in more depth something about my current living situation.

The translation work I am doing for the International Labor Office means nothing to me personally, of course. I do this work mechanically, while remaining absorbed in my own interior issues. A while ago, when writing about the changes in the pattern of my own daily existence, I began to express how keenly I was influenced by the various layers of the spiritual relationships I have experienced because of the place where I grew up. For me, this examination constituted a return to that first step in the cycle of my spiritual journey. And I realize afresh how deeply this journey, in turn, is related to my relationship to "work." As to whether or not I can begin to establish some progress in my personal efforts with any fixed rhythm, it seems, in fact, that I have begun to experience a sense of a sharp disharmony within myself, paired with an intuition that I will somehow need to return to Japan. Plus the certitude that, sensing so strongly the fact that any progress in my own work has been blocked, I believe that it has not been an error for me in coming here to Geneva. Nevertheless I cannot help but feel that this same sense of disharmony has now manifested itself here within me in Geneva as well. But this kind of mental confusion may ultimately help me all the more to ferret out the real truths that lie within myself. At that point, I am convinced, this interior meaning will become apparent.

Geneva in February really shows no special characteristics. It is simply a city at the edge of a frigid lake. Last Sunday I went to visit the castle at Chillon, passing through Lausanne and Montreux. The cold waters of Lake Lausanne were blue and clear, so much so that it seemed one could easily pick up the rocks and stones that lay down at the bottom. By the edge of the lake, at the spot where I ended up, there were benches set up for viewing the sights, arranged as though in some large park. On the other side of the lake, the various peaks of the snow-capped Alps seemed to press in, standing steep in the thin mists surrounding them. The quality of nature in Switzerland, almost artificial, clean, pure, everything as neat as a pleasure garden, somehow arouses a sense of desire in me. How delightful it would be, it seems to me, to have a lover and to walk here with a woman, almost as two children might. True enough, love may well contain any number of artificial, boxed-in elements. And even if you remove all such accessory components, there still remains a basic problem, as far as I am concerned. Because at present I really do not believe that I could respond to some unexpected, some new encounter with love. And even putting aside the question as to whether or not I could truly endure such emotions, there is still one basic issue I must consider. I have now come closer to accepting the inference that love is not a question of sensations or emotions but of volition. Yet in the end, is that really all there is to it? I would like to stare into the depths to grasp my true self. Just as a lover would seek to know the real nature of their partner, so I would like to know the deep truth about myself. As for me, I now only feel a sense of desolation.

Looking over the surface of this cold and solitary lake, I feel separated from my own feelings, as though they were mere reflections from some distant world. The issue for me is that the time has now passed for me to continue to wish for some new developments through my contacts with the outside world. This conviction seems to have deepened in me. I have witnessed an inner change, as I move from my perception that, as the moments pile up in the flow of time, even love itself, which is certainly one way of making human contact, is fiercely brief in duration. I now come ever closer to the belief that it is volition itself that propels that emotion along. And it seems that this inner change has clearly become a crisis for me as well, a development of an apparently enormous scope. Thus I can no longer simply sit at my desk to reflect objectively about the human spirit, or even about the basic nature of the human condition itself.

I wrote to a friend of mine this morning. I told him that I have been forced to reflect on the fact that, when examining my past, I seem to have found myself acknowledging a cooling in my relationships or my love with others, whoever they may be. Yet at the same time, is it not so that the lover feels a selfish satisfaction proportionate to the extent to which the person is loved in turn by his or her partner? When love is entirely egoistic, is not the partner, at least at first, made to feel a sense of satisfaction? There is no doubt about it. I have already lost most of my real friends. Yet I know that this must be, and so I have no regrets. This fact bears little if any relationship to the true value of a human being, one way or the other.

I was standing on a bridge just at the spot where the clear waters of Lake Lehmann become the Rhone River, as it flows off in a westerly direction. The faint winter sunlight touched the very depths of the river. The bubbling water, deep and plentiful in multiple layers, moved gently along. White seagulls, wild ducks, with their glossy heads, and a flock of small black grebes all flew between the bridge and the surface of the lake, while many swam on the surface of the water. The seagulls played gleefully, looking like bits of white cotton. Occasionally they dipped down and pulled up small fish they had seized. Some of the black grebes, with their yellow bills, were mixed in with the long-necked white swans. Altogether unaware of this ancient, timeless motion that constitutes the lives of these birds, modern sophisticates unheedingly continue to ride the trains and buses that cross over the bridge.

More than two years ago, I found myself standing at one edge of the swamp at the Camargue, still a desolate spot despite the crisp fall air. Before my eyes, the Rhone River, seeking to reach the sea, now swollen with water, quietly eddied into pools as it flowed past me. As I watched the water lapping up towards the sandy soil at my feet, I waited for the ferry to come back from the other shore. I suddenly brought to mind an image of myself, in all my loneliness. Did this flowing water disappear all the way into the distance? Such images sharply brought to mind the flow of my own existence. These feelings in turn seemed closely aligned to what might be termed pure sorrow. What was the nature of that emotion, one that indeed I did not truly understand? This remained a void to me, and yet I felt no remorse. What I felt was deeper than any mere contrition. As I sought to pursue the precise nature of this sorrow, I found myself moving beyond the Camargue, then beyond Paris as well, then England, Holland, Belgium, and Spain and Italy, even the Mediterranean, Djibouti, and India itself, all the way back to Japan, moving through some far distance in time and space, the extent of which I was not able to grasp. These feelings in me continued on until dusk had settled in.

This sorrow, which somehow seems intertwined with my very destiny, gives rise to so many feelings in me, and a deep, deep gentleness that embraces those I love, clear to the depth of their beings, as well as countless other feelings of my abuse and cruelty to those who have been close to me, and my wishes to devour them. There is surely no need to write here about my past, cluttered up as it is with so much sadness, so much so that may seem devastating. And as for my past, why cannot I escape from this burden, which seems to cut into my shoulders with such a smarting pain? This sadness seems to lie at the root of my character, a layer already present even before I was touched with any ideas of morality, or of Christian belief. I witnessed a manifestation of this same inconsolable sadness in the face of the statue I saw at the Campo Santo at Pisa, where the word describing her complaint, "INCONSOLABLE," was carved on the space beneath her. How far will I be forced to carry this burden? I now begin to understand, as did Rilke, the significance of this stubborn need to contemplate one's early years. If I really examine the realities of such a sadness, brushing aside any fleeting sense of sweetness, as I actually contemplate my life, will I be able to bear up under the burden? Or will I no longer be fit for the task?

The other evening, I had a dream. In that dream, I visited my mother, who was living in a shabby old Japanese-style house. When my mother was a student at Gakushūin, she excelled in her studies and was known for her talents as a tennis player.[2] On her slender, elegant face there remained a trace of loneliness that moved across her features; she was a person of nobility and integrity. Thinking of my mother made me feel in turn the anguish of nostalgia. And I came to comprehend that this sense of loneliness has flowed from her to me. It was as though some elements of the nobility found in the old feudal system had materialized in her very soul. Quiet as she had always been, I some-times found myself forgetting her very existence, but now, I began to understand how my own existence is rooted in hers. It is not a question of simply my being my mother's son, but rather that my mother's exis-tence retained the capacity to bring about the crystallization of some form or other of love in me. She was a woman who by nature appeared to be cold; she seemed to have no great affection for dogs, cats, or even children. Yet for certain persons, certain youngsters, there was a gentle-ness, arising from an overflow of just that sadness, that seemed to flow out of her. I myself, from the beginning, have never taken much interest in such matters as charity, benevolence, or social justice. My feelings of sentiment and attachment tend rather to concentrate on certain par-ticular persons I have known, those whom I have loved or remember with fondness. And as I await some crystallization of my own feelings, I have as yet no sense of their existence. Do my instincts require that I reach such a point of saturation before I can respond? It seems to me that such is the kind of space in which I now exist.

This space that my soul inhabits, depending on its contours, has the possibility of materializing into any number of different forms. And the qualities of that space, depending on the range of those forms, can create configurations that may remain a mystery to me. By way of example, if I am attracted to the paintings of the Venetian school, it is because, in my case, I have a sense I must possess something in common with that particular world of color. And I feel to an even greater extent a deep attraction to the music of Bach. El Greco captures such affinities for me in a truly striking way. Yet just what does this crystallization of a soul's space actually represent? I think again in turn of the emotions attached by Rilke to the very stars themselves. When I dig even deeper into the significance of this "crystallization," my mind is drawn to the way in which Valéry used this term. For him, there exists a process, a shifting between homogeneity and the "crystallization" of those quali-ties inherent in the nature of a particular space. Having written this much, I am immediately struck with the extreme nature of such ulti-mate issues. These are ones that I have been studying in the works of Pascal and Descartes for some twenty-five years or more.

Then too, as far as I am concerned, these distinctions can also serve at the same time to provide one genuine definition of "civilization." In other words, civilization, saturated with the sorrow of each correspond-ing space, crystallizes into forms that can and do become a source of joy in the fullness of time. By the same token, in the midst of that joy which has been created, there will also be a space where sorrow overflows as well. Or, perhaps one might say that sadness represents the homogeneity of the soul, while joy represents the crystallization of forms. The method of Descartes, particularly as concerns both his skepticism and his analytical skills, reveals that he wishes to manage a return to the condition of homogeneity as it affects the soul so that, depending both on insight and spontaneity, such a materialization can begin. This is what gives meaning to a civilization, and, at the same time, involves various issues of universality, individuality, and the nature of the Divine.

In each period—classical Greece, Byzantium, medieval Gothic, and, more recently, in France—the spirit of each age has been clearly manifested in historical terms. And within such spaces, which continue on to extend themselves outwards and grow larger, any single "human being," who has no special privileges, can nevertheless maintain himself as a unique individual, one unlike any other. Whatever the expansion possible within this continuity, or however extended that expansion may be, each individual, without any special prerogatives, must somehow struggle to gain some consciousness of a personal identity. And such an individual, in making an attempt to somehow or other achieve self-affirmation, in response to their own deep and primal desires, will find themselves powerfully pulled along with a force that cannot be resisted. When that individual does achieve a personal consciousness, one that cannot be replicated, and never could be, then their convictions take ever deeper roots.

We know that, however millions of human beings there may be, we remain absolutely certain that we are uniquely ourselves and cannot simply be replaced by another. I feel joy over the fact that human beings know of the limits imposed upon them, and yet I feel a certain sadness at this situation as well. This is because such a self-consciousness calls forth both unhappiness and hardship.

To be a human being is, first of all, to experience sorrow. These days I find myself absorbed in reading the Greek tragedies. The skies of Greece, so filled with sadness and silence, yet filled with brilliant sunlight, what do they bring to me? After the discomforting atmosphere of modern Europe, what is it that I might learn from these ancient spaces that open up before me? I had thought that there were no connections at all between Greece and myself. Or, at least, this is what I thought until recently. Now, however, I begin to feel the call of Greece somewhere in the depths of my being. When I see at the British Museum the Parthenon frieze or that of the grave of Halikarnassus, with the nearly cruel purity of their curving lines, or, when at the Louvre, I observe the standing statues, older even than the sculptures of Phidias, standing in great silence as though they were virtually sustaining pillars themselves, I find I recognize in all of them some root principle, some prototype, which reveals in turn a still greater sense of purity within any common-place concept of that term itself, one that takes my breath away. I won-der whether, in my case, I will actually be able to take consciousness of the true nature of such purity. In any case, at this moment I do not wish to articulate here any conceptions of Greece I may have. For despite the fact that heretofore I felt I had no connections to that civilization, I now realize that Greece has indeed had a surprisingly strong effect on me in so many ways. But I have come to understand as well that it will take me a considerable amount of time for me to fully grasp the true significance of this fact.

I have been writing a bit here about my inner feelings, to the point where my shoulders have grown a bit stiff with my emotions; so now, making use of some notes I found in my traveling case from two years ago, I would like to write something about Spain.

Memories of Spain, recollections that come to me in winter-bound Geneva:

> When I think of the extremities toward which human beings can extend themselves, I remember the adventures of the poet Mar-cel Martinet, a disciple of Romain Rolland, on the snow-covered Alps, on the cliffs of Bretagne, and the sheer drops at Plogoff, be-low which the waves of the Mediterranean come crashing in. This winter, I failed in my attempt to go still further on to Roscoff. Yet quite by chance, I did manage to arrive at a spot near Lake Lehm-ann, at the foot of the mountains, and so to Geneva.

Here, everything is absolutely clear, clean, and cold. This is true for the mountains, the lake, the town, indeed even for the hearts and minds of those who live here. Nevertheless, looking out of my hotel window in Geneva, I don't particularly experience any particular sensation of being anywhere near the lake itself. Beyond those white gauze curtains, beyond the darkened plaza, the neon lights blaze forth vividly in red, green, and yellow, and in front of them pass buses and streetcars. I hear human voices. A night scene typical of any station plaza in any city in the world.

Spain! The bald Extremadura mountains, above the desert sands, the limitless blue sky, enveloped in heat, where birds do not even fly—I would plan to go from Algeciras to the straits of Gibraltar, then to the sheer gray cliffs of North Africa, to those refuse-strewn villages, and the women with their hard, cool skin; yet none of these adventures, as far as I am concerned, are capable of stretching my soul to its limits. These experiences would constitute, rather, pleasures that would of themselves be filled with sadness. Indeed, at such moments, the soul itself dissolves altogether in the midst of pure sensation and so reveals itself in the realm of appearances. Without interpretation or explanation, flesh itself becomes the emblem of the soul.

In the Spain I know, the highest movements and rhythms of the soul are made manifest in the realm of pure sensation. Three years ago, in the Luxembourg Gardens in Paris, I have a happy memory of one particular spring day, when everything was bathed in that soft spring light and a light breeze was blowing. That is where you and I made a promise to travel to Spain together, a vow that so far has not yet been kept. And that, despite that fact that I have traveled so much since that moment in time. In the end, I was forced to make the trip alone. I undertook the voyage to serve as an interpreter at a conference which I couldn't refuse to attend, and all the while I was there I could do nothing but think of you. So I suppose I could say that I have visited Spain, but for me it was just as though I had never been there. This is because, for me, to truly see that country would have been to experience it together, as if with our one pair of eyes. So it is then that I am able to write so little, in terms of any record of the state of my own emotions.

Milan, March 3

In those impossibly busy days of the conference, I was robbed of any free time. In addition, I caught a cold, suffered a sore throat, and felt altogether miserable. The days passed without my writing any letters at all, and for a period that lasted virtually half a month. Nevertheless, during that time, I did find I was able to develop certain impressions and speculations. However, let me put off writing my responses to Spain for a bit, and let me address still another subject.

On the subject of "journeys," I did have time during the conference to visit Saint-Cergue, and was able to see Mont Blanc, on the far side of Lake Lehmann, its peak glittering above the clouds. This was truly an extremely significant moment for me. When the conference was over, I left for Bern, where I stayed for three days in the home of H, who was in charge of the legation there, and I was able to visit Adelboden, a ski resort not far from Interlocken. From Berlin I went on to Basel, where I saw the upper reaches of the Rhine. There was a fine Holbein in the museum there. This morning, I left Basel, took the St. Godard tunnel, and entered Italy at Lugano, arriving at the main station in Milan this afternoon at 3:47.

The train took about an hour to go from the shores of Lake Lehman to the mists of the Jura mountains. There, from the balcony of the Hotel Europe Central, high above the sheer cliffs, I looked out beyond the lake, covered in a thin mist, where, above the clouds, I could spot the main peaks of the alps, following in a line one after the other. Above the right edge rose the high, white glittering mass of Mont Blanc, soaring up in the pale blue sky of early spring. Looking at the sight, I began to think over the significance that mountains have always had for us as human beings. Looking at the mountains, for me, brings a kind of deep, true joy, touching my intimation of my own existence, a sensation unrelated to the passage of time. As I wrote to you previously, in this continuous cycle of homogeneity and crystallization, the ocean represents the former, and the mountains a symbol of the latter condition.

While I was in Bern, I observed from the balcony of my friend's house, far off in the distance, the silhouette of the Jungfrau. Here is the spot where the great European rivers, the Rhone, the Rhine, the Danube, the Po, and others, begin their courses, flowing into every corner of Europe. Yet such an image remains only an image, certainly as pertains to any natural phenomenon. Such depictions were an inspiration for Rilke, who wrote of waters given birth in the spray of the waters of the Adriatic Sea and crystallized in him when reaching all the way to the high cliffs of the Alps, an image that was to sustain him in his inner life. Filled to the brim with sadness as he was, he tenaciously walked forward, on and on.

It was in Bern, as I made my way among those gray houses now touched with the pale beginnings of spring, that I began to reflect on all the places in Europe I had not yet seen: East Germany, Poland, Ingermanland, Russia. And I thought in particular of the gloom, the sadness, and the powerful ardor of that vast country. Of course, my impressions are altogether subjective. Which reminds me that, on the train going to Adelboden, Mr. H remarked to me that that Berne resembles very closely the towns in East Germany. And then I thought of Dostoevsky. He was the writer who managed to arise from within a defiled Russian society, with its limitless melancholy, in order to create a representation of the highest reaches of the purest kind of love. I had become a devoted reader of Dostoevsky even before coming to France. My soul was able to enter into his world without hindrance. And now, I believe that I can understand the sadness he depicts to an even greater degree. Some time ago I published the book *Notes on Dostoevsky*, a work of mine for which I have a special fondness. At that time, I had not yet distanced myself from Christian ideas. I have since come to feel that he provides a mirror for my own soul as I move through my entire existence. Now, as I write this, I am reminded of the film made by Louis Jouvet, late in his career, of Graham Greene's *The Power and the Glory*.

Greene, in our own period, has deeply absorbed the spirit of Dostoevsky. He is a writer of unique stature. I have always hoped that you might read other of his novels. I have the greatest respect for what Jouvet has taken from Greene's work, and I would be pleased indeed to know that you could sense the closeness that Jouvet feels for him. In Bern, an icy thin snow is falling thick and fast, and I am in a bookstore beneath a glittering bright arcade, where I just bought several books, *Letters of a Portuguese Nun*, an edition of the letters of Abelard and Heloise, and *The Song of Solomon*.

Paris, March 24, 1956 (Saturday)

So much time has gone by that I can't manage to remember when I last wrote to you from here in Paris. During that intervening time, when I reflect on the changes that have come over me because of a growing maturity I have experienced, then what follows in not simply a continuation of what I have written before, but something altogether new, I am convinced. From the autumn two years ago until today, the progress I have achieved has brought with it a plethora of new reflections. And I do not yet know what they may truly signify.

Many sights: the Strasbourg cathedral, in a gray winter sky (Claudel called it a "rose cathedral"), its interior dominated by the yellows in the stained glass windows, as the rain and sleet fall steadily near the Rhone, standing high in the unappealing dusk, where cranes and storehouses stand at the quays; or the clumsy cathedral at Saarbrucken, rising darkly in the snow, a structure that barely manages to achieve the Gothic style; the Saar river itself, which flows past so many ruins left over from the war; or the church of Notre Dame La Grande in Poitiers, its long form, with its countrified look, standing astride the plaza on a quiet spring evening, spacious and bright—these Romanesque cathedrals, with the rich light flowing at ease into them through the stained glass windows,

their piled-up stones of white, cut with such precision in their angu-
lar fashion, in these quiet towns, themselves made of stone—so many
sights. And thus it is now, when summer comes, that in one corner of
my soul a green space suddenly opens out before me, and a variety of
reflections burst into life; these moments grow distinct in my mind and
become still more subtle. Now they begin to flow within me as though
there were no other path for them to follow. And they continue to flow
on. They will surely do so until the end of my days.

On a day when autumn had deepened, I found myself standing on the
plaza in front of Chartres cathedral. I looked up at the figure of Christ
on the façade, so filled with a sense of the Void. I then began to examine
the profound beauties of the stained-glass windows, which do indeed
beggar description. At sunset, I heard an evening mass performed with
Gregorian chants, while those verdant colors from the windows seemed
to bathe me in their shades. Then there was another occasion, in Bruges, when I stood in a corner of the park, when all the leaves had already
fallen, with the rough and freezing wind blowing, well below zero, as
I observed the structure of the cathedral, which seemed to approach me
like some enormous vessel. The canal was frozen over, and the pebbles
there made a clattering noise as they skated across the icy surface. And
then there are, of course, in Paris the changeless Notre Dame, the dark,
blackened Saint Séverin, and the church of Saint-Médard, resting in
silence in a busy square.

So yes, I have begun my life again here in Paris. By now, four months
have already passed. I have begun to seek out those emotions that first
lay within me during the prior time I lived here. The flow within me of
those prior experiences has now begun to assert itself again; there was
one stream of memory in particular that came alive in me last summer, one that seemed to spread itself out under the space of those blue
skies. I came to a consciousness that this was a kind of tributary within
the greater flow into which I had been absorbed, one that seemed to
increase in volume, expanding before me. Yet precisely, what did such
movements truly represent? What was their real nature? This is something I will perhaps only come to know in the future, perhaps the distant future. It has been as though, in my whole prior life up until now,
the water from some melting snow had moved in endless small rivulets,
pouring into rivers and valleys alike as it thawed, so that in this way
each stream began to join the larger flow of my own experiences. I do
not yet know what I might call the beginning of such a diffusion in
my interior being, in these endless gyrations. But I do know that the

process has begun, and that perhaps it is only because of this new movement that I can truly feel joy and genuinely experience sadness.

As I wrote in one or another of my earlier letters, these prior experiences—first, watching the Rhone as it flowed along, drifting into the vast swamp-like sands of the Camargue, then at the northern corner of Lake Lehmann, where the water birds were sporting in the water, so clear even to the very bottom, or when I visited the spot where the Rhone seems to begin its journey, or again, at the moment where I saw from the plaza the cathedral of Chartres rising up in the glittering afternoon light—all these memories took me back through time. Yet how is it that I can only recall the actual sensations themselves and not their deeper significance?

When I return to the sight of those things that never are subject to change—insentient nature, unmovable stones, piling up—I become conscious of these feelings in me of dissolution, of gyration. And so it is that, while still without achieving clarity, various strands in my existence start to connect, to solidify, and now begin in turn to relax, to slacken, then separate and set about again to revolve, to move about; my whole being, engulfed in this circling motion, now begins to achieve increasing moments of clarity, so that I can at last begin to feel that this flow, this movement, is all of a piece and inevitable.

So now, in this vast blue space, there is for me more light than color, more shafts of light than mere light itself, or, to put it another way, more strong points of light. These points now grow in number, they expand, and it is now possible for me to gather these innumerable points of light into my very being, so that I may join in that larger flow of light. I realize full well how imperfect, indeed how beyond the limits of possibility, any expression in words of these feelings must remain. I am convinced, however, that these feelings do not simply represent a phenomenon of nature or of my particular mental state. In the space between the Object and the Self, as each succeeding moment comes into existence, the Self sets out to make every effort to surpass itself, step by step, and with infinite patience; and just at that moment when some real progress is made, then, from within the Self, as it continues on with its daily existence, a certain separation now slowly begins to occur, and with it a certain sharpness and clarity. When that moment arrives, the Self, which has been leading an existence estranged from the true Self with which it was born, will now, on the contrary, find itself now attracted and enfolded, as it begins to be absorbed into that larger whole—all this is a phenomenon taking place inside the Self. It is precisely this phenomenon that might well be termed experience, something that therefore can only be undergone once in a lifetime. I have in recent days firmly come to grasp the nature of this process in so many ways. I use the words "once in a lifetime," yet the precise definition of this experience for each person may well be different. I firmly believe that within the span of this experience lies the meaning of any life led in sincerity. In that regard, I am describing quite a commonplace conception. It has none of the grandeur of art, of learning, of religion, or any other such thing; without such a base, however, we risk remaining without significance, and without value, so that life itself in fact becomes a falsehood, mere vanity, nothing more than a joke. Without this experience, in terms of fidelity to the Self, any true, unique meanings risk instead being merely reduced to the kind of words that can merely express nothing more than what are in fact painful delusions.

The apparently limitless sorrow captured in that flood of light that can be found captured by Van Gogh, or in the music of Bach, which within its jovial melodies seeks a harmony with the stern realities of life, or in the writings of Dostoevsky, which reveal within his ardent sense of freedom a sense the overwhelming miseries of humanity, or the sight of the spire of a cathedral, thrusting up with strength, thin and black under a half-leaden sky, or the grandeur of Aristotle's metaphysics—all of these are attempting to express the same object, all are making efforts to carry the same message, are they not?

As for my trip back to Tokyo from July to the middle of November last year, a number of central changes occurred, a process that has revealed a real ripening within me. I have no need to write anything here about the specific reasons for my return to Tokyo. It is solely the "meaning" of what happened to me that is significant. It had been a pending question for me for some time, this matter of my returning to Tokyo. Had it simply been a social matter, or some other similar circumstance, I might well never have made the trip.

I believe it was sometime in May. It was a cloudy afternoon, and I was in my room. I was sitting at my desk. I don't recall if I was in the process of writing something, or simply reading—my memories are not precise. But the fact that the day was so dark remains clear to me. The curtain was half-pulled across the window, so that the room was all the dimmer.

At that moment, for some reason or other, my thoughts idly turned to Japan. Suddenly, I had a sense of a bluish space all around me. The kind of deep, deep blue space that you see when you look down below you while on an airplane flight. But this was a small space, an intense space. And it was certainly true that when I had traveled to Japan by air, I did gain a sense of just such a deep blue below me in that vast sky. I am fond of reading about air travel, and so it may have been such descriptions of a plane climbing ever higher in the stratosphere, so that all both above and below the plane assumes a deep, homogeneous blue, that may have made such a powerful impression on me. Indeed, rather than a sense of the blue atmosphere, it might be more accurate to say that I envisioned a kind of blue cluster, filled to the brim with light. In any case, it was a beautiful, a powerful impression.

It was at that very point, I can declare, that Japan truly came into my consciousness. I had an intuition that this small, radiant blue space had begun to ferment within me, coming to grow and differentiate itself in endless ways, then began to generate a meaning, magnifying itself until the actual image of Japan began to layer itself into this larger image. It was then that I came to realize with great intensity just how much I love Japan, how much I am able to love Japan. Some may dismiss this moment as a mere dream, an idle fancy. But this was no fancy, no vague reverie. Rather, I would describe this phenomenon as something quite abstract. To the last degree, this sensation represents a kind of conceptual diagram inflected with my own emotional sentiments.

At that instant, I suddenly remembered that, some five years ago, the art historian Y had shown me in Paris a set of six lithographs by Alfred Manessier of Christ's passion and resurrection. These works, while created as far as possible in a contemporary mode of expression, revealed in each a singular purity of emotion. Indeed, it might be said that these works represent a kind of modern animism. The fact that the Soul seems to permeate, and without exception, every corner of these abstract designs, however surprisingly, and however justly, allows the spectator to understand the primal nature of his or her own consciousness. Of course, my own human experience has been different from that of the artist, so I haven't any right to lay claim to any particular interpretation. Still, at that instant, the truth remains that Manessier's vortex of remarkable colors forced themselves into my consciousness. That much is certainly the case, I can safely assert. And it goes without saying that this space inside my consciousness could give rise in turn to a sense of the Japan of my era, the Japan in which I was born and raised. And I do want to stress that it was just at that particular moment that such feelings first came into my consciousness. This was not a sensation growing out of some sort of intellectual reflection. Nor did I arrive at these thoughts through some special experience of my own. Thus it was then that, unexpectedly, I discovered the Japan within myself while in Paris.

I felt no unease or irritation about going back to Japan. Most Japanese, when they come to Paris, say that they would like to remain for an indefinite time, and I believe that for most of them this is an honest opinion. I have no reason for feeling any differently myself. Whatever one's particular personality, there is no need to have settled on any particular explanation for the existence of this feeling. One reason that allowed me to resolve to return to Japan without any sense of unease was because I knew that, apart from the fact that I knew I would soon be returning to Paris, I had already managed to create within me, as I wrote above, that basic consciousness of an internal space. And I knew as well that, even before that sense was born within me, I realized that I had come to feel altogether comfortable living here in Paris. For so many reasons, I felt a sense of gratitude for this conviction.

My Air France plane was soon already over the smoky, calm Mediterranean sea, first flying over the rough sandy landscapes of Arabia and Iraq, then over India (which had already yielded too much of its verdure) then over Indochina. Finally, on July 5, after a noon stop in a sweltering Manila, my plane at length set out toward Tokyo. All day long, looking out my round cabin window, I watched island after island as the plane moved forward. This was not some ordinary sentimentality on my part. Nor a simple sense of delight. Nor simply a consciousness of natural beauty. Rather, that alluring sense of luminosity that appeared in my consciousness now seemed in the twinkling of an eye to grow larger, expand, adopt a precise configuration, then divide itself up again in a complex fashion. Indeed, it was this process that provided me with a such a source of profound beauty.

From the west, a layer of radiant white clouds covered these islands, stretching on and on from north to south. Here and there a break in the clouds allowed me to catch a glimpse of the earth below. Here was not the simple beauty of nature. Here was a homogeneity of human endeavor that pervaded the land, the beauty of a human culture. This was the first time for me to witness such a sight of this kind of beauty since my plane took off from the Italian peninsula. Now, a layer of dense black clouds began to move intermittently underneath the bright clouds that lay above them. This movement made me think that it must be raining somewhere off in the far distance. Going beyond the storm, this deep blue sky, limitless and silent, seemed to contain the turmoil and peacefully engulf the entire pliant archipelago. No magnet could have pulled my eyes from the sight.

So began my stay of three and a half months in Japan; when this period was finished, I boarded a plane in late autumn. On the evening of the eighteenth of November, I landed in the outskirts of Paris as a light drizzle was falling. And so I began again my life in France, an existence correctly planned to a fault, yet not always hospitable, hard, even merciless. I felt myself tightening clear to the core of my being. I could feel the startling density of this culture.

At two in the morning of the twenty-fifth, I find myself, as usual, writing to you in my rented room on the fifth floor of my lodging house on the Rue Abbé de l'Epée. Yesterday I went to observe with care the Egyptian collection at the Louvre, a rare occasion for me. I have not been there for a long time. The lectures on literature I have been attending ended several days ago, my teaching duties at the Asian language school had finished as well, and the Easter vacation has now arrived. So I am feeling a bit relaxed and am able to sit and write to you.

Despite the fact that it is the middle of the night on the Rue Gay-Lussac, some kind of vehicle goes by every few seconds. On the left-hand side of my desk is a book containing lectures by Tsuda Sōkichi on the *Kojiki* and the *Nihongi*, as well as the notes I've taken on Japanese literature, all piled together.[3] Above them there is a kind of clumsy tin stand, which throws shafts of reflected light in my direction. Nearby is an old alarm clock, which, while broken, still manages to make a sound at unexpected moments. Behind all of this is a box of sweets, brought from Japan, a textbook on the Japanese language, a book on Japanese literature by Michel Revon, a book on Chinese traditional medicine, Husserl's study of phenomenology, notebooks, an attendance roster for my students, and a small dictionary, the *Petit Larousse*. On the right, a radio receiver, a detailed guide to the Louvre, an anthology of poetry from the *Kojiki* and *Nihongi*, several kinds of histories of Japanese literature, an address book, a Japanese–French dictionary published by Sanseidō, an ashtray filled to the brim with the remains of so many Gauloises I have smoked, and the Larousse dictionary of synonyms, all scattered about. Facing me is a jar of honey given to me by J, and a painting from Rome given to me by M of the ruins of the temple to Athena at Delphi. Now I really do think it is time to truly start writing to you.

These days, whatever I've been lecturing to my students, I have been reading some ancient Japanese poetry. I found this particular poem of great beauty, so I will attach the text here as a way to finish my letter.

The divine prince of eight thousand spears,
finding no wife to pillow in the country of eight islands,
hearing that there was a wise woman
far away, in the country of Koshi,
set out to pay court to her,
came here to pay court.
My sword thongs, still untied,
my mantle still untied,
at the wooden door where the maiden sleeps
I stand, pushing and shaking,
I stand, pulling and shoving.
On the green hills thrushes are calling;
birds of the field, pheasants echo;
birds of the garden, roosters call.
Damn them all, all those calling birds!
Won't someone hit those birds and shut them up?
This is the way the story's told
by the low-running fisherman messenger.[4]

The style of these ancient poems, which seem to depict the islands of Japan from some far-off vantage point in the upper reaches of sky over the Pacific Ocean, reveal a certain homogeneity in their tone. This image of witnessing such a scene from a great distance differs from the way in which other places in the world might be observed for example: the heaviness found in the southern countries, a mixture of pallid and dark, with their blackened sea water, or the rough sands of Mesopotamia, or Cyprus, or again Athens, composed, like Corinth, of hard stone, or even the Western European countries, with their lofty densities. The image of Japan in these poems, rather, shows a sense of abundance, one bathed in a clarity of light, gentle in its extended length, homogeneous, wrapped in a blue space, which itself spreads outward. The impressions that these poems evoke and the tonality expressed in their depiction of the birth of these islands concur altogether with my own personal response to these images.

Paris, March 26 (Monday)

As far as I am concerned, it seems that even after that decisive moment in which I felt I had managed with one intensive stroke to seize hold of my path, time still continues to pass, yet I still find myself unable to accomplish anything much.

One evening, as it grew dark, I found myself walking by the Jardin du Luxembourg. A bitter wind was blowing under the gas lamps, just as all the young sprouts of the chestnut trees were opening out. Then I passed the Senate buildings, went on down the Rue Touron, and followed the meandering Rue Saint Sulpice, which turns off to the left. The unusual towers of the church there gravely towered up into the dark sky. I have so often remembered my impression that the style in these towers were built seem somehow inferior to those of a cathedral in the Landes area of France, which lies on top of a hill, far above the swirling activities of the port. Those reveal a greater, a true vitality, giving me an impression of something akin to certain Asian architectural styles. Turning the corner of the Rue Mabillon, I moved toward the Rue du Four, where the old apartment buildings, all clustered together, emit a thick odor distinctive to Paris.

I arrived at Number 8, and following along the handrail as I descended the stone steps, I tapped on the door of Mr. S, which faces a small interior garden, also fenced with stone. This is the atelier of a bookbinder I know, and this space calls to my mind Rembrandt's painting [*The Philosopher in Meditation*]. Here, everything is quiet, somber, as though a unique moment had arrived from the distant past, one which has appeared without falsification, a space that opens out in this silent light and seems to envelop me.

It was just a moment such as this that has allowed me to reach a deeper understanding of the words "to exist." A profound comprehension that this primal condition exits prior to any other possibilities, such as "to learn" or "to make," even prior to the very act of "living" itself. As for consciousness, experience, or even thought itself, all those elements of one's ongoing life, a comparison with this far more profound and prior "existence" seems inevitable, no matter however artificial, prone to fallacy, even ludicrous such a comparison may appear to be.

And one can only shudder at the pain we human beings must undergo before we can manage to catch a first glimpse of this primal "existence" as we slowly come to understand it. Indeed, such an understanding can only come from the totality of all our own actual human experience.

Each human being lives in the company of others. This makes me think in turn of an old Scottish tale:

> In the midst of a stormy winter night, a group of soldiers are sitting in one room of a castle, stirring the fire as they continue their night watch. Suddenly a small bird flies in from the outer darkness into the room, and, an instant later, flies out again on the other side of the chamber into the night. The king speaks. "Such is the life of a human being," he says. The light, which has quietly been spread about, now gradually tapers off and quickly dies out in the darkness beyond.

There is nothing that represents the opposite of "existence." If there were, it could only be "to die." What a fearsome opposition. And what a stillness this represents. Only such experiences as love and friendship, when they come to us human beings, can remain the only exceptions to that frightful silence.

On top of a crude wooden table some large carrots, potatoes, cabbage, bacon, and a few other things which, having been steamed, are now all piled on a plate. Nearby is a pot of *soupe de poisson*. A large round loaf of bread has just been cut. This all resembles the kind of favorite meal that any Parisian might enjoy, yet it is different as well, more redolent of a touch of the real France, the endless rolling countryside that spreads out between the Pyrenees and the Massif Central.

A large bus passes with its green lights, its diesel engine chugging away in the depths of the night, when there are few people about. It stops at the corner of the Rue Vieux Colombier. I board the bus and go back to my room.

When I wrote to you a few days ago, I used the words "shafts of light" and "points of light," but I am not sure that these phrases are altogether accurate. These terms may be too visual. My words of explanation may seem a bit complicated, but I would now prefer to use the terms "pure sensation," or rather "sensation in a pure state." All true experience, and in consequence, all thought, begins from this point. I am not sure just how I can explain this. But if we make efforts to delve deeply into the matter, both in detail and in a larger context, then what I refer to is that moment when the larger truth of reality itself recedes behind the details. Therefore, this state of pure sensation is not subjective in nature, but, deep as the very nature of sensation itself. It thus manifests itself in a strict relationship with the object in question. This is surely the "point of light" to which I have been referring. Such is one kind of symmetry that is possible in sensation. It can be compared, perhaps, to several sounds joining together.

This reminds me in turn of the subject of the sublime Trinity fugue, written for pipe organ by Bach. This theme, composed of six notes—E-flat, B-flat, F, A-flat, G, A-flat—reveals a purity of emotion that incorporates just such a pure state of sensation. These are not merely subjective feelings, but because of the musical freight the music bears, these sounds take on a limitless individuality. There were surely no other composers besides Bach who were able to develop themes, as he did, into such musical structures. Such is the truth that defines the individual. As I suggested earlier, the continuation of an experience can be the same as the essential experience itself.

Well, let me put an end to this theorizing, which I scarcely can understand myself. What I am trying here today is to make an attempt to explicate what I have come to understand as the nature of that starting point from which all my own life efforts have proceeded.

What attracted me to Bach when I began to play his music as a young person were the sensations I experienced when I heard, while playing a gigue of his, the musical modulations when whole steps and half steps were entwined together, producing a cluster of sensations. When I experienced this while I was playing along, it seemed to me that I could see the face of the composer, with all its special and particular qualities. Thus a line in Pascal's *Pensées*, a particular section in Descartes's *Meditations*: both, in the sense I previously described, became the point of departure for my studies. By this I don't mean to suggest that this was the result of any sort of troublesome intellectual research. Rather, this was the development of a systemization of my own experience, nothing more. And such being the case, I was eventually able to develop within me the kind of patience needed to carry out such complex intellectual research.

Today was one of those beautifully clear days. Last night, after I got home so late, I lay down and immersed myself in reading the *Kagerō nikki*, and now, after a whole day has passed, my powerful reactions to that text have still not dissipated.[5] As a matter for my own personal homework, as it were, I have been glancing through many of the Japanese classics—the *Kojiki*, the *Nihon shoki*, the *Man'yōshū*, writings dating before the Heian period, then diaries from medieval times.[6] In doing so, something has begun to crystallize in me. It will be many years before I can grasp the significance of it all. However, even before I can attempt to achieve this level of comprehension, there is an important problem I face. It is the question of the significance of the kind of concentration of human experience that constitute our "culture." This matter, in turn, is directly related in turn to issues of tradition. And the fact that tradition has such a powerful meaning. Is this not because, objectively speaking, both the substance and the contents of our emotional responses seem somehow fixed and certain? Therefore, the issue becomes the real nature of that certitude. I myself believe that such certitude is in fact secondhand, and mediated.

All of my remarks here have become quite complicated, but the essence of what I want to say is that, as culture involves the use of subjective concentration and diligence. Yet to put it another way, if human vanity is involved, then there can be no true forward movement at all. For example, at the time when the cathedral of Rheims was built, the animals that collapsed as they hauled the stones to the top of the hill as they continued on with such diligence, reveal a far greater humanity than their masters, for it is they who were participating in the creation of a genuine "culture." Still, I believe there is little good that can be done in thinking over and over again concerning such fine points, and I have no interest in pursuing these thoughts any further.

March 27 (Tuesday), fine weather

Yesterday evening I received a request from the European branch of NHK to give a talk on the occasion of the 360th anniversary of the birth of Descartes.[7] Here is a gist of my remarks I recorded today in their offices at the Rue Grenelle.

Descartes was born on March 31, 1596, in the town of La Haye, located on the left bank of the Creuse river, in a westerly area of southern France, exactly 360 years ago. It appears that there are celebrations of this event all over Europe. As far as I am concerned, the lasting significance of Descartes lies in his unflinching efforts to throw light on some of the most difficult of human problems. The spirit of Descartes, the so-called Cartesian spirit, can be said to represent the spirit of France itself, but most of his admirers have not truly reflected on the deeper meanings involved. For it is not simply the fact that, all these centuries later, his work is still being taught in the classrooms in the philosophy departments of universities around the world, but that the issues he raised must remain central to all who engage in any kind of serious reflection. This suggests the breadth of his powerful influence.

Valéry wrote that, without Descartes, the act of thinking itself would be virtually impossible. Alain wrote that in studying the work of Descartes one comes in contact with the greatest of teachers. In Sartre's writings on freedom, Descartes's speculations on his personal concept of free will cannot be separated from proofs of the existence of God. And it goes without saying that, in terms of university faculty and researchers, the contributions of Descartes continue on in significance even today.

For me, it is Descartes who discovered, within himself, and indeed within every human being, the fact that each of us knows we exist by the process of thinking. It is he who earned the honor of firmly establishing this universal principle. Furthermore, to put the matter another way, Descartes must be esteemed for the fact that he was the one who, at one given moment in the flow of his own experiences, was able to seize anew a sense of the essence of the universe as it opened itself out to him, and as it came to reveal itself even as it extended even into the future. Moreover, there is also the fact that Descartes approached his sense of this developing structure of experience with a sense of passion on his own part. Such academic categories as Idealism and Materialism may be convenient, if somewhat crude, categories of academic philosophy, but they reveal little of any true significance. As for the articulation of any such fixed classifications, Descartes opposed any such abstractions because of the very existence of those passions that are found in real life itself. This conviction represents the ardor of one individual, one ordinary human being. In the famous *Discours de la méthode* [*Discourse on Method*] of Descartes, the vivid appearance of the author as an ordinary man is well-sketched in the first and second sections, as well as in the fifth.

On November 10 of the year 1619, Descartes moved to Ulm. At that time, he took the rank of a young commissioned officer under the command of Maximilian I, elector of Bavaria. At that period, he took a profound interest in the already flourishing studies of the natural sciences, and in particular, in the fields of physics and mathematics. On that famous evening of November 10, he had a dream, a revelation. It as though all the knowledge in the world could now be contained in one lexicon, here intensified, providing for him the sense of some central point of unification, so that, for him, a cognizance of the whole world could now be organized afresh. Moreover, he was convinced that this new world, in whatever eventuality, does in fact correspond altogether with the actual world as it is. Indeed, it is clear from his writings how passionately he felt about these abstract insights. The core of his vision involves the fact that he revealed a fresh concern over the heretofore-accepted views of the natural world. He could now examine that world through the purity of his own sensations, allowing him to make use of the methods of deductive reasoning as a basis for deepening his thought, as can be seen in his *Principia philosophiae* [*Principles of Philosophy*], where his system came into full fruition. Here, this purity of the human spirit is not limited to any particular closed mathematical or philosophical system but now allows for the development of any variety of human activity. For Alain, Descartes's method of philosophical speculation greatly expanded our ability to experience the sculptural arts and literature. Valéry, in his writings on Leonardo da Vinci, for example, found that Descartes's methods provide a highly successful strategy for analyzing the pictorial arts. And in my own view, it seems to be true that, as far as Valéry was concerned, there is little substantive difference between Descartes and Mallarmé.

Therefore, the best way to grasp Descartes is through his own personal experience rather than through the examination of some fully developed philosophical system. Thus, as concerns his metaphysics, he can be seen as testing the savants at the Sorbonne, while at the same time his ethical system aroused the concerns of many. Today, achieving a greater understanding of Descartes's conception of the actual realities of human existence represents, I believe, the most advanced aspect of contemporary research on this philosopher.

There is no need here to go into a lengthy description of the thought of Descartes, but one element in his work that has particularly attracted me personally is his explanation of the nature of morality. Observing his expressions concerning morality in such phrases as "the self-sufficiency of the ego," "high-mindedness," or "having no fear of death" and others, I cannot help but identify certain meanings in consonance with Eastern thought in his description of the function of self-denial. This view bears a strong relationship to his own basic intuitions, so that, based solely on those intuitions and his personal experience, he was able to give meaning to his own existence. The basis for Descartes's need to base his happiness on his own self-reliance was dependent in turn on his ardor for an abstract consciousness of the existence of just such a pure state. And this pure state, for him, did not only involve the creation of abstractions from the complexities of reality. Rather, these abstractions were supported through his intuitions precisely *because* of that sense of reality in which he was able to envelop himself. The quality of his perceptions was determined by the way in which he faced the actual world.

So it was that Descartes, by finding within himself the kernel of a whole world, and by striving to attach equivalent abstract values to the world around him, was a philosopher who could truly open himself up in all ways to that world.

It is well known that Descartes disliked settling down and often moved his residence from place to place. He was a lonely traveler. Still, he was not an adventuresome voyager; his only movements were in the most civilized countries of Europe. He turned his attention to France, then Holland, Germany, then later to Italy; in Holland he roamed about incessantly, readily changing his residence from place to place; in the end, he arrived in Stockholm, where he died soon after. I have never attempted to follow in his footsteps, nor indeed have I had any particular interest in doing so. Still, while traveling around in Europe myself, I have occasionally visited places where his own path had taken him.

While in Paris, during the period from 1626 to 1628, Descartes became increasingly estranged from his friends and apparently led a solitary life. I imagine that, walking along the banks of the Seine, the sights we now experience today must remain not altogether different from those of three hundred years ago. Tugboats piled high with coal move slowly up and down the river, soft rays of sunlight filter down from the thin clouds covering the sky like threads of silk, enveloping the white stone churches and other buildings. Near the stone pavements running along both sides of the river, pigeons throng together, and seagulls cross paths as they fly over the wide, flowing waters.

Then too, when taking the train toward the plains of Touraine, the area of France from which he came, one can see that the scenery soon takes on a rural air, so different from the suburbs of Paris, and the view is now filled with all sorts of bushes and trees, or fields, all part of an undulating landscape; here the waters of the Loire flow so gently that it is hard to determine whether or not the water is moving at all. The riverbanks are covered with the drooping branches of elm trees, and the beautiful plants by the riverbank are soaked in the moving flow. The multicolored sky is streaked with white clouds spread like thin silk threads, and there is no sign of any human presence in the fields.

When I visited Amsterdam, where the philosopher spent time as well, my arrival took place in the middle of autumn. The water was in motion in the darkened canals, and the lights of the city were reflected there in a charming fashion. It must have been the same in the seventeenth century as it is today, I imagine. The city itself was immaculate, and, as soon as you turn off the main roads, very quiet. On either side were rows of houses, with their fronts all rising up in pointed structures, all constructed in characteristic shades of brick, lining up one after the other, while various boats moved soundlessly up and down the canals. Occasionally a drawbridge would go up or down to accommodate them.

Descartes was nurtured in the midst of these quiet natural surroundings and within a culture of scrupulousness and caution. From here he made a fresh attempt to construct the basis for a new culture, one built on the idea of a restoration of a pure state, that of an abstract conception of humanity fully enveloped in reality, created from sensations and filled with ardor. And this pure spirit became the kernel of a new civilization, one that, in various ways, still continues on to the present day.

March 30 (Friday), Good Friday

A muggy day. I already have taken my evening meal at a restaurant at the corner of the Rue St. Germain and Rue St. Jacques, then dragged my weary feet back to my lodgings. When I turned on the switch of the radio, I soon heard a touching and familiar chorus from Bach's *Saint John Passion* (a performance by the chorus of the choir of the church of Saint-Guillaume in Strasbourg), which flowed over me like an incoming tide. Three years ago, at Westminster in London on Christmas morning, I heard a hymn-like piece that led me back to my childhood. When I hear one of the *Passion* settings of Bach, it is not simply a question of my listening to music that is sorrowful in itself. This music leads me to understand the totality of a whole universe, one redolent with grief. Thus, once permeated with these sounds, I begin to wonder where I am, and what the significance of this music I now hear with such a sense of deep emotion. This experience hints to me of the weight of the burdens I bear. Today, this response has been murmuring within my heart, again and again, ever since this morning. "Time stretches out far in the future, so then patience." So, it is that I now feel this sense of time, which stretches far into the distance, here transformed into a specific period of time I myself must pass through. And as a result, there is born in me a sense of patience and self-denial, and to a depth I have never experienced before.

March 31, 10:00 p.m. (Saturday)

While I was writing my most recent letter to you, I had a visit from I, the philosopher, who came from Munich to see me, and so I never completed it. So let me continue on writing now.

Last night, I and I went for a walk along the boulevards late into the night, ending up in a plaza that adjoins the Seine, where we made our way from its eastern tip in order to come as close as possible for a good view of Notre Dame. For some reason or other the lights on the cathedral were so dim that only the façade jutted up in the darkness. I have retained strong memories of where the paths can be found on both sides of the river, now lost to us in the darkness. These days, I realize that, as far as my observations of cathedrals and churches are concerned, their special characteristics have been somehow distorted, seemingly now a bit dim and faded. The term "cathedral," in my present consciousness, seems to me to follow a path from Carolingian to Romanesque, from Romanesque to Gothic, then from Gothic to structures built in the Renaissance, quietly revealing a complete shift from one style to another.

As for me, I have been inordinately fond of the Romanesque. And the high point of this style was surely the somewhat countrified cathedral in the town of Avila, near Segovia, in Spain. Then in France, there are in particular the Romanesque churches in Poitiers and Saint-Gilles, which I never grow weary of visiting. Still, there is surely some arbitrary risk in my choices. Indeed, I do not know why I was originally attracted to the beauties of this style. What captured my allegiance (and the same may be true for so many others who admire the Romanesque as well) was not dependent on the outward form of these structures. There are doubtless many others, of course, who find themselves attracted by the outward appearance of these churches. And I take my hat off to them. But such was not the case for me. I eventually came to grasp precisely why, in this style of architecture, the walls were so thick and the window openings were so small. I could imagine the spirit of Christianity somehow trapped within these walls; and that this one singular spirit began to grow and spread from such buildings, eventually to conquer the world, developing to the point where differences between the Self and the external world were no longer altogether so important. This understanding suddenly came to me one day in Paris when, as I was passing by the church of Saint-Étienne-du-Mont, on the Rue Clovis, I noticed the large windows in the Gothic flamboyant style and the flying buttresses that held up the walls of the building. At that moment, thinking over the profound meaning of such styles, I now seemed to grasp the real nature of these deeper connections, so difficult to articulate, all the more keenly.

As for me, I have, and with my whole spirit, now come to acknowledge that, putting aside the question of styles altogether, I am drawn ever closer to the inner spirit which gave birth to all these styles. So now, for me, these various forms of architecture, including the Gothic and those created in the Renaissance, all these forms of Christian architecture, lose the significance of their external differences. All revert to a higher state of pure form. Just as each person sees themselves in the category of a "human being," and every man imagines the visage of his mother as the face of all women, so, I would like to believe, I can recognize this deeper style that engulfs those superficial differences.

April 1, evening, Easter Sunday

How many times, since coming to Paris, has it suddenly occurred to me on some afternoon or other to pay a visit to the church of St. Denis, in the northern suburbs of Paris? Looking up at this square building standing in the corner of the square, so washed by time, and now so blacked, I am somehow struck with an ineffable sense of melancholy. In olden days the location for the tombs of the royal family, the church now looks somehow abandoned in a corner of this quartier in a working-class district. Today, the desolate church tower seems to rise unsteadily below a leaden sky.

Inside, I came into the middle of the evening mass for Easter. In the choir seats there were only a couple of old people, joining their prayers with the sound of the organ. For those who know the history of the past glories of this church, this present desolation is more than merely sorrowful. Even now, the sound of those hymns takes me back thirty years ago to the Catholic chapel in Tokyo's Kudan area.

In the transept of St. Denis, I looked with care at the beautiful, aristocratic twelfth century stained-glass windows installed there. Why is it that, despite the fact that I have come here many times before, I never before paid much attention to them? They have a beauty quite different from those produced in the ateliers of Chartres or Bruges. I realized that I had never until now taken account of their deep blue hue, with their golden borders. I became keenly aware of just how much time and patience are required to grasp the true nature of any single object.

Despite these observations, however, today this church as a whole does not create an image of beauty. And I don't believe that my impressions are based on effects of the weather or on my own sense of personal well-being on any particular day. As various aspects of the churches in France go in and out of focus in my mind, my impressions have become, in fact, all the more vivid. Thus, conversely, both the significance of the individual elements and of the whole have become all the clearer to me. And because my inner spirit has become increasingly able to define more precisely its own nature, I can be freed from the various forms by which it has formerly defined itself. Now, my freed and liberated sensations can continue their responses without hindrance, and with a lively response. And so, indeed, the essential nature of the human structures of humanity itself now have become clearer to me as well. As for myself, I therefore sense a certain leeway, and I feel more relaxed as I come to discover in myself a fresher and keener response to the exterior aspects of these churches.

Perhaps I sense you may find in these letters, written to continue on with the thoughts that I have been expressing to you for so long, a new sense of my difficulties in properly expressing myself to you. There is an important reason for this. For as I continue this correspondence, it seems to me that I have somehow veered away from articulating what remains for me the central issue at stake for me. I am having trouble expressing what is really in my heart.

In fact, I seem unable as yet to grasp the precise nature of what, in fact, I really do wish to express. To explain this in simple terms, I have been made to feel that, in fact, a whole new horizon is now opening up before me. And what does this horizon represent? Specifically, it seems that the past is slowly flowing back into the midst of the present. Moreover, I believe that a path to the future may have begun to be provided to me as well. This has truly been an invaluable experience for me. It is not simply a matter of recovering my dim memories of the past, but rather of the past again directly flowing back to me into the present, so that I can discern what still has value, and what remains important, so that I can take up just those particular things again, while becoming indifferent to all that now has come to seem meaningless, contemptible, or superficial. Thus, I can at last take consciousness, as I cross over time, of my essential nature and of the real importance of the experiences I have been through. This is not a matter of mere reminiscence, particular memories of "the good old days," or any sort of sentimentality, but rather something more astringent, less forgiving. It is to adopt an unsparingly analytical attitude, making use of the appropriate means to analyze each entity according to its own standard of worth. As for the process of taking apart the past, on the whole I admire to the highest degree those entities which are able to oppose any exhaustive analysis. Or, perhaps it would be better to say that the appearance of such an entity should elicit my admiration. By the same token, it must be said that these are rare. That fact alone makes me respect such exceptions. It is in this spirit that I believe I can understand the respect that the philosopher Alain had for the philosopher Jules Langneau. We use such terms as "admire," "assessment," "scorn," or "indifference," yet these words are not so simple as they seem, a fact I am slowly beginning to understand for myself. Even such extreme terms as "love" and "hate" are by no means easy to deal with in such terms. Therefore, even should the past come flooding back, its reappearance alone is not of significance in and of itself. Rather, this represents the fact that I *myself*, as I was in the past, am now brought back before my eyes again. And this bears no relation to any personal decision on my part, one way or the other. It is the actual past itself, in all truth, that must provide for one's ultimate judgment of oneself. And at that moment, none of those various images of that past, in and of themselves—whether they relate to the things one loves, one hates, one respects, one scorns—can either be denied or simply considered as still remaining up for discussion. They are now already fixed and certain.

Yet this level of understanding represents no more than a first step. After this, how best to proceed? I do not know. The very thought is intimidating. This must be the reason why the certitude comes into being that a human, despite all his limitations, can be converted into a God. European culture, itself the result of an accumulation of countless powerful experiences, has endured endless cycles of human involvement. When I first came to fully realize the nature of the complex process involved in this ferment, I found myself somehow assaulted with an unhappy sense of despair within myself. The meaning of such words as "history," "tradition," "the classic"—how was I to respond to them? These came to present an intrinsic, enormous weight for me.

In the case of Montaigne's essays, for example, what is revealed there represents not only a recording of the cycle of his own personal experiences during his lifetime, but a leisurely exposition of the entire movement of European civilization in his period, as well as the outpouring of the new ideas that followed. Such writers who contemplate morality, down to Marcel Proust, continued without pause to participate in this process. It was through my observation of Rilke's sharpened sense of his own morbid emotional sensitivities, the unusual depth of his introspection, and his thorough egoism, that I began to fully grasp the phenomenon of such paradoxical relationships in European culture. At any rate, Rilke was forced to finish by enduring them.

So it is, then, that my admiration of the stained-glass windows at Chartres can only remain a superficial response on my part, and it can only be with a certain sense of despair that I can try to imagine the radiance of the depth of a soul truly encompassed by that thousandfold depth of beauty.

Paris, April 6

Today it is gray and overcast. This afternoon, I went to the Ministry of Education on the Rue Grenelle for my payment and then went by the Rue de Notre Dame de Victoire to have my voucher cashed at the Prefectural Bureau. These days I have a lot of bills to pay, so my original travel plans for my spring vacation to visit the river basin areas of the Danube could not be realized; too bad, but there was nothing to be done about it. As I was hoping to meet Heinemann in Koln, you can imagine how complicated my feelings were when I received a postcard from him anticipating my visit.[8] My plans for this Easter vacation were to begin in Koln, go through Ulm and Munich, then go from Saarbrucken and Vienna and finish by visiting Venice and Rome. Given the fluidity of my financial situation, however, the best I can do is to make some shorter visits to some regions within France itself.

Crossing the Rue Mabillon, I was hoping for a brief meeting with my friend L, who was here from Völklingen in the Saar, but he was worried about a possible bus strike, and did not come, so I walked on in the direction of the Quartier Latin.

Tomorrow is my time to study with my instructor H, and, thinking to buy some tofu, I went around behind the Panthéon, then went up the Rue École Polytechnique and arrived near the church of Saint-Étienne-du-Mont. The forward section of the structure, jutting out from a row of stone houses that looked as though they were ready to tumble down, loomed before me under a gray sky, its massive shape a mixture of the Flamboyant Gothic and Renaissance. At the time I thought to myself what a joy it was to have such a building right here in Paris.

Dusk had now fallen on these streets, and there were few passersby. Occasionally, an automobile would arrive from the direction of

Maubert, then turn around and disappear again. Is it because the area is so hilly, perhaps, that there are no large buildings in the area? There are random store fronts here, a Chinese restaurant painted in red, a trading company, with large glass windows covered with gauze curtains so that the inside is obscured, and a small café at the corner, just what you would expect in some suburban spot. Yet this is only one corner in Paris, soaked in today's unremarkable atmosphere in this gray city. I could hear music coming from somewhere or other. Yet this delightful moment too soon vanished altogether.

When I turned the corner at the plaza by the Panthéon, a cold wind was blowing and my thoughts soon turned to other matters. All of these buildings here—the Panthéon, the Lycée Henri Quatre, the Saint-Geneviève Library, and the Law School—have left no real shadow on my consciousness. Coming out of the Place de L'Estrapade into the Rue Saint Jacques, I went into a small restaurant, my accustomed spot, to have a meal.

It's finally time, I think, for me to write something again about the sense of dread I have felt in Paris. I must be careful to point out that these problems are altogether my own, and they do not relate in any way to others. And these serious problems are connected to the fact that I have lived in this city for such a long time.

Just short of six years ago, toward the end of September, I boarded a French steamship and made the long journey to Europe. Before boarding the ship, I was quietly terrified. Should I give up the project altogether?—I said this to myself as a joke. My professor, Watanabe Kazuo, laughed, then kindly said to me, "Oh, go ahead and go, at least to see the roofs of the houses in Marseille!" And he began to teach me some everyday phrases in French so that I could get around.

The section of the voyage that I enjoyed the most was the passage from Saigon through Singapore, until we arrived at Djibouti. I felt some unease about the West, but at that point, I still felt that it was somehow far, far away.

Paris, April 9 (Monday)

I feel somewhat ill today, and despite the fact that this is the beginning of the academic calendar, I telephoned to the school office to say that I needed to take off the entire day tomorrow.

I didn't feel up to cooking something for myself, and so, in the afternoon, I went as far as the old Prado snack bar to eat some lunch, and then I returned to the area by the side of the Sorbonne, a neighbor-hood that Rilke mentioned. I learned that Heinemann was back from Germany, and apparently ill with a cold, but despite that, several people were coming to see him, so that he surely would not be able to get any of the rest which he so badly needs. Some sort of fatigue and lassitude seemed to sink into me, both in body and in mind. As though the whole landscape was shrinking, compacting, changing as if seen through a lens, and without a trace of sentiment, some mindless shift was begin-ning. Now, in turn, my sense of the nature of the outer world began to be filled with countless illusions and hallucinations.

When I reached the corner of the Rue Soufflot and the Rue St. Jacques, the Panthéon somehow looked grotesquely huge to me, mak-ing me feel as though the Rue Soufflot itself were a blind alley. Yet this sensation seemed accurate to me, so that the plaza on either side of the Panthéon appeared to be drained of energy, in line with my own feelings.

To resume: after the ship passed through the Suez Canal and entered the Mediterranean at Port Said, the water and the atmosphere alike seemed softer and more transparent, surrounding us in a sort of haze. My uneasiness now started to rise, and I began to feel a sort of helpless despair. Passing through the straits of Messina in the depths of the night, where both sides of the passageway were brightened so beauti-fully with countless lights, I felt something approaching a total lack of any emotion. I felt like turning my eyes from the sight. I can find no way to explain these sorts of feelings to you. Even though I told myself that this was Europe, I felt myself unwittingly plunging into a place somehow dangerous for me to go, and indeed, realizing that I had in fact already done so.

Thinking this over, I realized that of course I was not the only one with such feelings and reactions. There are, at bottom, many who share such a response. This is surely because, when face to face with their own culture, most people do hold a number of feelings in common, includ-ing certain darker sensations, including their perceptions of the exis-tence within them of a certain coldheartedness in the conduct of their daily lives. In such circumstances, human kindness can no longer be relied upon, so that, above and beyond a person's economic value and his labor, one's intuition suggests that there may be no further mean-ing to life. There is a sense that, although human feelings do exist, these feelings themselves, when thrust into the midst of an unfeeling social system, cannot be directly relied upon. But I did not grasp the import of such things at the time. So, driven by some sort of apprehension and uneasiness, I finally arrived in Marseille.

Since then, almost six years have passed. I have been able to analyze within myself these feelings of unease and dread, and I believe that I can say without exaggeration that I have been able to pinpoint the nature of those feelings through a certain process of coalescence within myself. In the interim, I have been pulled about by new sensations, and I have tried to embrace them. I have generated fresh responses concerning the relationship between man and Nature that have now opened up before me. Many interpretations can be placed on those feelings. Yet as far as I myself am concerned, this process has truly ignited something within me. Still, I cannot get beyond my initial response. For just when I first begin to feel a sense of tranquility in myself, my sense of unease inevitably returns again.

Six years ago, I found a space within myself, quite accidentally and in a haphazard fashion, which revealed to me the possibility that this vague but powerful sense of dread might possibly at some point be extinguished. Within the flood of sensations I was feeling at the time, however, it was clear to me that at that particular moment the means to do so were as yet still hidden within me. I had the feeling of a painful isolation among all these buildings of stone, inside them and outside of them as well. Yet at the same time, those sensations, and so many others like them, seemed to be no more than surface manifestations piling up in various ways, suggesting a still deeper unease. Essentially, however, these exterior objects merely existed in and of themselves. There was absolutely no will within them, in and of themselves, to intimidate or frighten. Yet in my exhausted state of mind, the Panthéon looked as though it might confront the wide Rue Soufflot and bring it to ruin, and then at that very moment when, fatigued as I was, I observed all of this in a state of apathy, everything seemed to return to nothing more than its original shape. And, in the midst of my observing this shift, I suddenly became aware of the existence of some indescribable beauty. True, I cannot be sure that this was really so. Both my body and my spirit were so fatigued that I could not be certain that such beauty had any objective existence.

At the beginning of these letters you may remember that I referred briefly to "Listen to the voices of the sea" [kike wadatsumi no koe].[9] I wrote there of the beauty to be found in inanimate nature as reflected in the eyes of those who confront death. As for myself, at this moment I certainly cannot compare myself in any way to those praiseworthy and brave young souls. Yet I feel that even now I now can begin, however dimly, to sense such beauty as reflected in my own eyes as well. It is not a question of simply understanding the essence of this beauty, or of capturing a sense of it, but rather, literally, as I say, to find it "reflected" in me. At such a moment, Nature and the outer world are no longer represented to me as subjective or delusional; I escape this state and can now see in myself a reversion to a proper sense of objects as they actually exist. This change represents for me not merely a perception of how things look as they appear on the surface, but suggest a deeper, essential reality that lies beyond exterior and interior alike. And at such a moment I do believe that some actual change comes over me, a change possible because I have become able to grasp the relevant aspect of any object that seizes my attention.

I found myself staring absent-mindedly at an elegant group of apartments built of stone near the Champ de Mars. Across from the Eiffel Tower, the ordered shape of the Palais de Chaillot could be seen, situated on a rise in the land. Between them quietly flowed the Seine, filled with young fish swimming upstream, both banks filled to overflowing from the melting snow. I sensed a limitless distance between this scene and myself. This year, when I visited Notre Dame and Chartres, with a friend, or when I visited the Cathedral at Perugia, with its jewel-like chancel, no music now comes to me from them. In how many centuries, in how many tens of centuries, how many shifting streams of time have we observed them drawing close to us, even if by chance? And what essential connection might they have to us? Whatever we may be thinking, whatever we might be expressing, what real meaning can they have for us? When something, in and of itself, is made manifest to us, then its reverse, fierce and indifferent, soon appears as well. Only Nature, unique in itself, can serve as the common factor to illuminate such a depth of solitude. Surely such thoughts and desires must have been in the heart of the geographer Élisée Reclus, who travelled the world. Still, the problem is by no means as straightforward as that.

Paris, April 12 (Thursday)

A heavy, cloudy day. This morning I had to take care of some issues concerning my apartment and I went to the Sixteenth Arrondissement, which consumed a good deal of time, so that it was an hour and a half before I could finally make my way to the Café Dupont in the Quartier Latin. I had only thirty minutes before the lecture was to begin, so

I wolfed down a pâté sandwich and a café-crème and entered the right-hand door of the Sorbonne

As I wrote to you previously, I have found the issue of Nature very much in my mind for some time. The idea that "all Nature is one" does not suggest that we can therefore conclude as well that all humankind is one; and even if this may seem to be so on the surface, such an elementary conclusion would be trivial at best, it seems to me.

What a disparity there is, for example, between the desolation of the Camargue's swamp-like areas and the desolate coast that abuts the Sea of Japan. And such a disparity does not arise merely through some subjectivity on the part of the viewer. At the same time, the cause of this disparity, if we observe the situation objectively, does not seem altogether inherent within Nature either.

Five years ago, when I landed in Nice, having taken a plane from Bastia on Corsica, I witnessed the Mediterranean at sunset, with clouds to the west rising as if on fire. Four years ago, I crossed in the early evening from Algeciras in Spain to Tangier, on the African shore. In the rough waters, dolphins, joining together in groups, swam together as though chasing our ship between the high cliffs that separate Spain from Africa, where the colder waters of the Atlantic Ocean flow together with the darker waters of the Mediterranean. When I returned the next morning, the mist was filled with golden light, in the midst of which the sky and the sea alike seemed to blend together as in a dream. The houses and mosques in Tangier seemed to float up like some mysterious vision. The sight seemed to make me feel intoxicated, yet at the same time I had the sensation of something cool, firm, and unyielding. From Western Europe to the Far East, whether witnessed by sea routes or land routes, the shifts of Nature reveal such differences. So I can only think that Nature, in so many differing regions, has organized itself in response to endless varying conditions. I feel, therefore, that I am not mistaken when I emphasize a special connection between the Mediterranean and Western European culture.

Last year on the plane, on an afternoon in the middle of July, as we entered the portion of the ocean in which Japan lies, I could see into the far distant western horizon and found myself breathless, completely absorbed in the beauty of my country's islands spreading north and south across the water. What is the precise nature, then, of this sense of beauty that I experienced? The basis for this phenomenon represents a feeling that, at least with my poor abilities, lies beyond any words I can summon up, but one that expresses a sense of a limitless affinity. It was as though I felt I had separated myself from the ocean and had melted into these distant islands, and then to become completely absorbed in them. Or so it seemed as I pressed myself to the window of the plane for so many hours, unable to tear myself away. These sensations resemble those about which I wrote to you in my last letter concerning the enormous privileges with which this country has been endowed. It is precisely as though my very existence had crystallized in my presentiment of that affinity that I now was beginning to experience. It seems to me that here I am attempting to express something that until now has remained beyond the realm of mere reason itself. As for the real nature of these islands—in their nature, humanity, art, and culture—are they here not all made manifest? And further, having lived abroad for so long, I believe that I can now unexpectedly apprehend them objectively, from the outside.

It seems to me that these qualities can doubtless be observed in those elements of feeling that make up a part of any genuine state of reality. Any sentimentality, however, corrupts the true nature of art and cannot protect the integrity of either an objective or a subjective view. So it is that a truly gifted artist is surely one of those few whose sense of self allows him to summon the level of powerful energy needed to express reality as he finds it, in terms of his responses generated within the midst of his own culture. One true meaning of the word "solitude" surely lies in this. Dostoevsky is one who can provide a unique example of this phenomenon. And I believe that I can find these qualities as well in the writings of Rilke.

Rilke was born in Prague, but in his early diaries written in Florence, the agitated nature of his responses from his own inner being to his external environment is vividly depicted. And it is at this moment that a new sense of time began to flow within him. His diary finishes with the following statement. "As for ourselves: we are the ancestors of a god and with our deepest solitudes reach forward through the centuries to his very beginning. I feel this with all my heart!"[10]

In just the same year as Rilke wrote these words, the writer Oscar Milosz, born on the Baltic shores of Lithuania, roamed the world and, under a foreign sky, attempted to forge his own sense of being. Yet he lacked that élan that, as in Rilke's case, sought in a total thoroughness of spirit to extend itself outward in order to seek out the birth of such a god. There is therefore a certain sentimentality in the nature of the loneliness that Milosz felt he had experienced. There is a strong odor in his work of what was to him the foreign smell of Parisian society, a somehow stunted subjectivity, that makes his example altogether different from Rilke's. There was not a particle of this attitude in Rilke. Milosz was thus no more than a descendant of that god.

I have somehow drifted away from my discussion of Nature, but in short, the view that all Nature is one doubtless derives from the influence of objective, scientific conceptions, yet this perception cannot serve as a simple common denominator capable of creating any intimate ties with humankind, it seems to me. In my own interior consciousness, Spain and the Baltic Sea occupy different spaces. The Adriatic Sea and the Tyrrhenian Sea have always been distinct. I have always had a strong yearning to see the desert, the beauty of which the writer Louis Hémon portrayed with such skill. Or just as Levi-Strauss has described in exceptional detail the nature of the culture in the Amazon river basin, providing details far beyond any simple curiosity one might have had about the area. I am profoundly attracted to the rough terrain of Spain. But the homogeneous nature of the landscape of France, so close by, remains the premise on which my feelings are based. Concerning Africa I find myself very attracted to Ethiopia, Egypt, and the whole region of North Africa. One reason may be because of the presence of such a variety of ruins, as well as the fact that this area is connected to so many ancient spiritual traditions that developed there. Yet indeed there may be no such essential reason for my response. Any basic intension on my part must be related to the specific qualities of Nature found there. And it is precisely those qualities of Nature that have allowed for the preservation of those ruins and those ancient cultures. Indeed, I cannot imagine that there might be any other cause for those attractions.

Today, in a somewhat hurried state, I took the bus from Trocadéro to Cluny and found myself observing from the window the great beauty of the Abbey of Saint-Germain-des-Prés. I had the strong impression that this structure had been constructed fully in the Romanesque style. The surfaces of those small pieces of the stone from which the tower is constructed are truly beautiful. And the Vault of Heaven below the summit of the tower looks to be of great delicacy.

As I left the Place Sorbonne with Heinemann, Martin and the others after the lecture at the Sorbonne was finished, the surrounding buildings looked all the darker because of the falling rain moistening the stone, and I found something agreeable about the sharp sound of our shoes on the pavement. My obligations thus concluded, I drank a delicious café-crème before returning home to do my own work, recalling that at this moment you are somewhere in Italy. As I watched the bustling boulevards, it seemed to slip my mind that I had no friend here beside me. And within myself, a quiet consciousness arose in me, as if a series of phenomena were pulled together into some magnetic field, falling in order and arranging themselves appropriately in a group. As soon as I returned home, I finally answered the letter of Monod-Herzen and sent my response off by special delivery. I felt much relieved.

Today, unusual for me, I felt a cold coming on, certainly a disagreeable feeling.

Once the lecture was over, I finished eating a light lunch around noon. I somehow felt faint, a sensation that still continues. I dropped in for a moment at my friend S's house, on the Quai de Gesvres, then took a bus home to the plaza at Saint-Sulpice. Today, nothing I see seems able to penetrate my consciousness, neither the church itself, nor the red flowers of the chestnut trees in bloom, nor the green verdure at the Jardin du Luxembourg. This surely is because I was caught in a draft two evenings ago while watching a movie at the Rue Bonaparte. In the evening Heinemann kindly brought me some medicine, and once I had taken it, I began to feel better. Then later in the evening, as usual, my friend N came by and we continued our reading of Husserl's phenomenology.

These past two weeks, my spirit has been strongly seized by an admiration for the work of Édouard Monod-Herzen. My chance encounter with this scholar and artist has truly been an important occurrence in my spiritual life. I am as yet not prepared to write much about this, so I can do no more than simply mention that fact here.

He is now over eighty years of age, and he continues on with great energy to carry on with his writings on art as well as his work as a metal sculptor. Since his first esquisses were presented to the Académie de Sciences in 1896, his written speculations have also piled up, one after another, constituting the work of half a century, culminating in the great work of his lifetime, *Principes de morpologie générale*. Since the book's first publication in 1927, changes and additions have multiplied again and again until this year, 1956, a revised edition was published by Gautier-Villars.

When examining the nature of Beauty, if you divide your observations into three parts—creation, analysis, and synthesis—then his work can be examined as follows. His sculpture is the first category and his scholarship in the second. Such is the reason for the fact that some of his work is on display at the Musée des Arts Décoratifs, although I have not yet seen these pieces. As a writer on aesthetics, his central assertions are based on the application of scientific principles to the phenomenon of art, thoroughly penetrated by his particular concept of Nature. And his vision of Nature does not stop at any commonplace view; rather, his is a concept of Nature based on human and social phenomena as well, a Nature as conceived by such men as Claude Bernard and Pasteur, who make use of scientific proofs, as well as the views of Nature as understood by Fabre, who used as his basis for his views of life in Nature on his study of insects. Or again, the views of Nature as unified by those concepts of human society that appear in the study of world geography espoused by such scholars as Élisée Reclus, or going back even to the concepts of Nature so central to the thought of Rousseau and the Encyclopédists. Reading Monod-Herzen's works, I was not only struck with the peerless nature of his speculations and the crystalline focus of his expression, but I realized with intensity the fact that I had not yet become aware of the variety of such issues concerning the relationship between Nature and Science.

At one point, Monod-Herzen invited me to dine with him at a restaurant, and while on the way, as we were riding together in a taxi, I questioned him about a subject concerning which I have written to you previously: the nature of the psychological process that had brought about a fusion in my mind concerning my various apprehensions concerning church architecture. He remarked immediately that this did not represent any subjective psychological state but rather an objective one, and he urged me to read carefully his essay on tradition and the rules of harmony. In this study, beginning with his analysis of a plan for the construction of a niche for the Eucharist in the Brussels museum, he examines the proportions of Romanesque and Gothic architecture, adding a very precise and clear analysis of the nature of the transition from one to the other. Not only did he prove to me that my own psychological process was not a pointless one, but he made me understand as well that, in the case of any psychological phenomenon, an analysis and consolidation of that phenomenon must be undertaken by relying on a scientific range of vision, involving strictly objective terms, in order to establish its validity, before attempting any leap towards observing any spiritual meaning directly. Monod-Herzen has spent some sixty years of his life in such analyses. In addition to his heretofore little-recognized efforts to manage such a strict protocol during this long period of time, now, just at the moment when such psychological elements have come into value again, his thought forms the foundation of the kind of psychological criticism proposed by Malraux and others. One of his disciples, the young physicist B, and others as well, are working in the area of aesthetic research, yet at least in this particular sense, I affirm, they have still not yet surpassed his *Principes de morphologie générale*.

In examining the various experiences that have come to me since I have been in France, Monod-Herzen's work has helped me on so many occasions to avoid reaching any superficial conclusions, for which I owe him an incalculable debt. For this, there is no way I can thank him enough. I believe that he has been able to make me move more slowly in fixing my ideas, certainly a good thing for me. Indeed, the deeper meanings in the work of such writers as Valéry and Alain suddenly becomes understandable to me when examined from the angles he proposes. And it has become clear as well as to how the "scientific" literary research of Ferdinand Brunetière and Gustave Lanson can now perhaps come to be appreciated.

Monod-Herzen's attitude towards life is bright and lively. He is the son of Monod, the famous historian, and on his mother's side of the family, she herself was the daughter of the famous Russian historian Alexander Herzen. When I leave Monod-Herzen's workplace, near the Avenue Châtillon, I inevitably feel keenly that his example might well serve as the root cause for that sense of awe I have when I think of France. This is not awe or trepidation in any usual sense, but rather a virtual sense of apprehension I feel precisely because of the nobility of his warmth and human kindness. Yet how very difficult it is to truly absorb his thinking into oneself. Is it a question of Nature or of Learning? I feel keenly the matter of how traditions have sunk so deeply into this country, have they not, over so many hundreds of years. In that sense, I have come to understand that my convictions over the sense of apprehension I may feel are justified and transcend any mere animal or instinctual response.

By the same token, as for my chance meeting with this scholar, or rather, the understanding that came to me as a result of that meeting, when I speak from the depth of my own interior life, I cannot deny in fact I feel that such an understanding was somehow bound to occur to me at some point in my life. This is because as my own experiences have continued on, I have kept attempting to seek out one particular configuration in which I could anchor my own particular situation. So that, in the end, no accidental outside influence played a part.

One of my mentors, the philosopher Ferdinand Alquié, has done superb research on Descartes, yet when looking at his two-volume account of his outline of philosophy, more than half seems to privilege psychology. And when it comes to those matters of significance the author wishes to convey, then rather than adopting the usual abstract arguments, he allows his insights to put down deep roots into Nature, revealing how his insights in turn derive from just such sources. Previously I had vaguely come to grasp this principle at work in his writings, but after reading Monod-Herzen, I came to realize the great importance of Alquié's psychological approach, which I believe has led me in turn to understand one aspect of a whole tradition of French philosophy from Maine de Biran to Bergson.

Paris, May 10, cloudy

So it is then that my views on the substance of French culture, which heretofore have been so oppressive to me, and in so many dimensions, have now undergone a transformation inside my own mind. Now I can see that European culture could by no means simply be successfully imitated from the exterior, nor merely studied on the basis of some undemanding appreciation. For that culture represents no shallow, unremarkable phenomenon. All I can do myself, therefore, is to pursue the path I have already undertaken, clear to the very end.

Once I came to understand this issue clearly, my apprehension of the denseness I felt in Paris quickly began to alter. Although I continued to internalize some issues, which remained a burden, at the same time the atmosphere that had previously enveloped me suddenly became much lighter. In fact, everything about me came now to seem perfectly normal. I was no longer oppressed by what lay outside myself, nor did I succumb to any wayward impulses. Indeed, I had been wondering just how long I would have to go on living while embracing this heaviness within myself. Now it seemed no longer necessary for me to continue to question whether I might ever be able to reach a state where my own ideas might come to be truly clear and refined, or if I might die with this heaviness still within me.

I have witnessed myself in what way a renewal of any potential thought (or experience) I had brought into being might be kept from slipping away. The past flows backward, the outer world moves inward, and then again, the interior moves out into the world, as all flows to the future. And could this process represent Nature raised to a higher power? And indeed, if such is the reality of Nature, then must not everything be left to Nature's own natural ripening? It was in just such a frame of mind that I, in that space we call time, faced forward as I sat at the stern of the ship, as though I were looking to the rear. As the future came into being, it seemed to spread itself without limit just at the moment when it faced the past. There was no way that a mere passenger could by himself change the speed of the ship. And this movement continued on. Without mercy, implacably . . . This is what I found so frightening. With constant work and patience, those two crucial qualities that Rilke has identified, we must adopt the calm attitude that time does not exist and only eternity is real. Such does not represent some mere theory of fate or destiny. Rather this is proof, as he writes, that we are entirely the sum of our experiences.

Six years ago, as I sat at the stern of the liner *La Marseille* staring at the vast ocean, stirred up by the ship's propeller as the bubbles spread further and further whitening the water, I could never have dreamed that my own experiences would have assumed the form they have presently taken. And my own feelings toward the realities of the ocean itself, the past and the future, now seem to be reversed.

After several days of fine weather, today there are thin clouds spread across the sky. The temperature is a bit cool. On the day of the Feast of the Ascension, a holiday here, there are few people on the streets, and the area in front of my window is deserted. Occasionally you can hear the sounds of traffic on the Rue Gay-Lussac. In my view, this deep silence of Paris is only superficially replaced by such noise. As I regard this sober face of Paris, it is hard for me to believe how much time has already gone by. Just how thick have been the curtains that have frustrated my eyes?

Paris, August 5 (Sunday)

Since I sent my last letter, virtually three months have gone by. And during this time, I have slowly made some steady progress concerning the issues about which I wrote to you on that occasion. Now it seems to me that any particular reality, or indeed reality itself, allows for no other real possibilities than those I suggested to you. If I examine myself closely, I believe that I have now come to understand a number of things. Yet the simple act of examining and supporting those "shifting marks" in my consciousness turns out to be the most difficult effort of all, so that concerning such issues, which arrive on a seemingly daily basis, I must make an constant effort to overcome them, so that there may come to be as little a divergence as possible between my consciousness and the actual world outside me.

I read the following in a book about architecture:

In the case of a drawing or painting, the arrangement of light and shadow might be perceived as a difference between dark and light. Thus, in the field of architecture, in any particular building, the principle of contrasting fullness and emptiness might also be termed the principle of dark and light. . . . If density becomes dominant and emptiness lessens, a graver emotion is engendered, and the observer immediately feels a vague sense of unease. In this fashion, the viewer may be taken by imagining the difficulties of those who feel themselves somehow imprisoned in such a space, and the resulting fierceness of their lives. Such persons cannot hope to see others, or to be seen by others . . . [after some omissions in the text, which I am leaving out, which concern the nature of Chinese houses, the author continues on as follows] As for any family secrets, in a house without interior walls, it is the screen that serves to protect them. Thus, by means of such a trifling object, the real and peaceful happiness in the mundane life of those who live in such spaces allows them to breathe freely. Under such restricted circumstances, however, true poetry can develop no further than as a showy sentimental attachment.

The fact that European architecture has developed from the heavy walls and tiny windows of the Romanesque through the Gothic, then to the Renaissance and Classic styles followed by the Baroque, even until today's further conversion to the style of Functionalism, is by no means accidental. One can speak of similar developments as well concerning the evolution of the character of European thought. There are, of course, quite a number of issues connected to this simple observation. But the true nature of Europe is surely captured in the fact that early on, in the midst of this closed architecture, the sense of the individual began to develop and open out with intensity in a spirit of communal love. Therefore, despite the existence of today's architecture, which faces into the light and the outside world, there still remain a number of restraints on the contemporary Self (and I would count Existentialism among them). That is, some of these essential possibilities still may be included in the various ways in which contemporary man can conduct his life. All this explains something quite fundamental to us. And, as this movement from the closed to an opening out must follow a strict and methodical order, there will always remain something quintessentially European about the nature of that process itself.

Still, this phenomenon is not simply limited to the European experience. For the way in which culture is manifested in the midst of all our daily lives is a matter of basic importance in any society. Without this process, our very thoughts and ideas could not exist. Of course, it is foolish to place European thought and Asian thought in any simple opposition to each other, because it is basically impossible to detach in some abstract fashion the assumptions of any culture as they are manifested in daily life. Rather, the matter devolves into our daily life and our own personal experiences. This is by no means a simple matter to think through, however. For those experiences and emotions that sustain our thoughts are vitally necessary for our very existence. Without them, any sort of useful debate is meaningless. As a precaution, I must state that at the moment when a particular thought is created and is ready to be expressed, it is by no means necessary that the presence of Europe should be a point of reference. No such external matters need be taken into account.

What is involved here is nothing like, say, the urge to admire a flower. Rather, a thought develops in tandem with the felt harshness of life in which one looks neither outwards nor permits any incursions from outside, as if the mind were lurking behind some fiercely protective wall. In this regard, there is no resemblance whatsoever between the attraction one feels for a flower and that force that sustains those shifting elements of the ego. . . .

Paris, August 6 (Monday), cloudy

Today, although we are still in August, it is cold and cloudy. It began to rain around noon. I have been thinking again recently about the deep impression that Samuel Beckett's play *Waiting for Godot* made on me when we saw a performance together. I recently heard on the radio that the New York performances of the play in English were very well received there as well. The commentator remarked that "This is the great play of the postwar era," and whatever the ultimate justice of this remark, I believe that certainly in the past decade, at least, if one were to choose to outline one truly important aspect of the spiritual situation here in the West, Beckett's work can certainly provide a striking example of the connections between the Existentialist idea of "here I am in the world" as it relates to the situation of contemporary mankind. But for me, the most important issue concerns the question as to where, for better or worse, the Self can be situated in the midst of the present circumstances found here in the West. In my own case, for those of us who were brought up lacking the background of this long spiritual tradition in the West, there remain dangers that must be acknowledged. Nihilism and Existentialism alike grew out of the European tradition, while in the Japanese case, such a development was by no means inevitable. We must acknowledge the fact that the meaning of these terms may therefore be different for us.

In other words, this situation in Europe arose because, even after the collapse of classical traditions, European culture continued on as a consistent whole until the beginning of the twentieth century; even now the remnants of that culture remain strong. Thus, these older conceptions still inform and protect the new principles of contemporary reality on which we now base our lives. In that regard, such philosophies as Existentialism, while not a strict continuation of earlier ideas, make little sense unless its melding with earlier cultural values is understood. Husserl's phenomenology and Monod-Herzen's morphology can only exist because of a conscious effort to examine in depth this inevitable merging with older aspects of European culture. At the end of this long expanse of two thousand years, and with the spread of European culture from its beginnings to the Middle Ages and far beyond, these points of fusion have been successfully achieved, and now the next steps stand ready to be taken. Yet for we who do not possess this background, what relationship do we have to these new developments? It is said that Japan never went through a modernizing process. Moreover, in terms of spiritual values, what in the West is termed the Middle Ages never arrived in Japan. Our ancient history extended itself into the center of our thinking, and this continued on until recent times. Since coming to Europe, I have come to recognize that in Japan these gaps are truly grave. I have found that it is only because of the beginnings of the flow of a new consciousness with me that I can now locate any real relationship between myself and Europe at all.

In one sense, this may be only a question of how this situation affects me personally. It is not simply a matter of being discouraged about something, unhappy over something, even joyful about something. There is nothing to challenge or gainsay those facts in themselves. Yet at the same time, there are moments when the simple purity of the human feelings of affection and emotion need not be sustained by any received ideas or customs and so are freed from them. There are moments as well when we are called to awaken. This not a question of any mere reaction or resistance. Here I can catch a glimpse of a freedom unrelated to any kind of personal selfishness. It is this in turn that forces me to draw closer to Japan.

Having arrived at this state of understanding, I suddenly find that I have again begun to enjoy walking from one area of Paris to another just to look about me at random.

August 29 (Tuesday)

From Orange in the Vaucluse, on a bright and windy day

The last time I wrote to you, I mentioned that since coming to Paris six years ago, I have now suddenly taken to walking about in the city. As a result of this, plus the fact that I have recently been hampered with a good deal of business that needed to be taken care of, I managed to come south before I had any chance to write to you again.

I have been walking with M, a psychiatrist friend of mine, in a virtually obsessive manner, around through every area of Paris. I had never guessed the extent of the beauty that these streets hold. From this, I can now understand for the first time that our human sensations as they pile up, however slowly, as we construct our own individual human histories, seem also to expand those histories, do they not? I thus came to learn that sensations become experiences, and then further on, that they can fuse into thoughts, so that in this way they can take on still other dimensions. Accordingly, from those that relate to our close contact with specific concrete things, those sensations come to develop in us a sharp power of discrimination and so are able to help shape the history of the growth of the Self. And so it is that, accordingly, these experiences and thoughts, refined and tempered, become mature.

As for these new discoveries in Paris, I will write about them at some other point and will not continue on here. But to briefly summarize, Paris, for me, has resolved the issue of an anonymous universe.

Yet, what does Paris actually represent for me? Surely not Notre Dame, nor Sacré Coeur, certainly not the Eiffel Tower, none of those famous places. And certainly not those important buildings or areas that draw so much public attention, either for aesthetic or historic reasons, such as Saint-Germain-des-Prés, St. Pierre, or St. Julian. Nor for those colorful popular areas that attract so much of the population. Indeed, I don't find myself attracted to any of the spots that have certainly made Paris such a place of renown. Rather, I have been discovering those places in Paris that possess no significance beyond themselves.

There is no easy way to explain my attraction to such locations. It would require a whole realm of letters to explain all of that to you.

In any case, in those unrecognized areas of the city, among the various things I notice on the streets and corners—church towers, domes, columns, windows, protruding beams, entrance doorways, façades, roofs, stone facings—it is these that more often arouse my interest than many of the famous sites in the city. To put this another way, now that I have become sensitive to those elements of analysis that comprise my emotional response to this urban atmosphere, my feelings can now be freed from the burden of what is acknowledged and famous. Such a connection is no longer needed. This shift in my interest, this transformation, began with religious buildings, then castles (including forts), then moving through communal structures to ordinary individual dwellings. And I came to understand as well that as I examined each individual structure, I could now clearly understand the wide variations that existed among them. Still more crucial, these are areas I had never before appreciated for their sheer beauty.

One day, quite by chance, when I was looking at Notre Dame, I was so struck with the splendor of this structure that I completely lost any consciousness of myself. What I grasped in this instant was the truth of the fact that each element of these interior variations within the Self can transcend the personal to fuse accordingly together as one. And so it is that a true beauty of the whole, and not simply of each part, comes into being. This process does not merely represent some simple synthesis. In the eyes of one who has to some extent grasped the various details involved, even if these elements might suggest a synthesis, thus making a cohesive whole a logical possibility, the actual process of achieving any such actualization still lies elsewhere. The process I am describing here is not simply based on my own observations. This phenomenon which gives rise to my feelings, in this sense, may simply represent the truth.

This world of unnamed shapes, sounds, colors, and words spreads outward, and by analogy to other categories as well. From there on, this becomes a world where names themselves disappear. At that point, however splendid any particular thing or quality may be, no mere name can encompass its essential nature. As for any more profound significance, surely it a matter of defining the nature of the actual space in which it exists. In writing to you earlier, I remember mentioning that even one experience can serve to define the Self, but, as I wrote on that same day, this is what defines the nature of Time as well.

Any point of departure develops from the state of one particular sensation. Within my own consciousness, when such a point of light can first be analyzed, it splits up as though divided by countless thousands, so that one important point of arrival becomes the Self. At this moment, the outer world flows backward and becomes Time. On the other hand, this is not the outer world in any usual sense. Now, even a single category can reveal many possibilities and so has become Space as well. Names disappear, and categories and definitions take their place.

It was in this frame of mind that yesterday evening I boarded the mail train for the south. Tonight, I am staying in a hotel near the station at Orange, and outside my window the express trains from Paris to Marseilles pass continually, and at a frightening speed. It is now 10:30 at night.

Earlier this morning, in midst of the vague light of dawn, my train followed along beside the banks of the Rhone. On the surface of the water, swirling about into eddies, the dense morning fog began to lift, although I still could not make out the opposite bank. You know how very much I find myself attracted to such vague and shadowy scenes— the mouth of the Rhone, or the bleak swamp-like Camargue, and the area from Belfort through Langres to Chaumont, or the endless blooming flowers at Corrèze, and the vast fields of eastern France, all the way to the black deserts of Andalusia in Spain. . . .

Yet now, the situation for me has become a bit different. My own existence can now be somehow disentangled from the flow of the Rhone and I can achieve my own essential reality. To speak more precisely, it is just as if, in the midst of all that has remained so vague, I now have developed a powerful feeling, an enormous yearning for something more directly related to myself, and those feelings have grown ever stronger. Yet at the same time, there has indeed been a change in me, for I seem to have matured in my ability to separate my outer and inner worlds. Such were my thoughts watching the Rhone as it turned westward and passed the bridge at Pont Saint-Esprit, as I looked vaguely at the old town on the other side of the river, still shrouded in the morning mist.

Although it has been only a day and a half since I left Paris, I feel as though many months have gone by. Here in the south of France, in the midst of this strong sunlight, seemingly so dense, not thin and transparent, Nature casts such powerful and protective shadows. In the short time since I have been here, I feel that this light has penetrated me to the core. This clear atmosphere acts like a powerful tonic on the fatigue I was feeling in my body from the stress of city life.

Yesterday I spent all my time walking around the town of Orange. The houses, constructed from stones of brownish limestone, have small windows and expansive wall surfaces. Most of these low buildings are painted green; with their venetian blinds closed, they seem hushed and silent under the strong sun. The famous Roman amphitheater is constructed of piled-up stones that reveal the color of dried mud. The façade rises a severe thirty-six meters in height and dominates the entire center of the town, confronting all comers. Aiming towards the clouds drifting in the blue sky, the structure juts up, unmoving. To the right, as if somehow dormant, lie the ruins of a Roman gymnasium, encircled by a brook. My impression of these ancient Roman remains is that they are relatively unremarkable; in particular these ruins suggest some sense of roughness. Such words as "integrity" or "unfeeling," spring to mind, with little further interpretation required. As for other ruins in this area from the Roman period, such as the Maison Carrée, the Temple of Diana in Nimes, and the Amphitheater at Fréjus, I recall that each gives a much softer, gentler impression. The same is true for the Triumphal Arch here in Orange. For example, the triumphal arch which stands near the ruins of Glanum, near Saint Rémy, elicits a much more delicate response in the spectator. Looking at these impassive ruins, I found myself unexpectedly mulling over my impressions and observations. Roman ruins of this sort (or rather, "Gallo-Roman") are most prevalent in the south of France, but they cover the entire country. In Paris there still remain the ruins of a square bathhouse at the corner of the Boulevard St. Michel and the Boulevard St. Germain that I pass by every day. Of course, I often reflect on the fact that the Gauls, the ancestors of the French, were soon to perish, facing the danger of absorption into the heretical Roman Empire with its Mediterranean culture. Yet they still managed to retain their culture and resist that absorption. Within their own strong hands, unpolished and rustic, they succeeded in slowly beginning to build their structures in an unsophisticated fashion corresponding to their own character. And it was of great importance that they chose Christianity over and against the heresies of ancient Rome. Naturally they had no interest in building pagan shrines or entertainment arenas. I am struck by the fact that these tribes, while they had before their eyes a number of superb structures, constructed from the Merovingian period through the Carolingian period, still continued to pile up those coarse stones in an artless and naïve spirit.

In the Paris region of Oise, as you enter into the area of Picardy, there is a small village of Morienval, said to be the birthplace of French

Gothic, where there stands a countrified eleventh-century Romanesque church, its ceiling supported by stones, a strategy that will soon become adopted in Gothic architecture. The remains of this Benedictine abbey for women, built at the command of Charles le Chauve, reveal a square stone building that dates back to the time of Dagobert. This structure, which serves as the entrance, consists of piled up stones, without windows or ornamentation, and reveals in an artless fashion the basic human resolve to work steadily in order to repulse the ravages of nature. But those square buildings made up of such piled stones have in and of themselves already given rise to a certain kind of beauty. At the entrance of Poitiers there is an eight-sided baptistery, dating back to the fourth century, which reveals a similar kind of allure. A small number of the remains of such buildings dating from the Carolingian era are scattered throughout France (the old cathedral at Vaison goes back to the Merovingian period; beginning with St. Bertrand, in the Pyrenees, cornerstones for this type of Roman basilica, from the Rhone area outward, began to be placed throughout France), followed by those of the Romanesque and Gothic periods. Even we outsiders can easily seek them out. By the same token, this development, in and of itself, was not so easily accomplished, as there were many complications back and forth before this style could eventually came to full fruition. And there is certainly no denying the influences of Byzantine and Arabian architecture on these structures as well. The basic cause for these developments, however, comes from the fact that the Gauls, arriving from the north, brought about the construction of this type of structure on the basis of their own lived experience. Their sensibilities, because of the intrinsic peculiarities of their ways of thinking, gave rise to a particular sense of space they had been compelled to discover. However, other influences from the outside were bound to bring certain definite distortions in that homogeneous, anonymous sense of space, so that merely copying from one generation to another would not prove sufficient. And in the Renaissance, an important period that marked the conclusion of these developments, when the level of civilization had reached new heights and a denser complexity, was it indeed not the case that an appreciation of the beauty of Greece and Rome could now be truly acquired for the first time? This is because the West had, in fact, now inherited the ancient culture of the Mediterranean, which required several thousands of years in order to mature and then ripen again within this new environment. Nevertheless, Western culture, having finally achieved such sympathies, still continued to maintain its differences, qualitatively speaking, from that ancient civilization. It was this process of growth that first gave rise to medieval culture.

These observations are not simply the product of my personal speculations derived from some sort of deductive reasoning, and so of necessity based on only scant evidence. The products of each of these civilizations, one by one, speak to us directly through the ruins that remain behind. Ideas are not based on a system deriving from any one single supposition alone. These deepest secrets must be teased out from the midst of the relationship between one set of objects after another, so that our abilities to truly perceive them requires a high level of skill.

Today I went to Carpentras (the word refers to both the name of the town and of those who live there). This town, like Orange, has been colored by its history, ranging from Roman times up to the present, with deep roots stretching back to the Gallo-Roman period. As the earlier tourist season has past, the autocar I boarded had only two or three local passengers. We now traversed the fields surrounding the base of the famous Mt. Ventoux, formed from the westernmost tip of the Alps, as we drew closer to Carpentras. It is difficult to know what kind of description I can provide for this sun-drenched moorland. The land gently undulates up and down, where occasional patches of scrub grow in a luxuriant fashion. *Platane* trees, low, and with thick trunks, spread out their bright green leaves toward the sun, in contrast to the darkened foliage of the surrounding bushes. Here and there are small fields. Sunflowers are everywhere and in prodigious bloom. Because it is still summer, my autocar crosses one small dried-up stream after another. There are no shadows in sight. Mt. Ventoux, standing alone in this wilderness, now seemed closer, those gentle slopes around its base now clearly visible. In the small villages on the way, Sarrians and Jonquières, the houses, built of square stones, stand all in a line, as if asleep. The clean, cool air coming in through the car window was tinged with the odor of myrtle and lavender. Tiny bugs were darting about. I suddenly recalled that it was in Carpentras, my present destination, that the naturalist Henri Fabre retained so many personal connections. I remembered that at the end of his life, when he lived in retirement in the village of Sérignan, not far from Orange, Fabre, having spent his whole life in the study of insects he now considered as friends, had by now become renowned as a scientist, his character established at the highest level. He would observe insects moving in the clumps of grass, and with his wide-brimmed hat, his clothing soaked from the heat and with a net in hand, he would dart from one spot or another. The old man's glance, as severe in its way as the sight of Mt. Ventoux itself—what was it that he perceived in this shadowless wilderness?

Presently the autocar pulled into Carpentras. The town seemed surrounded by hills, all well-filled with tile roofs dotted in red.

Among the various things I observed in Carpentras, there are two I would like to tell you about. No, three. First, the arch dating from the Roman period set into the wall at the back of the cathedral of Saint-Siffrein. Next, the view over the Vaucluse from the high ground in front of the Espérance church. Finally, the Gate of Orange.

As for the Roman arch at the rear of the cathedral, one might assume that it had always stood on that spot, but in fact this is no longer truly an arch, since the original stones had been part of a prior structure that preceded the church (which is in Gothic style) and now inserted into a section of a wall, itself the remains of a Romanesque construction. This partial arch-like structure is attached to the side wall, now part of the priests' quarters. Standing on the path by the east side of the church, one can easily see the difference between the Roman arch, the Romanesque wall, and the Gothic church itself, the huge wall itself supported by the transept, all blended together. The Roman arch helps to support the Romanesque structure, which in turn has been put to use as a part of the newer Gothic church. Examined from a purely commonsense point of view, there is little more to observe. From a formal aesthetic point of view, this ensemble lacks any unity in its composition and the results can certainly not be considered beautiful. Yet in fact there is manifested here an overflowing sense of beauty, one far removed from ordinary considerations of that term. It is easy to see that those builders who were concerned with reconstructing the church were certainly not planning for any aesthetic results through their efforts. But it cannot be denied that, through the use of those variations provided by such a diverse collection of materials, a genuine kind of harmony has been created from these disparate elements. Here, these enormous Gothic walls, the rough, thick, and substantial Romanesque walls, and the firm semicircle of the Roman arch all work together, making use of the methods and materials appropriate to each. Here, in this radiant light and limitless airy space, a kind of rough beauty comes into being. Within the same natural environment, the spirit of each age manifests itself, one following after the other. This truth in turn brings about various speculations on my part. Walking around the church, it appears to me that the bottom half is in Renaissance style, so similar columns and arches appear again. I felt that indeed I had observed with my own eyes a turning point during some thousand years of history. Here I saw one moment in the progress in the life of a civilization. Here was the vital, living proof of the movement towards the universal. Within the creation of that simple half-circle of an arch, how much of the heresy of the ancient pagan world stands here revealed. Those who made up the population of this area, passing through so many centuries of Christianization, became able during the midst of this process to rediscover again their own true nature. This ancient society has put down deep roots in civilization, far surpassing what ordinary people might imagine. So I thought to myself as I walked around the church, forgetting the time altogether.

What we take from this, I believe, is a profound understanding of the fleeting nature of any task we believe we ourselves can accomplish. Still, those things that transcend us are made manifest to us only by the very act of their passing through us. To those who would write history, a multitude of factors must be fused together. But being able to grasp and extract such real meanings in the midst of ordinary reality is all the more important. And all the more difficult.

The second thing that struck me in Carpentras was the view from the garden in front of the Espérance church, one that provides such a striking prospect on Mt. Ventoux (the land used to be under the jurisdiction of the pope). From the plaza in front of the Hotel Dieu (now a hospital) at the southern edge of the town, the road, lined with splendid old *platane* trees veers north; then, as you walk to the east, you come upon this area, which rises some hundred meters above the flat land below. Behind there lies a small area, something like a park, which situates the church in the background, so that the eastern edge becomes the spot with the most commanding view. It was two o'clock in the afternoon when I found myself standing there.

Along the side of the terrace, paved with small stones, there are two long iron benches installed. The framework of the terrace in the front has been constructed from square stones, and the view directly ahead provides a distant view of Mt. Ventoux and the villages in between, Bedoin, San Pierre-de-Vassole, and others. This is precisely the scenery of Cézanne. On the day of my visit, a cool wind was blowing from the east. When the wind stopped for a moment, everything around me suddenly seemed to grow warmer. The space was now filled with bright light from a painfully burning sun. The flow of this shining light was absolutely clear and now cool air moved within it. Above the stone balustrade, a lizard was running about, occasionally lifting its neck to gage the situation in the vicinity. Near the north of the terrace were two more long benches, where three old ladies sat silently holding their knitting materials, wearing dark hooded garments. Behind the terrace there was an extensive flower garden. Above the flowering portulaca, an automatic sprinkler continuously sent forth a fine spray of water. Looking to the front, the tips of the branches of fig trees revealed themselves all the way to the top of the railing, extending upward from where they were growing out from the middle of the cliff below, along with other branches of a tree with slender leaves that resembled those of an oak. Looking through these branches I had a clear view of the low hills surrounding Mt. Ventoux. And on the other side I could see the waterway, built apparently sometime in the late eighteenth century in order to bring water to Carpentras, supported by hundreds of stone arches; the long horizontal line of the waterway divides the surrounding scenery into upper and lower sections. The space above is a world filled entirely with brilliant light. The rough surface of Mt. Ventoux ascending into the mist of the moving clouds, seems to etch its own curving silhouette in the sky. The space below the line is filled with groups of scraggly shrubs scattered up and down on the Earth's surface, providing a home for deep shadows and luxuriant foliage. Throughout are scattered small houses, with their red roof tiles, that seem to appear then disappear, and it would seem that over this endlessly bright panorama a kind of diaphanous veil had been spread in order to give a soft appearance throughout. There is nothing here resembling the kind of harshness that might be expected in Spain, Corsica, and similar places, or in those countries on the southern side of the Mediterranean. Here the feeling seems altogether less brilliant and more restrained. Everything seems more relaxed, and there is nothing rough or crude. Every object is soaked in the soft light that fills this gentle space. And in fact, this characteristic lambent atmosphere is not limited to southern France. In the moors of the Franche-Compté, the fertile fields of Normandy, the hills and the valleys of Burgoyne, indeed in all those spots of rural beauty in France, everything seems covered with an invisible sheet of thin silk. What is most remarkable is surely the color of the half-covered sky that spreads itself over the whole area of the Ile de France surrounding Paris. This sort of veiled space removes any raw appearance and gives rise to a sort of indirect and softening beauty. Any strong or opposing color receives this neutralizing effect and so enters into a greater harmony. It not simply a matter of some sort of enveloping mist. This half-veiled quality is somehow able to seep even into the midst of a clear sky and surely represents a special characteristic of nature in France. Those who live in this atmosphere will surely find themselves affected by it, would they not? I believe this to be an element in the very womb of French culture that gives rise to its underlying tone. This quality is made manifest in painting, sculpture, music, and in literature as well. And even on the occasion when a foreign culture is absorbed here, the most disparate elements are somehow gracefully welcomed in.

When Gide set out to write his treatise on Dostoevsky in his own particular fashion, he stressed that his was to be a psychological interpretation, and as a result, a number of critics in Japan took exception to his treatment. Whether a matter of psychology or not, when the ideas of the Russian writer were reflected within the mental space of Gide, there is no denying that a certain distortion, a certain ambiguity did occur, so that Dostoevsky's thought began for the first time to flow in consonance with French thought, just as, when one musical key is shifted to another, the creation of a half-tone is involved during the process. At the same time, there is an opposite effect when attempts are made to comprehend and appreciate French civilization from the outside, which can be a perplexing task. I would like to identify those various conditions as representing one kind of special space inherent in French civilization. I cannot imagine French culture or civilization without these particular spatial characteristics.

If all of such analysis results in a mere understanding for the sake of understanding, then this phenomenon has no larger significance. From my own point of view, however, if one particular element that makes up a civilization involves the relationship of that civilization to the conditions of Nature, then for me France is a country that is truly blessed. Perhaps, on one level, this may simply be taken as a matter of course. After all, the development of any culture is, in its very essence, deeply entwined with Nature. Essentially, what is most important here is the fact that the French created a civilization altogether in accord with those conditions; theirs is thus not the ordinary concept of "Nature." As I write this, I am thinking of the culture of the Heian period in Japan.

The prospect of Mt. Ventoux is changing.

In the middle of this bright, strong sunlight, I now found myself standing absolutely still, turning over so many thoughts in my head. I could somehow gather these thoughts and hear them in my mind, yet in fact, my real impressions remain scattered and confused. All the objects I saw, however reflected, seemed to invite so many reveries in me. Above the top of the cone of Mt. Ventoux, at such a great distance from where I stood, I could witness shifting shadows, probably from the moving white clouds. There, in the midst of that clear atmosphere so charged with light, France's heaven and earth seemed to virtually touch one another.

Since the time of France's initial dynasties, which began with the legendary emperor Merovaeus and lasted some five centuries, and in the fifteen hundred years since then as well, it may seem on the surface that, when examining the diverse and profound workings of this culture in terms of the splendor of France's continuous engagement with the world, Nature may seem to have played no more than a small part in this everlasting flow. Yet Fabre, while a middle-school teacher in Carpentras, and later, when he retired in Sérignan, compiled with great diligence his data and records on the plants and insects of the area. It was directly from these efforts that his own thoughts and ideas emerged, spreading out from those living forms he studied, reaching to seek out afresh the moral nature of existence itself. This is nothing more than one simple example.

This scene now before my eyes has never changed since distant antiquity, a fact that speaks to the character of a human culture able to set down such deep roots into Nature. Now, if you remove the cultural and philosophical phenomena in order to study what lies still below them, what kind of significant meaning remains? This issue goes far beyond any study of natural phenomena. I am now myself at a considerable distance from my own country, and so I find myself in this same position. If I set out to look into myself, I am now able to examine whatever prior conceptions of Self or of Nature I previously possessed from fresh and unexpected angles. By the same token, this does not mean that my former ideas may simply crumble away. This is because these sorts of impressions and feelings may not touch the Self directly.

The third thing I saw in Carpentras that I wanted to describe to you is the so-called Orange Gate, which lies on the road that leads north toward the town of Orange. As you know, I never weary of looking around everywhere while waiting for a bus or some such. And so it was that I espied this tower now serving as a gate, with quite a thick and sturdy appearance. Built in the fourteenth century, the structure is not that ancient, but it is an impressive seven or eight meters wide and must surely be roughly thirty meters in height. The tower itself is built of square stones carefully placed together and is crowned with crenellations and loopholes, so that it looks at once all the more both fierce and dignified.

Be it in the case of this tower, or in the arrangement of the stones in the cathedral I mentioned above, we may be startled or moved by what we see. But we must be able to imagine as well what forces produced the kind of questing spirit that sought to bring about these developments.

Exhausted as I was, I continued to ponder over these ideas one after the other as I turned them over and over in my mind. When I got back to my hotel and thought about all this, it seemed an extremely important fact to me that such human skills in fact do constitute another, a second Nature.

Orange, August 31 (Thursday)

Beautiful weather, quiet and with no wind.

Today I spent the day in Vaison-la-Romaine (simply the name "Vaison" may actually be correct, as this is what the natives call it). It was a day very profitably spent, and I am no longer sure where to begin to write about my experiences. The village is located in the lower slopes of Mt. Ventoux, and the phrase "la-Romaine" is used because of the existence of so many Roman ruins there. The original excavations, which covered a wide expanse, involved the reconstruction of the original village just as it had been in ancient times. That original village stands as it was, and only the vacant land around it has now been excavated. As the area is very large, it is said that there still remains a considerable area that has not yet been examined, suggesting that the original town was surely of a considerable size. The original town must have dated from the first century BC. Even as early as in about the sixth century BC, Greek traders were apparently already sailing up the Rhone river from Marseille, so that there were urban settlements here going far back in time. I am referring to the site of the village of Saint-Bertrand-de-Comminges, a town of similar size that served as the administrative center for the Roman government, the Oppidum Convenarium. Five years ago, I visited the well-known site of Glanum, near Saint-Rémy-de-Provence, and returned there again two years ago, but the size of that area cannot be compared to this. Burrus, the tutor of Nero, is said to have come from this area. The ancient city is spread out on the slopes of the hill that faces south overlooking the river, which runs through the center of the village. On the opposite hill lies the medieval city, and to the left of the ancient settlement can be found the modern sections of the town. It is unusual, I think, to find an area on this scale where the ancient, medieval, and modern sections are piled one on top of another, lined up together in one spot.

I won't say much about the oldest sections, since you know them for photographs, but the half-circle of the theater, located on the slope of the hill is compact in shape and truly beautiful. The structure rises as though made of steps mounting up and up at extreme angles. The seats, made of stone, are arranged in exact concentric circles, and the effect is truly arresting. I never tire of looking at them. The qualities of rigid stonework seem to agree with the exact geometry of the construction itself, creating a harmonious whole.

The white stone pillars, gates, and walls, slightly blackened from the wind and the rain, are lined up in perfect order, creating this open and spacious urban space. Then follows the crowded enclosed areas of the jumbled sections below the medieval castle. Finally, you reach the less-organized modern sections, which are without any character at all. The only commonality between the three is that all are constructed from the same materials and so rendered more interesting.

Yet for me, what catches my attention the most, when I consider the contrasts between these three urban areas, is the old cathedral itself.

Quite weary by now, this is as far as I can manage to walk today. Having visited three cities, Orange, Carpentras, and Vaison, in three days, I find myself completely worn out. I will try to continue this letter tomorrow.

September 2 (Sunday). A beautiful, clear, and windless day. From Sommières in Gard

Yesterday, and the day before that, I found myself so weary from all my travels that I never managed to continue writing. Two days ago, I had first planned to go to Sérignan, then suddenly changed my mind and took the 12:47 train to Marseille, changed trains in Avignon, and arrived in Nimes about 2:30. I visited Nimes once before five years or so, by autocar, but I have no precise memories of that visit. I spent the day walking around and looking at the various Roman ruins, among them the Maison Carrée, the Temple of Diana, the Gate of Augustus, and the arena. Tired as I was, my enthusiasm was hardly overwhelming, Still, I found the Maison Carrée and the Temple of Diana quite striking. I had completely forgotten about the cathedral, but as I stood before the façade, my memories came back. The building is a beautiful example of the southern Romanesque style. Just like St. Trophine in Arles, the cathedral in Nimes has a frieze in the Roman mode, but it is inconspicuous. The entire surface of the façade is without ornamentation and looks quite as severe and flat as a board.

I had forgotten this cathedral altogether and never remembered it from my visit five years ago. Now, standing before this structure, my recollections suddenly returned. Yet had I not come back to Nimes again, those memories would doubtless never have been revived. With only such scattered impressions, I stood in front of the cathedral on its narrow street corner and found myself rooted to the spot. My memories began to revive when I passed on my right the entrance to the museum containing Gallo-Romaine artifacts. From the entrance, I could not actually see the cathedral because of the narrow winding streets and thought it too much trouble to try. But in that instant when I pushed those feelings aside and stopped myself from entering the door of the museum, I suddenly remembered that in fact I had made precisely the same gesture five years before. I also remembered that, as before, and at exactly the same place, I had hoped to take a closer look at the buttressing and was disappointed at not being able to do so, thus invoking those earlier experiences again. And, in that same second, those experiences from five years ago now began to emerge from the fog of my forgetfulness, and I managed to recreate that earlier interior mental episode that had so far escaped me.

Yes, I certainly had been there five years ago. And my slackness and disappointment, all those past sensations I had experienced just prior to that instant, now truly took ahold of me again, and precisely because I could and did recall exactly those earlier responses. Concerning this phenomenon, I remember that quite some time ago I had read a relevant commentary by Alain, based on a citation from Montaigne. In such cases, if it seems that any particular trouble or disappointment had never actually occurred, it is doubtless because such things are simply no longer remembered. This is surely because if we posit the idea of a "recollection," this might well be because there remains still preserved, somewhere inside our heads, something resembling the negative of a photograph, so that the persistence (as here, for example, in the case of the cathedral of Nimes) of such a recollection is not limited by any particular stretch of time (five years in this case) but can always be reactivated when given the right circumstances. It can occur at any moment in time. Therefore, in this case, there was something within me that continued to endure.

It begins, first of all, with the Cathedral of Nimes itself (common sense would argue that there is no reason to doubt the existence of this church) as well as a self-consciousness springing from an ego possessed with an appropriate desire. Should not this fresh encounter therefore be able to call up just such a recollection? Of course, on many occasions one might remember certain things that may be troublesome, or memories that can serve as reminders of how often one has met with disappointments and despair. At such moments, however, one would still not necessarily remember the Cathedral of Nimes. Should these precise emotions and sentiments not repeat themselves, then, even though one might observe again the actual cathedral with one's own eyes, those memories still might not return. Indeed, perhaps one might still never even remember having been at the cathedral at all at some prior point in time.

Even under such circumstances, however, when I now look at the cathedral from the entrance to the museum, I am made to recall again my own sense of frustration and disappointment, as well as the fact that indeed I did experience all of this before. To analyze this situation more precisely, the fact of my being there five years ago does not constitute a "recollection" in and of itself. Rather, this is something that I have grasped through an objective mental calculation. Indeed, I had grasped Nimes itself in just the same way. And as for the fact that I stood in front of the cathedral in order to see it, I realize now that there was no reason why I would *not* have seen it. As I think over the matter (setting all of these details aside) I believe it was just under those circumstances relating to my standing by a church that led me to feel that frustration and disappointment. This led me in turn to recognize that such a situation had indeed existed before. These are the only actual facts involved. Moreover, there remains in me no sense of any expectation of the effort the muscles of my legs would have required to make in order to enter the museum, nor the certainty that no such a gesture to do so was recorded in the retina of my eyes. I simply acknowledged the existence in my consciousness of the actuality that this moment represented a second experience. Still, I do believe it is during just such occasions that the precise nature of the meaning of a "recollection" can be found. At this moment, however, I am not yet able to turn this analysis into any precise definition, so I will end my thoughts here.

I arrived in Sommières yesterday, but before I write about my experiences here, I would like to continue on with my impressions of Vaison-la-Romaine.

The old cathedral is situated on the right bank of the Ouvèse River, in a section of the old city. Construction on the cathedral, as with so many of the churches built in the Romanesque style, was actually begun much before that era, in this case dating back to the Merovingian dynasty of the sixth century; of course, the entire remaining building does not date from that time, but the three chapels attached to the transept certainly are from that period, allowing for some speculation they must date back some fourteen hundred years. Recent excavations reveal traces of a fourth century foundation, which perhaps may already have existed in the middle of the second century, well before the present church was constructed. The main building dates from the eleventh century and is in the Romanesque style. Later, portions were reconstructed still again in the Gothic style during the thirteenth century, when supports for the "Vault of Heaven" were apparently constructed. In addition, the four entrances, with Renaissance-style roofs and columns, were added later. White limestone from the area has been used for all this construction. There is no decoration and the whole building is simple and plain. Here in this one building all the chronology of Christianity can be seen in layer after layer, from the fourth century, perhaps even the second, up until recent times. Indeed, virtually all of Western history can be included in this span of centuries. The ancient stone that served as the chair (*cathedra*) for the first bishops still remains. The gravestones of believers from the second century have also been preserved.

At first glance, the church seems plain and without interest, but as you examine many of its facets, the structure becomes more and more beautiful. In this regard, the transepts are particularly striking. In the center is a chapel of square proportions. To the left and right, there are additional semicircular structures. The three were constructed to line up in a row. The rustic and unpretentious stone used in the construction reveals the darkened marks of fourteen hundred years of rain and wind and is truly handsome. These stones have been assembled together in a completely natural and logical way, so that they provide support for each other, and these building materials appear little changed from how they were originally found in nature. So, when they become old and crumble, they will look just as they would if in their prior natural state. Thus, should it suddenly become the time in time when they will naturally deteriorate, there can exist no means to force an extension of their natural life. The movement of Nature though the passage of time thus seems firmly carved in these stones, and they reveal the same kind of beauty that can be found in the faces of old people.

The remains of the Romanesque arches set in the outer walls of the main structure, which must have dated back to before the eleventh century, can be observed in the elegant curved lines that remain. The roofs on the outer structures are sloping and gentle, somewhat in the style of Greek architecture, and give an effect of quietude and composure. Because of the small windows, the interior is rather dark. The stones of the floor are thick, and the surfaces are rubbed away on those spots where so many have walked before.

This building, accommodating to the changes of the epochs as it went through these gentle transformations, can serve as a significant and powerful symbol of Western civilization. Such religious structures, although they exist in time and space, manage to transcend them as well; they are not only crucial for an understanding of European civilization but also serve as a manifestation of the rules and precepts concerning our essential human qualities, I am convinced.

As for the beauty of these ancient churches, there inevitably remain certain aspects of these qualities that escape any fully logical explanation. What this involves, in the deepest sense, is a matter of definitions, not merely a question of explanations. And as pertains to the beauty of these old structures, only a person born into the continuity that matches the realities of these commonly perceived conceptions might be able to explicate those characterizations. The power and beauty of French thought, I believe, has the ability to elucidate such definitions and so might bring into being the articulation of such conceptions. Indeed, it is precisely because of such abilities in such thinkers as Montaigne and Pascal that their greatness is evident. Such insights require time above all else, so that it can be difficult for us to differentiate between the lives of these writers and the significance of their thoughts. So it is that literature, the arts, even science, can come to find themselves closely linked together. Still, it does seem to me that any final definitions cannot, in the end, be truly rendered. Here humility must remain the basis for any understanding, I am sure. The great modern scientist Louis de Broglie has indicated that it was the writings of Paul Valéry that made clear to him any number of the universal scientific concepts of science, which in turn allowed him to grasp the significance of his own work. The powerful import of what is expressed here can never be exhausted.

The corridor attached to the north wall of the cathedral dates from the eleventh century and gives an overflowing sense of silence and a classical elegance. No railroad runs close to here. The monastery of this ancient town, where visitors no longer arrive, is surrounded by those thick walls of square stones. Only the swallows now provide an occasional movement, intersecting the sky above the garden, where a storm now spreads over a gray sky. With its deep roofs, the south wall of the monastery becomes the north wall of the church itself, and the three-layered roof looks quite beautiful from the garden. To the left one can see the thirteenth-century tower. In this corner, an even more profound silence exists within the reigning silence itself. Unlike the cloisters at Moissac and Mt. San Michel, the corridors here were once used by the monks, so there is an even greater sense of intimacy. The walkway is of the same type and on a similar scale, as those found at such places as the cathedral at Aix, or the old cathedral of Saint-Bertrand-de-Comminges in the Pyrenees. I am quite taken with them. But one must not think of such medieval remains as these merely in terms of simple contemporary tourism. Many such cloisters still manage to exist right in the middle of Paris today, near the Rue Saint-Honoré, Notre-Dame-des-Champs, and the Rue Gracieuse. Yet passing by the exterior walls, you do not realize that they are hidden away there.

I wrote that a consciousness of the Self can give rise to a certain homogeneity in the human spirit. In the case of such a church or cloister such as this, the faith in God that can still be found there, in quite a different way, provides the means for a self-awakening. This, in turn, gives rise to a different kind of homogeneity vis-à-vis the larger world. As for how these two come to be related together, would not the lives of the monks themselves provide some suggestions?

I have often read *The Imitation of Christ* of Thomas à Kempis, or the even older works of St. Augustine. In addition, I have been much attracted by the writings of the Christian mystics, and in particular I have sought out the *Theologia Germanica* of Meister Eckhart and the biographical writings of John van Ruysbroeck. Now, however, I have come to believe that all these books, while representing in some ways one particular apex of Christian insight, may present a considerable hazard as well. From the point of view of those who are not Catholic, would not such beliefs seem perplexing and virtually impossible to accept?

Still, I love the silence that inhabits these buildings. It is here that human existence can find a form that allows for the most open movement toward the Spirit. Any building, of course, can represent no more than one kind of symbol capable of representing that Spirit.

I came from Nimes to Sommières by car. It was clear from looking out the window that the earth in this area is barren and poor. In the fields, which are strewn with rocks, there is little to be seen under cultivation except for grapes and olive trees. The rest turns into vacant land, strewn with weeds and wild growth. Here and there are mounds of stones piled together into what almost seem to become small hills, and on them there is virtually nothing of any kind growing at all. Traveling through these continuous scenes of desolation, I arrived at Sommières and managed to set myself down at the summer home of my friend C, which I found at A and P Street. And thus I began what I hope will be a stay of two months.

Sommières, September 3 (Monday), beautiful clear weather and virtually no wind

The village lies on top of a hill, at the base of which the Vidourle River flows along in a gentle, meandering fashion. The castle is surrounded by the village, including a series of small plazas and narrow roads that move this way and that with no pattern or logic. C's house was built in the seventeenth century, a splendid home of four stories surrounding an attractive interior garden. My room is on the third floor, and my window overlooks the courtyard from the north. And because of this southern orientation, a calm light floods quietly into my room through the bamboo blinds. This stone house is solidly built, altogether different from the houses in Paris, with their thin divisions dividing up the rooms in their multiple stories. On the wide window ledges are planted pinks, and the stems of the half-wilted rosy and white flowers growing there lean heavily to the side. Now it is morning, and the sun now shines only on the northern wall. Above, the blue sky appears as a series of diverse squares. On the opposite wall, there is a corridor furnished with an iron railing, which apparently leads to the bathroom. The furnishings in my room are all quite old-fashioned, solid and spacious; there is no excess decoration of any kind, and the whole gives a pleasant impression. There is a storage room on the north side, completely stuffed full of C's books. I was glad to see that many of them are the Greek and French classics. It will be a pleasure to stuff myself full as I read these, along with the books I brought with me from Paris.

This morning I went for a walk and followed along the bank of the river. In the midst of the gently flowing water were growing some beautiful green plants, entrusting themselves to undulations in the moving currents, and a great number of fish were swimming among them. Some were more than a foot long. Apparently, this river is known as one of best-stocked in fish in the whole of France. I take great pleasure in watching the fish as they swim by, and so I stopped for a while by the bank to watch them. Fish that seemed to resemble trout were moving near the surface, and below them were other fish that appeared to be carp. Those on the bottom kept fluttering and turning, as rays of light penetrated the clear water, sparkling and shining. It seems there are also river sharks or pike called *brochet* in this river as well.

Here, in the outskirts of this village, there are also Roman remains. And it seems certain that, some two thousand years ago, the road from Rome to Spain, the Via Domitia, passed near this spot. The sturdy ancient arched bridge still serves the houses in the center of the village, just as it always has. There is a handsome tall and narrow gate at the Porte Narbonne.

I found quite a number of letters waiting for me when I arrived here. Among them were some from you. I have an image in my mind of you, looking at some beautiful Aubusson tapestry.

In the quiet of this room, looking past those drooping pinks to see the blue sky, that silence seems to have returned and now is everywhere. I do not yet know what this kind of silence represents. Nor is there any need for me to know. But it is only at this point in my life that I have been able to truly sense such a silence in the very foundations of my being. And I feel as well that I would detest any single disturbance that might come to trouble that silence.

It is now the evening of the same day. A little after noon today, C's old friend, a scholar of German literature, and his wife, who have also been staying here, left for Zurich, so now I am alone in this enormous house. Strictly speaking, though, I am not entirely alone. The concierge has opened a grocery store next door, and in the evenings he comes to sleep in a bedroom on the first floor. His fierce dog Merlin runs about all through the house. I use the phrase "fierce dog," but according to his master, the dog apparently howls in his haphazard fashion out of sheer cowardliness. The dog is large of body, and when he howls in his ferocious way, any one would surely be frightened and afraid to ever come inside. I am on excellent terms with him. While I am working, he comes close and lies down beside me.

It is such a wonderful thing for me that I am free to make use of this large study. The whole room is piled high with books. Virtually every work in the canon of the Greek classics can be found here, both in the original and in French translation. The study has a high ceiling and, in Japanese terms, is about thirty tsubo square.[11] It faces south. The floor is composed of large slabs of stone, and near the doorway, the footsteps of many generations have worn the surface of the stone away where so many have passed on through. Crossing in front of two other rooms on the way, you come out into the interior garden. On the north side there is a salon and a sitting room. In the middle of that room is a wide and sturdy desk well fit for working. On the south side, two large windows are open, facing the street beyond.

It is now the evening of the same day. Just a little bit before eight o'clock. After cooking and eating my own dinner, I went back to the study. The first of the letters I have collected together to put into this book is one that I wrote shortly before I left for Florence. That was in the autumn of 1952, I believe. When I come to realize that some four years have passed since then, it all seems like a dream to me. At the same time, it seems like an enormous length of time has passed. And during that time, I did go back to Japan for some three months. I still do not yet know precisely what meaning this span of time has had for me. At the least, I can say that I have been provided a period in which to undergo a process of analysis and synthesis. Through this, I have come to understand that the beauty of objects, and the nature of beauty itself, becomes a question that we human beings must pose to ourselves. It is just at that moment when we arrive at a sense of beauty that such an analysis and synthesis can begin. Such is the path we are destined to follow, like some preordained tracks in the earth, ones that now begins to vaguely appear on my own horizon. What is certain is that, for us as human beings, this beauty must exist.

So now, I can understand to some extent why Rilke made such an effort to go back to his childhood years.

These days I have been thinking of the matter of definitions. I am coming to believe that it can only be definitions (providing limitations, *définer*) that can confer truth to humanity. The essence of a definition does not lie in mere words alone. Words can only serve as a symbol of that essence. Through the process of analysis and synthesis, one can progress from one definition on through to the next. An artist, doubtless, through the modeling of their material, can attempt to create equivalent symbols. A philosopher attempts this with words. As definitions proceed, they deepen and expand more widely. And as these definitions come closer to perfection, they inevitably reveal a dimension of the spiritual. Needless to say, any such definition does not merely result from ideas conceived of in the head. Montaigne, in one of his essays, talks about various definitions that accrue to his conception of humanity and human existence, or at least he hints at them. But the process he describes differs a bit from merely an intellectual one that depends simply on those ideas in his head. In his thinking, it is human experience itself that is crystallized in such representations.

There is one more thing to add in connection with the idea of definitions: there is nothing new that we need acknowledge or understand. Each and every thing has already been known and accepted for countless centuries. But it *is* true that we can acknowledge the various definitions for them. During his time, the ideas of Proudhon concerning anarchism and socialism seemed new, but were these not merely his own definitions concerning those ancient conceptions of justice? This kind of thinking in Aristotle was developed in turn from the foundations laid down by fundamental ways of thinking shared among the Greek philosophers, and, in one particular sense, those conceptions affected Hebrew thought as well.

My travels are by no means finished. Indeed, they have scarcely begun. Yet even in this brief space of time, I have been taught many things by my experiences. And, to a surprising extent, these travels have brought a good deal of joy to me. I have encountered those who were in despair, those who have revealed some great goodness, and I have been struck by much that is beautiful. And just as it may seem difficult for us to actually realize what it is we plan for, our encounters are not always effortless either.

And they can appear to us even when they are least expected. In Paris, for example, I discovered the Wall of Philip II Augustus, on the Rue Clovis, which is located near the office where I would go to the University Dispersing Office to collect my monthly pay. While waiting for a friend at the Étienne Marcel entrance to the Métro, I happened to discover the Tour John sans Peur when I happened to look up through the roof. The Diana de Poitiers of Jean Goujon in the Louvre. Or when, from the village of Tarifa in the south of Spain I was able to spot the cliffs of Africa across the water. Or, the Library Reading Room at the St. Thomas Church in Strasbourg, where I felt the shock of seeing for the first time, among a vast pile of manuscripts, some examples of the early printed books of the sixteenth century, among them works of Calvin, Lefèvre d'Étaples, and François Vatable. Then again, at noon on a sweltering day in Paris, behind the Rue Vieille du Temple, when I was able to grasp the symmetry responsible for the powerful architectural beauty of the Hôtel de Rohan, which has left such a vivid image with me.

Yet powerful first impressions of this sort, however much learning or study I might subsequently undertake about these places or subjects, have never been made more compelling because of that scrutiny. When I first came to Paris, I was powerfully struck by the sight of Notre Dame, and, as I noted previously, that same sensation has returned to me again and again. Now, as I think about it, I have the sense that all was implicitly contained in those first impressions. And this phenomenon in turn is bound up with the essence of the significance of travel itself.

I feel now afresh the truth of the words of a learned monk of the Middle Ages, who wrote that "there is nothing in the mind that is not first in the senses."[12] Therefore, this truth, as it concerns us, quite naturally leads us toward an overcoming of the Self, for these sensations allow us to be in touch with what lies outside ourselves.

Postscript

By the Waters of Babylon consists of a collection of letters written between 1952 and 1956, and, with the assent of the recipient, have been collected together in one volume. Therefore, there are certainly inconsistencies in the nature of various statements that occur here. My title has been taken from a section in the *Pensées* of Pascal. The reader may attach any meaning to this that is deemed suitable.

Early Autumn, 1956, at Sommières.

Notes

1. More recent investigations suggest that works attributed to Orcagna may have been created by Buonamico Buffalmacco (active circa 1330).

2. Usually referred to in English as the Peers School, the school was founded in Kyoto in 1849 to educate the children of the imperial aristocracy. The school was moved to Tokyo in 1877 and remains an important institution of higher learning today.

3. Tsuda Sōkichi (1873–1961) was a distinguished Japanese intellectual historian who wrote on a wide variety of literary and cultural topics. For the *Kojiki* and the *Nihongi*, see note 6.

4. The translation of this poem attributed to Prince Ōkuninishi is by Hiroaki Sato and can be found in the section of poems from the *Kojiki* in Hiroaki Sato and Burton Watson, eds., *From the Country of Eight Islands: An Anthology of Japanese Poetry* (New York: Columbia University Press, 1986), 4.

5. *The Kagerō Diary*, written by an author only identified as the mother of Fujiwara no Michitsuna, is one of the great literary classics of Japan's Heian period (794–1185). There are several translations available in English.

6. Three of the earliest works in the Japanese literary and historical canon. The *Kojiki* (Record of Ancient Matters) is a compilation of historical and literary texts, myths, and other similar material said to have been composed in the eighth century. The *Nihongi* or *Nihon shoki* (Chronicles of Japan) is a lengthier version covering some of the same material and dating from 720. The *Man'yōshū* (Collection of a Thousand Leaves) is the first anthology of Japanese poetry, compiled before or during the early Heian period. Translations of all three are available.

7. The reference is to the Paris offices of NHK, the Nippon Hōsō Kyōkai (Japan Broadcasting Corporation), an organization analogous to Britain's BBC. Mori had given lectures on Descartes and Pascal while teaching at the University of Tokyo. His comments on these two philosophers were published in 1971.

8. Possibly a reference to Fritz Heinemann (1889–1970), a well-known philosopher who in his writings discussed many contemporary German philosophical movements. He was now back in Europe, having spent the war years at Oxford.

9. A reference to a famous collection of letters and other documents written by young students who were sent to the front in World War II. For some details on wartime diaries and their significance, see Donald Keene, *So Lovely a Country Will Never Perish: Wartime Diaries of Japanese Writers* (New York: Columbia University Press, 2010).

10. This translation is from Rainer Maria Rilke, *Diaries of a Young Poet*, trans. Edward Snow and Michael Winkler (New York: W. W. Norton, 1998), 78.

11. A tsubo is a little over three meters square.

12. Professor Michiko Yusa has identified the monk referred to here is St. Thomas Aquinas, and his statement is based in turn on Aristotle.

Mori Arimasa: A Philosopher in the Making

Michiko Yusa

Translated here by Professor Thomas Rimer is Mori Arimasa's *Babiron no nagare no hotori ni te* (*By the Waters of Baby-lon*)—or *Sur les fleuves de Babylone*—hereafter referred to as *Babylon* in this essay. It was first published as a single volume in 1957 in Japan.

Leaving home generally affords one to take a renewed look at their old environment, be it cultural, personal, or intellectual. Distance often makes things clearer. For Mori, it was indeed the case. He left Japan in 1950, as one of the six recipients of the French government's full scholarship, which marked the beginning of his intercultural journey abroad, through which he began to discover his roots. In his words: "I unexpectedly encountered Japan in Paris, and within myself."[1]

Mori was a prolific writer, whose writings extended from essays on Christian faith (because he grew up as a Christian); philosophy of the arts (architecture, painting, sculpture, and pipe organ music); schol-arly works on Blaise Pascal, René Descartes, Fyodor Dostoevsky, and so forth; translations into Japanese of works by Rainer Maria Rilke, Alain, Pascal, and others; a translation into French of Akutagawa Ryūnosuke's short stories; a textbook on the Japanese language for the French col-lege students; journalistic communications submitted to the Japanese media on such topics as contemporary global political situations as seen from the European perspective, or analyses of the state of contemporary Japanese culture and politics. Later in his life, when he resumed his annual visits to Japan, he was invited to give church sermons and public talks. Books that featured his participation in dialogues and public discussions were also all very well received. The present translated work belongs to a category of its own, a literary-philosophical genre Mori attempted in Japanese.

I. The Text

A distinctly fresh tone of his prose style that characterized *Babylon* caught the imagination of the younger generation of Japanese readers. It became a bestseller, and inspired countless Japanese youth.

The text is put together as a compilation of letters Mori composed to his confidant friend (whose identity is never revealed). One could argue that it is a sort of literary device. This setup can convey a very intimate personal feeling to the reader, who assumes the position of a privileged reader of Mori's communication concerning his innermost spiritual journey. Through his frequent travel to various parts of Europe—to Rome, Firenze, and so on, and his visit to major museums and historical sites—the reader was able to enjoy these places vicariously, deftly described by Mori. He traveled extensively, visiting Italy, Spain, England, Germany, Greece, southern France, and other places in between.

Babylon broke ground for a semi-confessional writing as a literary style. What separated Mori's work from numerous other Japanese predecessors whose work fell into the genre of "I-novels" was the depth of his spirituality, engaged in an existential quest. Unlike St. Augustine's *The Confessions*, his work is obviously a secular writing, but it succeeds in conveying the elevation of the spirit from mundane concerns to a higher and deeper realm of being.

Babylon comes in at least four editions with no textual variation:

(1) The 1957 edition, published as a single volume by Kōdansha.
(2) The 1968 edition, published by Chikuma Shobō. This elegantly bound volume contains two other sequel books, *Nagare no hotori ni te* (On the shore of the flowing river, first published in 1959) and *Jōmon no katawara ni te* (By the City Wall of Harran, first published in 1963). This is the edition I used in writing my essay.

(3) The 1978 edition compiled as volume 1 of the *Mori Arimasa zenshū*, (abbreviated *MAZ*, Collected works of Mori Arimasa), published by Chikuma Shobō. The *MAZ*, in fifteen volumes, is the comprehensive collection of Mori's writings, and thus scholarly citations are often made based on this edition. Already owing the majority of Mori's books published prior to the publication of the collected works, however, I simply cite from my 1968 edition.

(4) The 1999 edition compiled as volume 1 of the *Mori Arimasa essē shūsei* (Mori Arimasa selected essays), in five volumes, published by Chikuma Shobō, in paperback. The Rimer translation is based on this edition.

The Title of the Book

In his "Postscript" to the first edition (1957), Mori mentions Pascal's *Pensées* as the source of inspiration for the title of this book.[2] Pascal's passage reads:

> The rivers of Babylon flow, and fall, and carry away.
> O holy Sion, where everything stands firm and nothing falls!
> We must sit by these rivers, not under or in them, but above, not standing upright,
> but sitting down, so that we remain humble by sitting, and safe by remaining above, but we shall stand upright in the porches of Jerusalem.
> Let us see if this pleasure is firm or transitory; if it passes away, it is a river of Babylon.[3]

In his book, *Sabaku ni mukatte* (Heading into the desert), the sequel to *Babylon* and which Mori called the "Second Babylon," he talks about the symbolic significance of the river of Babylon (i.e., the Euphrates), along which Abraham and his father Terah traveled from Ur in Chaldea to Harran; after the death of his father, Abraham now seventy-five years old, set out, for the second time, for Canaan, the Promised Land (Genesis 11:27–28, 12:1–3, 16–18:21). For Mori, Abraham's second departure overlapped with his own personal spiritual journey. Thus, he adopted Abraham's journey, first along the river of Babylon from Ur to Harran, and then from Harran to Canaan, as the title of his book that talks about his inner journey.[4]

II. Mori Arimasa's Family Lineage

Mori was born in Tokyo on November 30, 1911, as the son of Mori Akira, the Protestant pastor, and Yasuko, the third daughter of the Shimizu branch of the Tokugawa family. Mori Akira was the third son of (the viscount) Mori Arinori (1847–89) and the princess Hiroko, the fifth daughter of (the duke) Iwakura Tomomi (1825–83).

To put it otherwise, Arimasa's paternal grandfather was Arinori, and the maternal grandfather was Tokugawa Atsumori (duke). Iwakura was his paternal great grandfather. We need to unpack this here

Mori Arinori and Iwakura Tomomi were both "founding figures" of Meiji Japan, who rose to prominence during the turbulent years when the political system shifted from the Tokugawa shogunate rule to the emperor as the head of constitutional monarchy. These men became the patriarchs of the illustrious families of Japan's prewar aristocracy, known as the "*kazoku*," a newly created social class, made up of former provincial lords (*daimyō*) and their relations, on the one hand, and the court nobles (*kuge*) who served the emperors, on the other. Iwakura was the architect of this new system, and he envisioned these two strands of powerful families—the former warriors and the courtiers—into the new rank of "aristocrats," modeled after the European system. They soon positioned themselves as the crème de la crème of Japanese society

Mori recalls his childhood environment in which he grew up, and how those aristocratic families lived in the "European" style:

> When I was a child, I used to take long walks along the dykes of the Yodobashi Reservoir, accompanied by my servant who held my tiny hand. Sometimes, I was taken to the military training ground in Yoyogi, where the Meiji Shrine stands today. Its construction was yet to begin then [the work began in 1915, and completed in 1920], so it was a wide, open ground.
>
> Aside from these long walks, I used to call on my relatives. My maternal uncle's home was in Aoyama Minami-chō; the home of my maternal grandfather [Tokugawa Atsumori] was in Sendagaya; my maternal grandmother's was in Ichigaya [the Ogasawara]; my maternal grandmother's younger brother's was also in Ichigaya [Iwakura Michitomo?]. Occasionally, I visited the family home of my paternal grandmother in Shibuya [the Iwakuras]. . . . My surrounding environment was something solemn and somber. . . .
>
> On these occasions, I always played Western-style card games with my numerous cousins, and enjoyed wonderful meals. . . .

At home, my paternal grandmother [Princess Hiroko] often showed me the photo albums. I saw many formal portraits of my grandfather [Mori Arinori], and other relatives of mine. Almost all the gentlemen were dressed in elaborate formal attire worn on special ceremonial occasions, while women were dressed in a Western-style long black dress, which was fashionable among the ladies of high society. . . .

Before my grandfather [Arinori] joined the Ministry of Education, he served as the chief diplomat to the United States and to the Great Britain. In those days, there were not yet Japanese embassies overseas.

My grandmother [Hiroko] and my father [Akira] both became Christians. Many of my uncles received their education in England.

Thus, I imbibed an old-fashioned aristocratic air as a matter of course . . . and lived a European lifestyle that was very unusual and unfamiliar to the vast majority of the Japanese people.[5]

As time went on, Mori developed close relationships with many of his relatives and he wove them into his world as his "vertical" connection to his roots. It was especially after he left Japan and lived in Paris that his appreciation grew how his ancestors actually informed his being. Someone who knew Mori Arinori's accomplishments recommend him to read the biography of his grandfather (it was in 1967; Mori was well into his fifties). He felt that through discovering his ancestors, "time reversed its course and flowed back from the past into the present." His younger sister, Sekiya Ayako, was especially close to her grandmother, Hiroko, and wrote a detailed account of her experiences growing up in this unique environment. Ayako's book is a precious information trove of the Mori family and the relatives.[6]

As mentioned earlier, Mori's discovery and increasing appreciation of his family roots began to form part of his philosophical reflection, as his life in Paris became more settled. The opening paragraph of *Babylon* in fact anticipates the importance of his family roots as his "destiny." We read:

Isn't it the case that how one's life unfolds and is lived is present, in essence, in one's childhood? I cannot help but be convinced of this, as I reflect on my present state of affairs and recollect my childhood memories.

If it is indeed the case, this "fact" contains not only painful memories but also offers an infinite sense of consolation. . . .

As you are familiar, in the Greek myths and in the Old Testament—to which the European spirit always returns whenever it exhausts its inquiry—temple priestesses and prophets made prophecies about those who would bask in glory or about those for whom tragic fate would await.

Why was it possible to make such prophecies, unless the entire life of the person was already essentially present in one's childhood?[7]

Lest it be misunderstood, let me clarify one thing here. Mori was not a "fatalist" or a "determinist," but rather, a realist. The knowledge of one's roots does not necessarily confine oneself to the past, but rather, the recognition of one's ancestral roots could bring about a new meaning of one's life—as was the case with him. His ancestral roots affirmed how deep his Japanese cultural roots were, even though (or especially because?) he was living on a foreign soil.

Through this sort of reflection, Mori developed a philosophical view of "time"—the only thing one can change is the past by enriching one's understanding and appreciation of it. Somewhat counterintuitive at first, this makes sense when we take into account Mori's experience of finding his ancestors (i.e., the past) and his acceptance and appreciation of what they accomplished. This in turn necessarily opened up a new existential dimension for him, full of a renewed and personalized significance of "heritage" and "legacy." After all, his ancestors lived during the critical moments of Japan's transition from the old Tokugawa regime to the new Meiji period, and were the major architects of the new social and educational systems. His great-great grandfather (Iwakura Tomomi) and the grandfather (Mori Arinori) were both men of interculturality, just as Mori himself was now finding that it was to become his destiny as well.

As early as May 10, 1956, Mori observed how temporality is closely connected with the totality of one's being. "The past flows back into the present; one's external environment revolves internally, while one's internal environment develops externally; and all begin to take a new course of 'flow' toward the future" (*Kako ga gyakuryū shi, soto ga naiten shi, sarani uchi ga gaiten shi, sore ga mirai ni mukatte nagaredasu*).[8] This conviction only got stronger in Mori, as we read his statement in his 1962 essay, "the end point of this ripening of time is for me something spiritual, going beyond the questions of mere epistemology or the nature of experience."[9] The future is shaped in this way, but the past that informs the present always accommodates the changing times and blends itself into the new emerging ethos.

In order for the reader to understand and appreciate Mori's world, I will go further into the specifics of his parents, grandparents, and a few of his close relatives.

Mori Arinori

Arinori was born into a samurai family in the Satsuma Province (today's Kagoshima Prefecture), and excelled in his study of English. Lord Shimazu Nariakira realized the need for a greater knowledge of the western world, and in 1865 dispatched nineteen young samurai to London to receive their training in science and technology. He was chosen among them and enrolled in the University College in London.

Even prior to his travel to London, Arinori already had a well-developed sense of who he was. Somewhat typical of those days, he drew up his personal motto (dated 1864). This motto, discovered among his papers posthumously, was quoted by Kimura Tadashi, who wrote his biography.[10] Mori quoted the grandfather's motto:

Be mindful of the essentials in life.

1. Always maintain yourself calmly.
2. Always leave room for critical self-reflection and correction.
3. Be patient in anything you do.
4. Avoid avarice and gluttony.
5. Control your sexual appetite.
6. Be a man of few words and focus on the essential affairs.
7. Leave to others' decisions concerning affairs you deem unimportant.
8. Eat and drink just enough to satisfy your hunger and thirst. Do not overindulge in food.
9. But make sure to take in enough nutrition to maintain your good health.

If you miss any of the above, you will fall into the likeness of a beast.[11]

By 1867, these young men in London had to think of their next step. At that time, a new door of opportunity opened:

Lawrence Oliphant, mentor and sponsor of the Japanese students, and formerly a member of the British legation in Edo, and Thomas

Lake Harris, the leader of the Brotherhood of the New Life, on a visit to England in the spring of 1867, offered free passage, room, board, and education to any of the Satsuma students who would go and live at the colony [at Brocton] in New York. Mori was one of six who accepted the offer.[12]

Mori stayed in New York and labored on Harris's farm, until he received the news from Japan that the emperor's government was formed in Edo (today's Tokyo). Arinori and a few others returned to Japan in June 1868 to be in the new government's service.

Arinori's living knowledge of the United States served him well. In 1871, he was appointed as the chargé d'affaires to the United States with the main mission of establishing Japan's diplomatic headquarters in Washington, DC, as the state embassy headed by Iwakura (November 1871 to September 1873) was to visit North America and Europe to work on the terms of unequal treaties. As part of their itinerary, their visit to Washington was fixed for February through July of 1872. To inform the members of the Iwakura Mission, Mori compiled the *Life and Resources in America* (1871), with his assistant, Charles Lanman.[13]

After successfully completing his first diplomatic appointment, Arinori returned to Japan in 1873, where he organized the Meiji 6 Society (Meirokusha), with like-minded progressive intellectuals such as Fukuzawa Yukichi and others. Their goal was to introduce Western ideas to the Japanese public. Arinori advocated the equality of sexes and higher education for women, among other progressive ideas, and in 1875 he married Hirose Tsune, by drawing up a matrimonial contract, with Fukuzawa acting as their witness. This civil ceremony was "followed by a lavish wedding reception that dazzled all of Tokyo."[14] When in 1886 the circumstances led them to annul the marriage, they simply voided the matrimonial contract, and each went on their separate ways.

Arinori was appointed to successive diplomatic positions to Qing China (1875–78) and to Great Britain (1879–84). Effective on December 12, 1885, he was appointed as the first minister of education (December 12, 1885, Meiji 18) by Itō Hirobumi. Arinori, then thirty-eight years old, implemented his vision of a new nationalized education system, under which all existing local schools were reorganized and absorbed into the centralized system by 1887 (Meiji 20). This had the most fundamental and sweeping impact on the modernization of Japan.

Iwakura Hiroko

Iwakura Hiroko (1864–1943) seems to have been the glue that kept the Mori family together through thick and thin.[15] Served by her two maids as the "princess," she kept her dignity until her death at the age of eighty-three. As the youngest daughter of Iwakura, Hiroko grew up in extremely privileged circumstances, in which Western-style education and cultural pursuits were a high priority. If her older stepsister Kiwako (born of a different mother) was of any example of those young ladies of the early Meiji period, it is not too difficult to imagine what sort of upbringing Hiroko had. Kiwako was fluent in English and social dance, as well as gifted in the traditional Japanese musical instrument, the zither (which she performed when she was in Vienna for Brahms).[16] Kiwako was praised as the "Flower of Rokumeikan" for her elegance and beauty—Rokumeikan was the hub of Meiji diplomatic social scene, where highborn aristocrats enjoyed their evenings of music and dancing.

In 1887, Hiroko married Arinori—for both of them it was their second marriage. Arinori had divorced his independent-minded first wife Tsune in 1886. Hiroko had been sent home by the Arishima family in 1885, leaving her two children with the former husband's family. It appears that in those days, divorce and remarriage were not uncommon among the aristocrats, and there was very little social stigma attached to a second marriage. Hiroko took care of Arinori's two boys from his first marriage, and a third son, Akira (Mori's father) was born to the couple in 1888. Scarcely nine months later, however, Arinori was fatally stabbed by an assassin on the morning of the promulgation of the Meiji Imperial Constitution (February 11, 1889) and died of the wound the following day. The man who committed this violent act had a written motive kept inside his kimono sleeve, which explained that he was upset with Arinori's stance on religious freedom in Japan, which seemed to this man to slight the ancient native Shinto religion. Hiroko carefully folded the formal Western attire in which her husband was stabbed, and kept it in a chest of drawers. Ayako remembers her grandmother once opening the bundle and showed her the bloodstained clothes, in silence, while her eyes spoke to her: "It may be good for you to witness the last day of your grandfather."[17] Arinori was then forty-two years old, and Hiroko was twenty-five.

Arinori's eldest son from the first marriage inherited the headship of the Mori family and the court title of viscount; Hiroko and Akira established a separate branch family to secure their legal independence. The widowed Hiroko and the young boy Akira came under the care of the members of the extended Iwakura family. Also there were friends who took pity on them. The professor Frank Muller (1864–1917) and his wife, among them, were especially important, as it was through them that Hiroko and Akira came to embrace Christianity. Muller came to Japan to teach English at the Naval School for Officers, and later at Aoyama Gakuin. He introduced them to the Presbyterian faith, and Hiroko and Akira came to know Uemura Masahisa (1857–1925), the Christian minister, who founded the Fujimichō Church. Under Uemura, Hiroko and Akira were baptized in 1904.

Hiroko in her widowhood found much consolation in her Christian faith, and spent a few hours in prayer daily. Mori recalls his grandmother reading the autobiography of the French quietist, Madame Guyon (1648–1717), with the help of a young American woman.[18] This book must have been *The Autobiography of Madame Guyon* (translated by Thomas Taylor Allen, 1897). Madame Guyon, widowed at an early age, was sustained by her faith in God. Hiroko must have found a moral courage in her story.

Mori also recalls that his grandmother read for him *The Stories of the Old Testament*, when he was just about the age when he learned to read "hiragana" (Japanese syllabary).[19] This book, written by the children's book author Nobechi Tenma, remained in his memory clearly, although it has largely been forgotten by the Japanese today.[20]

Mori Akira

Mori Akira (1888–1925) suffered from childhood asthma, which made it difficult for him to attend school. He was obliged to drop out of the Peers' School after the first year, and henceforward he was home-schooled by private tutors. Following his baptism, he decided to go into pastoral care as his vocation. He founded the Naka-Shibuya Church in 1917 in Tokyo and became its first minister. Two years later he organized Kyōjokai (Mutual Support Group), an association for Christian students. This was a network of university and college students—-both male and female. This group published its own journal, *Kyōjo* (Mutual support), which served as a catalyst to form a network of dedicated able students around Akira.

Akira died in 1925 at the age of thirty-six, from an aggravated asthma attack that weakened his heart. His dying wish was to bring together different groups of young Christian students in Tokyo to have a prayer meeting. Eminent Japanese Christians, notably Uchimura Kanzō and Takakura Tokutarō, in full agreement with the tenet, took charge of organizing the convocation, which was held three months after Akira's death, in June 1925 at Aoyama Kaikan. It is said to have been attended by almost 3,000 students.

Akira was a scholar at heart, an avid reader, and a thinker. He amassed a huge personal library, in pursuing his studies of theological doctrines, as well as of the question of the church and the state. His published writings were posthumously collected into a single volume, *Mori Akira chosakushū* (The collected works of Mori Akira), and a revised edition came out in 2020, when the Kyōjokai celebrated the hundredth anniversary of its founding. The lively activities of this group continue to this day. Such is the lasting legacy of Mori Akira.[21]

Mori Arimasa remembered his father as a stern figure, whom he always held in awe and respect. Akira was the embodiment of old-fashioned "parental authority," still very much in the air among the upper-class former samurai families in Japan. But he was also a highly cultured man, an accomplished violinist, and a lover of Western classical music. His hobby was river fishing, and Mori recalls that his father would often take him along to nearby Tama River. On one of those occasions, the whole family spent the afternoon on the riverside and enjoyed barbecue. Mori's mother and grandmother—proper aristocratic ladies—were seated on the red carpet spread out on the floor of the moored fishing boat, and enjoyed biting into freshly caught grilled fish.[22]

After the passing of his father, Mori inherited his study, which was so well furnished with books from abroad that he was able to start his serious reading and writing. This study in their spacious home in the Tsunohazu area of Tokyo became the prototype of how one should be physically laid out—with a solid desk, and the light streaming in from the left-hand corner, which layout Mori replicated in his apartment in Paris. In many unspoken ways, his father had a formative influence on him.

An important point to remember is that Akira's devoted colleagues took excellent care of the bereaved family. Mori's first published essay appeared in their journal, *Kyōjo* (starting in 1938). Years later, especially in the 1970s, when Mori began to make regular visits to Japan, Akira's old colleagues invited him to join their summer retreat of the Kyōjokai and asked him to speak at these gatherings. Among those

who took good care of the family were Shimizu Jirō and Okuda Shige-
taka. Mori always made time to accept these invitations, coming from
his father's former colleagues, for "the Kyōjokai is a group inseparably
bound to me."[23]

Tokugawa Yasuko

Tokugawa Yasuko (1888–1959) was the third daughter of the ten children of Tokugawa Atsumori and Toyoko (née Ogasawara). Atsumori
was the head of the Shimizu branch of the Tokugawa family, and her
mother was from the former daimyo family the Ogasawara.

Until she was eleven or twelve, Yasuko enjoyed a carefree life of a princess. She attended the Girls' Division of the Peers' School, where she
excelled academically and was a good tennis player. She took the piano
lessons from one of the most renowned teachers of the day. At school
she was adored as Princess "Yā" of the Tokugawa. Fortune is fickle,
however, as her father had to give up his court rank of duke in 1899,
for he could no longer sustain the enormous expenses associated with
such a title. Yasuko's mother returned to her Ogasawara family, while
Yasuko's oldest sister invited her to come along, and the two sisters
took refuge at a girls' boarding school run by a British Anglican mis-
sionary lady, known as Miss Brownlow, at Fukuyama (near Hiroshima).
During that time, Yasuko came to know the Bible and the Christian
way of life.[24]

In around 1910, Yasuko married Akira. Their son, Arimasa, was
born in 1911, and their daughter Ayako in 1915. Mori recalls that his
father and mother often played violin–piano duets at home. It was from
his mother that he took his first piano lessons, although his interest
quickly shifted to the organ and to Bach.

Mori's recollection of his mother was always tinged with wistfulness:

> My mother was academically gifted and a good tennis player. On
> her noble and narrow face, I always detected a hint of loneliness.
> She was a spiritually refined honest person. Whenever I think
> of her, I am filled with so much nostalgia that I go mad. When
> I think of her, I see that the source of my sadness traces back to
> her. If the best quality of feudalism can be described as "noble-
> ness," it was embodied in her.
>
> When I was young, her quiet presence at home often escaped
> my notice. But recently I have come to realize how greatly my

existence is rooted in hers. It is not because I am her son. Rather, my mother possessed the quality that crystallizes in love. To those who do not know her, she gave the air of being distant and indifferent to small children or pets. But in actuality, her gentle sadness overflowed towards people and things around her.[25]

Somehow, I would like to think that Yasuko's carefree spirit of the girlhood was who she really was, judging from the lively characters of her brothers, who were brave men of action, especially her oldest brother, Tokugawa Yoshitoshi (1884–1963). He was career military man, who was dispatched to study aviation at Henri Farman Aviation School in Étampes, southwest of Paris, in 1910. Once in Paris, he rented a motorbike to commute to school, so that he would be the first to arrive there, and have access to a plane to accumulate his hours of practice. He successfully completed his coursework, obtained the pilot's license, and returned home to Tokyo. He made his name in December of the same year, as the first Japanese pilot to fly an airplane, and in 1911 (the year of Mori's birth), he succeeded in taking the first aerial photos in Japan. In 1928, he was decorated with the court rank of baron, thus taking back the family honor lost by his father. Yasuko fondly spoke of this "pilot uncle" to her children.[26] Although Mori never directly spoke of this particular uncle by name, he seems to have been in the back of his mind. Take, for instance, the following episode. During one of his stays in southern France, he made an excursion from Sommières to Lunel on his rented moped, but the engine gave up in the middle of nowhere, and he spent a night under a starry sky, confronting his fear of death. The next morning, he found a way back and walked to Sommières, pushing and pulling his broken moped.[27]

III. Mori's Education and Academic Career

Mori's parents enrolled him at Gyōsei, one of the most prestigious private schools in Tokyo. It was founded by French Catholic priests, who belonged to the Society of Mary. Thus, at age six, Mori was introduced to spoken French at school. Later, he lived in a dormitory run by the French-speaking fathers. (Incidentally, the famous novelist Natsume Sōseki chose Gyōsei for his two sons so that they could learn foreign languages, but the father's optimism turned out to be unwarranted.) It was also at Gyōsei Middle School where Mori's interest in Pascal was piqued, when he heard Father Émile Heck (1867–1943), who enthusiastically spoke about the unique quality of Pascal's prose. This especially made an indelible impression on the teenage mind.

It was around this time (1927—when Mori was sixteen), the Fifteenth Bank, which was a national bank established with the funds of the members of the "*kazoku*" (the Meiji aristocracy), went bankrupt, and Mori's family lost the foundation of its family assets. With the assistance of grandmother Hiroko's elder sister's relative (who married into the Matsudaira family), he was able to adjust the family's financial portfolio, but many changes had to be made to their former style of living. Mori, his younger sister Ayako, mother, and grandmother moved out of their large house in Tsunohazu, in order to rent it out for needed income, and the four downsized in a small but fully functional rented house. The sixteen-year-old Mori came to assume the responsibilities as the head of the family. At this critical time, his father's friends and colleagues stepped in to render moral support to the family. On the day of Mori's graduation from the middle division of Gyōsei in 1929, Shimizu Jirō, a member of Naka-Shibuya Church, and who taught at the Peers' School, took the place of his father Akira as the guardian figure and accompanied him at the ceremony.[28]

Mori went on to the Tokyo Higher School (which was abolished under the Allied Occupation as being too elitist an institution), where he continued his study of French with the professor Watanabe Kazuo. When he entered the Imperial University of Tokyo, he majored in French literature and resumed his study with none other than the very Professor Watanabe. In his sophomore year, Mori succumbed to tuberculosis, possibly triggered by malnutrition, and he had to take an extended medical leave for four years from the university in order to convalesce (1933–37). When he regained his health, Mori wrote his bachelor's thesis on Pascal, and graduated from the university. He continued on to the graduate program (in 1938), and worked as a teaching assistant (*fukushu*). Because of his earlier bout with tuberculosis, and also he narrowly survived a serious case of typhoid (in 1940), he was excused from military service. During the height of the war years, he remained at the university, working as associate (*joshu*). This is the period described by Katō Shūichi.[29] In 1942, at age thirty-one, he married, and his first daughter Masako was born in 1944, but she died after brief illness in her eighth month. Mori never forgot the excruciating pain of losing his first child for the rest of his life.

In the last years of the war, Mori was offered a position of professor at the First Higher School in Tokyo, where he taught from 1944 to

1947. Meanwhile, Japan surrendered to the Allied Forces on August 15, 1945. In the early postwar days, Mori and his wife had their second daughter Toshiko, and a son Ariyuki. In May 1948, he was appointed to the position of assistant professor (with tenure) at the Imperial University of Tokyo. (It was not until the May of 1949 when the "imperial university system" was dismantled under the Allied Occupation, and the prestigious title "Imperial" was dropped from the official title of the national universities.)

As early as in 1938, Mori had already begun his public career as a writer (as we saw previously). By the time of his appointment to the position of assistant professor at the imperial university, he was already a widely published well-established scholar with much promise. By the fall of 1950, when he left for France, Mori had an astounding number of publications under his belt: over one hundred articles, twenty-three books (that included a Japanese translation of Pascal's *The Provincial Letters*, the selections from the *Pensées*, and a small book on Uchimura Kanzō, the eminent Christian writer and evangelist), several book reviews, and about a dozen roundtable discussions with leading thinkers.[30]

IV. France: The New Beginning, and Professor Jean Wahl

Following the conclusion of World War II, the French government resumed its fellowship program in 1950. Mori and five other fellowship recipients left Japan on board *La Marseilles* in August. After four weeks of sea voyage, they arrived at the port of Marseilles. In those days, Japan was still under the occupation by the Allied Forces, and the Japanese government had no sovereign status to issue a passport. Therefore, they each carried with them a piece of paper, which stated that the possessor of the paper was permitted by the Allied Occupation Authority to leave Japan to study in France.

Mori's initial intention was to complete his doctoral dissertation on Pascal, on which he had been working for some time. He also wanted to initiate an in-depth study of Descartes. However, as the ship neared the Port of Marseilles, his deep-seated anxiety began to surface in his consciousness. Would the kind of scholarship he had been trained in, and mastered, have a universal validity? Would it stand the test of French academia? This question had a deeper root—could one culture accurately communicate with another at the most profound and critical level?

As uncertain as he was, he headed north to Paris from Marseilles, and arrived there on September 25, 1950. His accommodation prearranged, he settled in a room at the Maison du Japon for foreign students. Among the first things he did was to contact the professor Lucien Foulet (1873–1958), the renowned medievalist, who was Watanabe's mentor. Foulet accepted Mori as a private student and read Montaigne with him once a week, but due to his advanced age, this arrangement terminated after a year and a half. Mori recalls punctuality regulated Professor Foulet's entire life. He soon found out that if he is early or late to the weekly meeting, even by five minutes, it was not a good idea.[31]

Mori also took the chance of contacting Jean Wahl (1888–1974), a professor of philosophy, without any letter of introduction. Carrying a one-page written research prospectus on Descartes's thought in his pocket, he knocked on the door of Wahl's office at the Sorbonne. Professor Wahl, after reading Mori's prospectus, said: "This is the kind of research I have been wanting to carry out myself. Do you think you can do a better job than I can?" To this, Mori responded: "Yes, I think I can." Thereupon, Wahl said: "So then, *you* have this project. I wish you all the best."[32]

With these words, Wahl took Mori under his wings and introduced him to his colleagues—both specialists of Descartes, Henri Gouhier (1898–1994) and Ferdinand Alquié (1906–86) at the Sorbonne. Mori joined the circle of Wahl's students, who read works by Heidegger, Husserl, and so forth, which met outside the formal university classroom setting.[33] Wahl also invited him to attend talks given at the Collège Philosophique, where Mori heard many cutting-edge philosophical discussions presented by young up-and-coming French thinkers. Through this kind of mixture of formal and informal social–academic interactions, Mori came directly in touch with the dynamic living world of contemporary French philosophy and literature. Mori called Wahl the "*onshi*, a teacher to whom he is deeply indebted."[34] It is unclear if Mori eventually produced the dissertation for Wahl on Descartes's notion of "Eternity and Moments," as his research turned into a much slower-moving project.[35] Wahl retired from the Sorbonne in 1967, but he continued to be in Mori's life, as he invited his daughter Toshiko, for instance, to spend time with him and his wife.

Wahl was a unique thinker and a poet. During World War II, being an outspoken intellectual Jew, he was arrested for his anti-Nazi stance and put in the Drancy Internment Camp. By a miraculous series of events, he was released from incarceration after three months, and fled to the Free Zone in southern France.[36] His friends secured him a passage to the United States, and he spent the rest of the war years in New

York and Mount Holyoke. Together with other French expatriates, he organized the "university in exile," which became the lively hub of displaced French intellectuals in the United States. He befriended American poets during his stay there and translated some of their works into French. After the war, he returned to the Sorbonne. He also founded the Collège Philosophique in 1946 in the Latin Quarter, as the alternative venue to the Sorbonne, where nontraditionalist thinkers were able to exchange their ideas.[37] Among those who gave their presentations were Jacques Derrida and Michel Foucault as well as Emmanuel Levinas, just to name a few.

Wahl's profoundly humane brand of existentialist philosophy, no doubt reflecting the plight of the war years, is captured in his poem "On Reading the Four Quartets."[38] Published in 1949, it was his response to T. S. Eliot's *Four Quartets*. The poem starts with:

> Better than praying on the tomb of the mother,
> Is to say yes to this world,
> And to seal it with our will.

In this poem, he alludes to his recent harrowing experience, which is not "redeemed, deceived, or healed," but he chose to embrace the world in its eternal pattern of what it is. In the darkest moments, it was not "renunciation or repentance" but "the taste of some moments preternatural, in nature" that got him through. I especially find the line "knowing the way of dispossession and loving it" stark and heroic at the same time. The poem ends with these lines, which are his reflection on what it means "to be":

> We see the pattern and live it,
> We live our own successive deaths,
> And this is living our lives.

V. Years of Economic Uncertainty in Paris

When the terms of the French government's fellowship ended, Mori decided not to return to Japan but to stay on in Paris and continue with his studies. He decided to leave his academic position at the University of Tokyo. Many deemed this move reckless, but Mori was compelled by what he called the "deep inner existential urge" (*naimen-teki unagashi*). Mori seems to be talking about something of the "intimation of the universal" that he intuited. It is to live life fully and authentically, by reaching out to the full potential of one's life, for which one is born.

If one is familiar with the "Ten Ox Herding Pictures" of Zen Buddhism, Mori now stood at the very starting point, "looking for an ox." Not knowing what he was looking for exactly, but sensing that something was missing in his life, he set out on the path of spiritual quest.

In Mori's case, he wanted to see if he could forget his cultural and personal "baggage" and start out afresh. Is there another way to live one's life free from the established status quo? He moved into a cheaper apartment hotel (with a kitchenette) in the Quartier Latin, which one could rent per month, and where a tardy payment of rent was over-looked so long as one paid up at some point.

It was out of economic necessity that he took up translation work. A big commission soon came his way thanks to the staff at the Japanese embassy—a translation into French of a novel by Serizawa Kōjirō, *Pari ni shisu* (*Dying in Paris*). This offered him a lump sum payment in cash.[39] It appears Mori's translation was further edited by a professional French translator, before it was published by Robert Laffont in Paris with the title, *J'irai mourir à Paris* (1953).

In the spring of 1952, or thereabout, the professor Nanbara Shigeru, the former president of the University of Tokyo, visited Paris on his way back to Japan from the Netherlands where he attended an international conference. He stopped by in Paris specifically to talk to Mori and to persuade him to return to Japan. Nanbara pointed out that it was his moral duty to return to Japan for the sake of his family (Mori had his wife and two children back in Japan) and for the university, but Mori had his reasons to remain in Paris. In the end Nanbara respected Mori's decision.[40] Effective March 31, 1954, Mori's position at the University of Tokyo was officially terminated, as he requested.

Mori's life was now firmly in his hand. The following is a glimpse of his daily routine shaping up in Paris in 1953, when he was putting his life in order. He found the time to go into the detailed description of his routine, when he was in London on his Christmas holiday:

> I get up at 5:30 a.m. with the ring of my alarm clock. I quickly wash, make coffee, and drink it along with a piece of bread. Then, until 8:30 a.m., I toil away on my translation into French of some writings on eastern medicine [a work commissioned by a medical

doctor at the Army Hospital]—this is to earn income.[41] As soon as I finish this, I go out and have a cup of café au lait for thirty francs at my usual café in the neighborhood. Then, at the corner of the Rue Saint Jacques and Gay-Lussac, or from in front of the Luxembourg Station, I take a bus, number 21, 27, or perhaps 81. I get off at the Palais Royale, walk on the Boulevard Richelieu, and enter the Bibliothèque Nationale. There I work until 6 p.m. on my research on Descartes.

For lunch I sometimes go to a small cafe nearby for a sandwich and a cup of coffee; sometimes I take my own lunch with me and eat it while seated at my chair in the Bibliothèque. Unless I leave to listen to lectures at the Sorbonne, or the Collège de France, or attend the talks at the Collège Philosophique, I always remain at my desk at the Bibliothèque Nationale, doing my research.

When I finish my work at 6 p.m., I board the bus again and get off at the Quartier Latin, where I eat at an inexpensive restaurant or simply cook for myself in my room. Then, from about 10:30 to 11 p.m., I use my time as I wish—preparing articles for various Japanese newspapers or magazines, writing letters, or reading books that interest me.

Once a week, I go to the Institut Panthéon for my lessons in French composition; twice a month, I go to the home of Madame M (an acquaintance of Professor Wahl) on the Rue Jacob to read Heidegger's text [*Sein und Zeit*] in German.

This is my routine from Monday through Friday, leaving me with Saturday and Sunday completely free to make use of as I wish. . . .

The simpler and more regular my routine becomes, the more productive I am [in my work]. That my life has settled into this kind of rhythm after my coming to France three years ago, and that I'm now in London for a visit for the first time, is significant for me, because I know that I can transfer this routine from Paris to London with no problem.[42]

VI. More Settled Life in Paris

In 1955, Mori landed a position to teach a course on the history of Japanese literature at the Sorbonne. He was also offered a position as a Japanese language teacher at the École Nationale des Languages Orientales Vivantes—facilitated by the professor René Siefferet. Things were looking up.

His marital situation back home had become unworkable by this time, and eventually the couple decided to divorce. Mori assumed his parental responsibility and summoned his daughter Toshiko to Paris. In order to make this happen, he needed the requisite funds to show to the French immigration authorities that he was able to afford a family member living with him. For this reason, he signed a contract to translate the short stories of Akutagawa Ryūnosuke, for the UNESCO translation series. This work paid him in advance, which enabled him to fund his daughter's move to Paris in 1958. Mori found an apartment large enough to accommodate his daughter to live with him.[43] This seems to have given him the joy of family life in Paris, after so many years.

As for the translation of Akutagawa, he initially completed the draft in 1957, but no sooner than he thought he was done with it, he was dissatisfied with it.[44] Snatching back the draft from the secretary of the UNESCO, he ended up toiling over the translation for the next several years, going over one draft after another. *Rashōmon et autres contes* (*Rashōmon and Other Stories*) was finally published by Gallimard in November 1965.

Through this work experience, Mori realized that in order to make a good translation, the translated work must read as if it had been originally written in the target language. In order to reach this level of readability, Mori mobilized his young friends and students—native speakers of French—who would read aloud to him the translation, while he fingered along the Japanese text. So long as both texts cohered, it was a good sign; when they did not, they had to stop to rework on the translation, until wrinkles were smoothed out. Ultimately, he realized that putting together the original and the translation side by side was the best (and the only) way to finalize a work of translation. Moreover, the key was not so much the choice of correct words (in a lexical sense), but rather to pay attention to the color and the nuance that each word conjures up, so as to convey the scenes and the atmosphere of the original work in a translation.

This is a familiar problem for many scholars whose work involves translation. Should one be faithful to the original, or can a freer translation be made? Mori found that it was necessary to go beyond a literal translation in order to find the "resonance" that could do justice to the original text.[45] I, however, tend to maintain that this is not necessarily applicable to philosophical texts, in which the train of thought of the thinker is more important than the color and the sound of words that conjure up images and evoke a certain atmosphere.

VII. Language Acquisition: A Bodymind Activity

While Mori honed his linguistic sensitivity, his awareness of the importance of language deepened. In his early days in Paris, he already knew that fluency in French was the *precondition* for engaging in serious academic work. He was quite fluent in his French, as he had been exposed to the language since he was six years old. But his French was not a "living and breathing" French, as he put it. Facing this fact squarely, he thought about the reason:

> When I began my research in France, what mattered foremost was that I improve my proficiency in French, even before I concentrated on my specialized field of research. . . .
>
> I had carried with me a certain method of language learning, which consisted in two "bags"—one bag was the world of Japanese language, into which I was born and raised. The other bag was French that existed as secondary to my first "bag." I was able to translate French literature into Japanese, but I could not compose a literary work in French with natural ease. French literature was something that I read by consulting my French-Japanese dictionary and my French-Japanese phrase books.
>
> It turned out that this method of correlating two languages "bags" relied on my Japanese language; and the second bag (i.e., French) was not a living language in the proper sense of the word. I think I was reading French as a sort of sign (*fuchō*). . . .
>
> I had to discard this old method in order to make my French come alive and enrich it. I needed to mature linguistically and present myself as a meaningful member of society.[46]

Language acquisition is a gradual and living process. Mori had already noticed as early as in 1957 that he no longer needed to translate familiar French phrases into Japanese because they made immediate sense to him.[47] How does this "progress" take place? He observed the following:

> For a long time I used to think that it was my rational faculty—that is, the intellect or the reason, and the power of memorization—that was paramount in learning French. But no. It became clear to me that learning French was like transplanting an organ. From the moment when a cell of little French is transplanted in me, and it successfully takes roots, this little French begins to imbibe the French language that is floating around me to "nourish and

stabilize" itself within me, and it starts to grow. There is no other way to learn French, unless one is satisfied with the method of language learning like "a translation machine."[48]

VIII. Language Teaching and Philosophizing: A Mutually Enriching Circle

Mori began to make his annual visit to Japan in 1966, as his life in Paris found its equilibrium. On October 11, 1968, during his stay in Japan, he looked back on his career of teaching Japanese in France, and thought about how it was related to his study of philosophy. Mori noted that contrary to what one may think, "my language teaching not only did not interfere with philosophizing but also it has given me much food for thought."[49]

Teaching one's own native tongue to a nonnative speaker is not a mechanical work, but it requires a well-balanced approach of clear explanation of grammar combined with rich and insightful presentation of cultural information related to the lexical items. To teach and learn a language is also a kinetic and rational activity at the same time. A philosophical perspective of how the mind works in this process is actually beneficial in language teaching. In particular, Mori's classes on the history of Japanese literature gave him the opportunity to read the original texts in ancient, medieval, and modern Japanese, and analyze them by being guided by philosophical questions. In this way, he discovered the perennial quality of the way of Japanese thinking in the works of the nativist scholar Motoori Norinaga (1730–1801), who struck Mori as a highly original thinker. He also discovered the writings of the Buddhist master Dōgen (1200–53) to be full of philosophical implications. Through his language teaching, Mori was unexpectedly developing a unique organic and concretely systematic way of thinking. The study of the history of Japanese literature turned into a history of Japanese thought—this kind of crossing boundaries resulted in their mutually enrichment for Mori.

His reading of Dōgen was especially helpful for him to understand the modern Japanese philosopher Nishida Kitarō (1870–1945). Mori's diary entries of 1968 are especially full of such references:

February 14, 1968: Upon reading Nishida's writings, I realized that having read Dōgen in order to prepare my lectures, I actually deepened my understanding of Nishida. This came as a real surprise. From now on, whenever I talk about "experience," I must reexamine the writings by Dōgen and Nishida carefully.[50]

February 17, 1968: I gave my 8 a.m. lecture on Dōgen at the Sorbonne. I'm growing ever more enthusiastic about reading Dōgen's *Shōbōgenzō*. His view of time is surprisingly profound, especially when I consider the fact that it was intimately connected with his meditation practice.[51]

IX. Mori on Nishida—Philosophy of "Pure Sensation" vs. "Pure Experience"

Mori's interest in Nishida Kitarō's philosophy began a few decades back. One of the earliest mentions of Nishida by Mori is his criticism of Nishida's notion of "pure experience." In his diary of January 27, 1957, we read:

> The one glaring essential shortcoming of Nishida's philosophy is that he postulated what he called "pure experience" as something a priori. But today, we have lost sight of this reality [and we no longer possess it].[52]

This curious passage indicates that Mori was laboring under the assumption that Nishida's notion of pure experience was some sort of socio-historical construct. This type of interpretation of "pure experience" as a "special (privileged) spiritual awareness" was an interpretation commonly held among the students of philosophy, going back prior to the publication of Nishida's first book, *An Inquiry into the Good* (*Zen no kenkyū*), in 1911. Nishida's former student from the Fourth Higher School, Kihira Tadayoshi, introduced Nishida as someone who sat zazen (seated Zen meditation) for a decade, in the *Journal of Philosophy* (*Tetsugaku zasshi*).[53] Born in the year 1911, the same year Nishida's *An Inquiry into the Good* was published, Mori may have carried a remnant of the air of the Meiji period; it is possible that he uncritically inherited the old-fashioned interpretation of what "pure experience" might mean, possibly understanding it as something akin to the "spirit of bushido" or the experience of "satori" (Zen enlightenment)—the sort of mental attitude which was still alive and embodied by many Meiji–Taishō intellectuals, statesmen, and those who belonged to the former "samurai" class. Mori was most likely looking back on the traditional samurai mindset that was no longer present in the postwar (i.e., post-1945) Japan.

Setting this quibble aside, Mori introduced Nishida to the French reading public in his essay in spring 1958, which he was invited to contribute by the editor of the journal *L'Age Nouveau*, who was among his acquaintances.[54] In this essay titled "Cheminement et direction de la pensée au Japon dans sa nouvelle génération d'apprès-guerre" (The direction of thought in Japan among the new postwar generation), Mori singled out Nishida as the most original Japanese thinker, who went beyond the usual Japanese academic practice of merely studying western ideas as a "philosophical" activity. He recognized in Nishida the profound attempt to fuse "rationality" and "existence," to reach the bedrock of philosophical insight that was in harmony with the native cultural sensitivity, where metaphysics and human existence fused into one:

> [In Nishida's thought] as the result of his indefatigable pursuit into the roots of affectivity and metaphysical passivity, rationality and naked human existence came to be fused. As far as I know, Nishida is the only one who deepened (*approfondir*) this specific tendency of Japanese thinking that penetrated into the core of that culture's metaphysical foundation.[55]

Mori continued to read Nishida as part of his personal philosophical studies. A striking remark is found in his diary of October 16, 1965, which starts out with the mention that the day before, Professor Wahl had invited him to attend a dissertation defense held at the Sorbonne for the doctoral candidate Mr. S, who presented his dissertation on Nishida. Mori's diary continues:

> As the defense was nearing its end, the chairman of the committee, Professor Lacombe, asked me to say something about Nishida. I basically said that we needed to clarify *sociologically* why he set out with the idea of "pure experience" as his starting point. As for the relationship between Nishida and Western thinkers, I mentioned that he dealt with Western philosophers only insofar as he needed to define his own philosophical stance.
> But as I think about what I said, I realize I left out one crucial point, namely, that Nishida's philosophical endeavor was a pursuit to give a coherent expression to the easterner's experience, to give it a rigorously constructed logical expression. As such it was a vast and profound, passionate, and almost an impossible task.
> Nishida himself stated something like that in the preface to his book, *Hataraku mono kara miru mono e* [From that which acts to that which sees]. If I dare say, his attempt was comparable to those

of medieval scholastic philosophers, who tried to give a logical expression to the Judeo-Christian experience.

Viewed in this manner, Nishida's philosophical attempt looms large indeed. That is, he attempted to raise the legacy (*isan*) that the eastern people inherited from their ancestors into a rational realm, and ultimately to a universal dimension. Who could deny then that whatever our ancestors accomplished had great value?

Nishida looked back to these [cultural and historical] roots in order to move forward. This "looking back" [as a posture] raised misunderstandings, [as it could be taken that Nishida looked to the past]. I think the true value of Nishida's thought will become clear slowly but gradually, and this must be so. I'm convinced of this. We should not overlook his profound inner urge that spurred him onto his work. If we overlook his inner urge, then I would imagine that any scholarship on Nishida would just be a pile of learned husks, full of empty analyses. It took me thirty years to reach this level of appreciation of Nishida's philosophical endeavor.[56]

Apart from Nishida's *From That Which Acts to That Which Sees*, Mori was reading other works by Nishida (including his lecture notes, "Introduction to Philosophy"), but I will pass over these for now.

In short, Mori came to revise his understanding of Nishida considerably over time. He came to define Nishida's "pure experience" as "the primary reality of the unity of subject and object" (*shukyaku gōitsu no genshoteki jijitsu*), as we find in his lecture he gave at International Christian University around 1970.[57] This, however, still does not do full justice to Nishida's philosophy of pure experience, but I will not go into this point at this time.

Instead, as an extended footnote, let me point out a few facts concerning Nishida's notion of "pure experience." The expression "pure experience" is actually something Nishida adopted from William James, who had described Henri Bergson's philosophy as one of "pure experience," and began to describe his [i.e., James's] own philosophical position as that of "pure experience." Two letters by James to Bergson are most illuminating on this point. On December 14, 1902, James wrote to Bergson, by giving his reaction to the latter's work, *Matière et mémoire* (*Matter and Memory*). James writes that the ideas presented in that work "were so new and vast" that it required him to go back to it for the second time, four years later. James informs Bergson that he just accomplished this task, and goes on:

> It is a work of exquisite genius. It makes a sort of Copernican revolution as much as Berkeley's *Principles* or Kant's *Critique* did, and will probably, as it gets better and better known, open a new era of philosophical discussion. . . . The *Hauptpunkt* acquired for me is your conclusive demolition of the dualism of object and subject in perception. I believe the "transcendency" of the object will not recover from your treatment.[58]

In the next letter of February 25, 1903, to Bergson, James writes:

> I am convinced that a philosophy of *pure experience*, such as I conceive yours to be, can be made to work, and will reconcile many of the old inveterate oppositions of the scholars. I think that your radical denial . . . of the notion that the brain can be in any way the [maker] of consciousness, has introduced a very sudden clearness, and eliminated a part of the idealistic paradox.[59]

Nishida was closely following James and Bergson, as his own philosophical interest was developing along the line of the "philosophy of pure experience," as James put it. Nishida used the term "pure experience" interchangeably with "direct experience," and he referred to the phenomena of consciousness under this term. A direct sensory datum, freshly given to the bodymind, gets filtered through the individual's consciousness. The state of pure unity, prior to subject–object distinction, does get separated into subject and object in the subsequent moment of reflection of consciousness, with the rise of the awareness of the presence of one's body as "here," and the source of the sensory datum "out there." I want to make clear that Nishida's philosophy of "pure experience" did not start out with the religious experience of "satori," or it represented some specific idea, such as the warrior's spirit ("bushido"), as Mori might have understood it to mean.

Another point I want to bring up is that "pure experience" has two directions—that of unification (including the unity of subject and object prior to reflection), and that of diversification and development. Mori came to recognize the former direction of unification in his later work, but the latter direction of dynamic unfolding somewhat fell out of his purview. Had he realized Nishida's philosophy of pure experience in its two aspects, Mori might have agreed with him and accepted the notion of "pure experience" as dealing with the same problem that

Mori was pursuing in terms of "pure sensation," which he came to develop somewhat systematically.

Moreover, soon after Mori's death, three sets of typed manuscripts of French translation of Nishida's writings were discovered among his unpublished papers. Nakamura Yūjirō, a Japanese philosopher, who was well acquainted with Mori, was asked to identify what they were. It turned out they were French translations of book 2 "On Reality" (*Jitsuzai*), and book 4 "On Religion (*Shūkyō*) "—both from the *Inquiry into the Good*. The third set of translations was a segment of Nishida's final essay, "The Logic of Topos and the Religious Worldview" (1945).[60]

This episode had a non-dramatic ending. These translations turned out to be the work of Professor Frédéric Girard, which somehow ended up among Mori's papers. A segment of Girard's translation was published in a special issue of *Cahiers pour un temps* (December, 1986).[61]

Further Diversion: Nishida and Mori

Mori might have been surprised had he known that Nishida crossed paths many a time with the people who had a special significance in his own life.

(1) On October 25, 1887, Nishida saw and heard his grandfather, Mori Arinori, who came to Kanazawa on the day of the official opening of the Fourth Higher School, to deliver the congratulatory speech in his role as the Minister of Education.[62]

(2) Nishida enrolled in the introductory French class at the Imperial University (fall semester 1891), offered by Emile Heck, who opened this course immediately following his arrival in Japan. (Father Heck is the person who talked about Pascal to young Mori at Gyōsei.) Nishida recalled that the class met early in the morning, from 7 to 8 a.m., so that by the end of the fall semester, the number of students had dwindled from thirty to seven or eight, and that Father Heck was a very kind and patient teacher, who conscientiously corrected his students' compositions. Nishida was among those who persevered through those early morning hours and completed the course.[63]

(3) Takakura Tokutarō (1885–1934), who was one of the closest friends of Mori Akira (Mori's father), had actually studied at the Fourth Higher School (1903–06). He was also a member of the boarding house, Sansanjuku (literally "three-three house"), which Nishida and his colleagues established in the thirty-third year of Meiji. Nishida's diary has the entry that he and Takakura had a deep conversation on January 9, 1906.[64]

(4) When Akizuki Itaru, another student who was close to Nishida, became seriously interested in Christianity, Nishida suggested Uemura Masahisa as someone to consult. When Nishida was in Tokyo for one year teaching at the Peers' School, he called on Uemura, and borrowed a copy of Rufus Jones's *Studies in Mystical Religion* [65] Uemura was the pastor who baptized Mori's father, Akira, and his grandmother, Hiroko. It is also likely that Mori himself received his infant baptism from Uemura in 1912.[66]

In this way, Nishida's path intersected with Mori's in more than one way. A further study will most likely unearth more intersections between Nishida and Mori.

X. Mori: A Philosopher in the Making

In this section I will choose two areas in which Mori was developing his own philosophical system. Not included in this discussion is his study of Descartes. A few remarks Mori made in his last years, however, indicate that his understanding of Descartes was moving beyond the model of usual Cartesian dualism, and moving toward the philosophy of "bodymind" as a unit. Wahl's reflections on this point seemed to have played an important role in Mori's interpretation.[67]

Nature, Culture, and "Pure Sensation"

Mori was fascinated by the role of senses (*kankaku*) as the gateway to the "Other"—to the environment, and to things beyond oneself. Moreover, Mori saw that this "Other" is actually immanent in the self as the self-forming experience. This is the "dialectical movement" he was interested in developing.

Mori's concluding passage of *Babylon* refers to the Aristotelian dictum, which was adopted by Thomas Aquinas: *"nihil est in intellectu, quod non prius fuerit in sensu"*—"nothing is in the intellect that was not first in the senses." For Mori, this was a good starting point of reflection. He wrote:

> I am reminded of the truth of the dictum that "whatever was not in the senses does not exist in the intellect." Moreover, this observation transcends the individual self. It is because the senses provide a direct conduit to that which is other than the self.[68]

Mori continued to develop his philosophy of the senses in his sequels to *Babylon*. He realized that the word "sense" or "sensation" could easily be confounded with the notion of "sentimentalism," "sensationalism," or "indulgence in the senses"—a life devoted to the pursuit of the pleasure of the senses. He thus distinguishes what he means by the "senses" from "sentimentalism," and so on.

> In order to form an ontological rapport with nature, one must not give in to the sensuous. To take the senses as the starting point of philosophical inquiry does not mean that the soul turns into "senses" (*kankaku-ka suru*). Rather, the proper relationship is the other way round [i.e., the soul becomes the cool observer of the senses].[69]

To look at one's environment through the filter of romantic notions would only obfuscate the clear perception of what one is actually seeing. Contained in these words is Mori's healthy self-criticism, for he was guilty of doing that when he first came to Paris and found himself infatuated with the city; he romanticized everything he saw through a tinted lens, which he eventually had to drop in order to understand France as it is.

This experience of idealizing or romanticizing famous landmarks is not unusual. Johann Wolfgang von Goethe, for one, experienced something similar when he first saw Rome. He soon realized the futility of superficial excitement, and reflected on it in this matter:

> My first amazement (*Staunen*) generally dies away into more of sympathy (*Mitleben*) and a purer perception of the true value of the objects. In order to form an idea of the highest achievements of the human mind, the soul (*die Seele*) must first attain to perfect freedom from prejudice and prepossession.[70]
>
> (Goethe, *Italian Journeys*, December 25, 1786)

In his attempt to purify his senses, Mori found the power of nature. One cannot will nature. Nature has its reality, and one has to find a way to become attuned to it. Mori's European sojourn involved many explorations of rugged nature, which he found untamed, unlike nature in Japan. In Japan, be it haiku or waka, the composition of poems over the centuries appropriated and "tamed" nature to such an extent that "nature" became so saturated with cultural memories and values, which in turn generated the experience of "nature" for many Japanese people. (He found the exception to this, however, when he Hokkaido, where he discovered untamed and naked nature.)

Mori's multicultural perspective led him to observe that the human sensory faculty tends to respond to nature through the filter tinted by human values, and in this way the inner and the outer environments become fused. Having realized this point, Mori adopted a fresh perspective and looked at such illustrious philosophers, be they Michel de Montaigne, Alain, Descartes, or Paul Valéry, who seem to be buried under the classics. He came to see them being ensconced in nature, although they assumed their place among human beings at the same time.[71] Mori drew the conclusion that ultimately, nature "shapes" human beings, who in turn respond to nature and find their "equilibrium" in nature.[72]

In the last decade of his life (June 1967), Mori discovered the Japanese philosopher Watsuji Tetsurō and his notion of "climate" or environment (fūdo). He found this notion very helpful, and adopted it to talk about "spiritual fūdo" in his writings.[73] Watsuji's environmental perspective no doubt resonated with Mori's reflections on the vital interconnection of culture, nature, and sensation.

Japanese Social Interaction as the "You–You Relationship"

Mori's keen observations on language led him to pay attention to the peculiar interpersonal relationship that he saw characterized the Japanese mode of communication, which he called "the you–you relationship," or "the second-person"-oriented linguistic behavior. He developed this observation circa 1969, out of his reflection on the state of postwar Japan, especially paying attention to its political and cultural fronts. He saw that Japanese cultural and linguistic behavior was progressively colored by this peculiar linguistic character of the "you-you" orientation. Let me unpack this point.

Resorting to the grammatical categories of the first persons (I, we), the second person (you), and the third persons (he, she, it, they), Mori

starts out his analysis with the general mode of interpersonal communication as follows:

> A human being, seen from outside, is a third person, an anonymous
> individual. Each speaker is the center of the meaning, which he/
> she tries to communicate to the other. When two persons engage
> in a dialogue, a conversation unfolds between the two. So long as it
> is a conversation, each dialogue partner is a "you" to the other per-
> son. In conversation, the third person becomes the second person,
> who is fully aware of being the first person as subjectivity.
>
> The speaker (the first person) is also a fully independent indi-
> vidual (i.e., the third person). The first person qua the third per-
> son comes to interact as the second person in dialogue. Thus, the
> relationship between them is essentially opaque and their mutual
> understanding is not guaranteed.
>
> If there is any element of certitude in conversation, it is due
> to the certitude of the language they speak. The spoken words
> (*kotoba*) are organized into an entity guaranteed by objective
> certainty, which transcends the actual speaker. These organized
> words of certitude take shape in the form of culture and society.
>
> The actual speaker, a human person, behind the words remains
> unknowable.[74]

Next, he turns to Japanese linguistic behavior. In the "I-you" relationship formed in the European languages, the accent is placed on
the first person, and independent individuals voluntarily enter into
the "I-you" relationship. But in the Japanese linguistic milieu, which is
permeated by the "two-term relationship" (*nikō-hōshiki-teki kankei*), the
demarcation line between the first person and the second person gets
blurred because "the second person" actually constitutes the "content
of the speaker, the first person." Mori does not mention the feature of
the Japanese language called "*keigo*" (polite language), whose grammar
is defined by the social position of each speaker, in relation to the conversation partner.

> To put it plainly, the first person, the "I" (*jiko*) in Japanese tends to
> get erased before the second person, "you," because the "I" assumes
> the role of the "you" in conversation with another "you."
>
> That is, I am always conscious of what "you" want to hear,
> and in the end, my self-identity is defined as "you" in relation to
> you, my conversation partner. This, then, is *not* a relationship of
> "I-you," but rather that of "you-you," wherein the first person,

"I," is constantly being erased. This is the daily social "experience" for the [adult] Japanese people.

This explains why, an individual in the Japanese linguistic environment is essentially a closed-off and private (*shiteki*) space, and not public (as defined in relation to a "you"). Each individual, bound by the consciousness of who is socially superior and who is inferior (*jōge kankei*), tends to tilt towards the direction of self-effacement (*jiko shōshitsu*). . . .

What happens to the third person in Japanese, then? It has the tendency to disappear altogether, along with the first person. It is because the third person is the first person in reverse. The third person, seen from outside, is the first person seen from within.[75]

Keigo, the honorific language, has two vectors—one is to elevate the other with the expression of respect, and the other is to humble oneself as the speaker with the expression of humility. These expressions can be on the lexical level (words), as well as on the structural level (reflected in the verbal and adjectival endings, and the forms of copula). For instance, the propositional statement, "X is red" is expressed variously in Japanese as "*Akai*" (propositional neutral statement), "*Akai desu*" (normal polite discourse style), and "*Akou gozaimasu*" (super-polite discourse)—depending on to whom the speaker is speaking and about what the speaker is speaking. As a rule of thumb, the longer the expression, the politer the statement.

When this linguistic habit of "you-you" is securely established within oneself, one's social antenna is also set to work. That is, one is constantly aware of "to whom I am speaking," and adjusts the level of linguistic politeness.[76] In an aristocratic family such as Mori's, the mother used to speak to her own children, and especially to her sons, in the hyper-polite language! "*Arimasa-san, kyō, irasshaimasuka?*" (My dear son, Arimasa, will you come to see me today?), for instance, was an ordinary style of discourse among those families. The son was equally expected to speak *keigo* to his parent.

During the Allied Occupation, this form of super-polite discourse came under criticism as "undemocratic," and the adoption of a less formal style of speech was encouraged for the Japanese people. Today, the connection between social class and speech style has disappeared to a great extent, but subtle traces of this old linguistic custom still survive to this day.

When it comes to business transactions, the skillful use of *keigo* is paramount. It is the lifeline of the business company, as a careless speech can offend the customer and lose their business. Someone close to me underwent a company-training program for six months when she first got her job. She became very skilled in answering the phone and interacting with clients that she became an invaluable asset at her workplace. Her training entailed not only the proper choice of words but also the proper tone of the voice, the softness and the clarity of the voice, and the pitch—all carefully modulated to make the other feel comfortable and important.

Mori was critical of the practice of this "you–you discourse" because he saw that it inhibited individuals from thinking for themselves and developing a healthy sense of self. He saw it also as detrimental for the country of Japan in the long run, if it wanted to establish a confident diplomatic presence on the global stage.[77]

XI. The Final Phase of His Life

By around 1969, Mori sensed that his inner and outer world had arrived at a new state of equilibrium, as his experience of life in Paris had fully matured, and things were coming together. He felt he was at the threshold of a new chapter of life.[78] He was a living witness to his own experimental hypotheses that experience is not a closed system but open—something that can grow and ripen. Experience is after all another word for life. He returned home to Paris from his three-month stay in Tokyo on November 2, 1967, with the new sensation that his world now began to draw an oblong shape (*daen*) with two foci—Paris and Tokyo, France and Japan, and more broadly, Europe and Asia.[79]

From 1968 to 1969, Mori talked about a radical mutation that was taking place within him. This intimation of something new marked the final phase of his life. In 1969, he was appointed to the position of visiting professor at International Christian University in Mitaka, Tokyo, where his duty was to give an intensive series of lectures annually. This academic appointment created a new rhythm of life, as he now had a reason to return to Japan annually, which rekindled many old ties he had once left behind. His reputation of a thinker-author with an international perspective, was reaching celebrity status. The beautifully bound edition of *Babylon* and its sequel volume (published in 1968 and 1970), no doubt played an important role in enhancing the image of Mori in the minds of Japanese readers.

In Paris, his years of contribution to the field of Japanese studies were duly recognized. He was appointed to the directorship of the

Maison du Japon in 1973—the very same place he began his sojourn in Paris in 1951, and this time as its director, not as a lodger. His children were all growing up, including his French daughter, conceived out of his brief second marriage to a French woman.

He began to look forward to his postretirement phase, when he could finally devote himself to his philosophical work on Descartes and to his organ playing. He was translating (into Japanese, I presume) Descartes's last work, *The Passions of the Soul* (*Les passions de l'âme*, 1649), which went beyond the body–mind dualism to a "third realm" (Wahl), which had as its sui generis principle the unity of spirit and matter (or the bodymind).[80] Mori's health began to falter around this time, however. He was unable to quit his lifelong habit of smoking. He first suffered from a major stroke in the summer of 1970, while in Sapporo. This dissipated his intellectual energy, needed to complete the project on Descartes. Jean Wahl died in Paris on June 19, 1974, at age 86, and Mori died two years later, on October 18, 1976, at age 65. He was surrounded by his family and devoted friends. His body was cremated at the Cemetery of Père Lachaise. The ashes were brought back to Japan by his daughter Toshiko, and interned in the family grave at Tama Cemetery in Tokyo. Mori thus concluded his long journey and returned "home" to rest alongside his parents. He was "able to die his own death, without fearing death."[81]

Augustin Berque, a geologist, who had Mori as his professor of Japanese at the Center for the Oriental Languages in Paris, 1967 to 1969, recalls that Mori was a popular professor among his French students, as he took delight in illustrating grammar points with cultural information, which he had at his fingertips. His students lovingly called him "Professor Savant." Berque, a recipient of illustrious prizes and honors, is now a retired professor of the École des Hautes Études en Sciences Sociales, Paris. When Mori was in Sapporo for his second visit in 1971, Berque also happened to be in Japan, and on one afternoon he and Mori had a leisurely witty conversation over a glass of beer.[82]

A Personal Note

"Is that Professor Mori?" I asked myself one evening, when I got on a bus at Mitaka Station in Tokyo. I was returning to my dormitory on the campus of International Christian University (ICU), after an afternoon of my part-time job. I was tutoring a high school student who was preparing for her university entrance exam.

Unmistakably, it was Professor Mori, as I recognized him from the photos on the cover of his books.

He sat at the very back of the bus, occupying the entire row of seats to himself, with a little parcel of "doggy bag" in his hands. It might have been a delicious dessert or whatever he was bringing back from his dinner. He was then staying at the guesthouse on campus—Fūrinsō (Maple Grove Guest House). That little white parcel strangely remains in my memory to this day, as well as Mori's serious expression on his face, guarding this white package of "treasure."

I was seized by the urge to go up to him, introduce myself, and shake his hand. But my shyness overcame me, and I just remained at my seat. It must have been the late fall of 1971—my freshman year at ICU. To this day, I regret that I missed this opportunity.

Even if I missed a personal handshake, I recall that I heard him play Bach on the pipe organ at the Seabury Memorial Chapel on campus. The occasion was sparsely attended, I remember, but somehow that lack of popular interest in the organ concert resonated with the kind of music he played—nothing fancy or showy, but austere and ascetic.

I also remember that I heard him speak at a university-wide lecture series, also given on campus, on a topic that far surpassed my young immature mind. Probably, he was used to that sort of impact of his talk on the audience. He just went on with his talk. Today, over half a century later, that image of Professor Mori, talking to the audience from the podium, comes back to me, like an abstract drawing of a non-conformist solitary thinker.

I end this personal note by mentioning Professor Paul Mus, who was the authority of Southeast Asian Buddhism at the Collège de France (and later coappointed at Yale University).[83] Professor Rimer married Mus's daughter Laurence. Mus's moving tribute to his childhood friend, "Paysans et paysages: Ense et Aratro," which he read in the *Esprit*, left a deep impression on Mori.[84] Especially poignant for Mori were the lines that described the independent and inventive character of the French peasants, who "did not need to read Descartes," because they already embodied how to think on their own and live their lives accordingly.[85]

I am struck by this remarkable coming together of various lives, as Professor Rimer, the translator of *By the Waters of Babylon,* and his wife Laurence, shed new light on the living connection that existed between Mus and Wahl, in relation to Mori (I cannot go into the details at this time).

What a surprise it has been to return to the living "waters" of life. My deepest appreciation goes to Professor Rimer, through whose present translation, Mori's most influential work that inspired many a young Japanese student in the 1960s and 1970s shines again, having gained new luster.

Notes

1. Entry March 24, 1956; Mori Arimasa, *Babiron no nagare no hotori ni te* [On the shore of the river flowing through the region of Babylonia] (Tokyo: Chikuma Shobō, 1968). This edition contains three works: *Babiron no nagare no hotori ni te* (first published in 1957), 1–130; *Nagare no hotori ni te* [On the shore of the flowing river] (1959), 131–298; and *Jōmon no katawara ni te* [By the city wall of Harran] (1963), 299–397.

2. Blaise Pascal, *Pensées*, est. Léon Brunschvicg, ed. Dominique Descotes (Paris: Garnier-Flammarion, 1976), 459. There are at least three main methods of identifying Pascal's passages of the *Pensées* adopted by different editions: B = Brunschvicg edition, L = Lafuma edition (the English translation by A. J. Krailsheimer, 1966 was made based on this edition), and S = Sellier edition. Because L (translated into English) and B (in French) benefit from the existence of the "concordance," I refer both to L and B to identify the passages.

3. Pascal, *Pansées*, 1966, 312.

4. Mori Arimasa, *Sabaku ni mukatte* [Heading into the desert] (Tokyo: Chikuma Shobō, 1970a), 47–49. This is the sequel to *Babiron no nagare no hotori ni te* (1968).

5. Entry of January 5, 1954; Mori, *Babiron*, 68.

6. Sekiya Ayako, *Ippon no kashi no ki—Yodobashi no ie no hitobito* [The lone oak tree—People associated with the house in Yodobashi] (Tokyo: Nihon Kirisutokyōdan Shuppankyoku, 1981).

7. Entry of October 8, 1953; Mori, *Babiron*, 3.

8. Mori, *Babiron*, 107.

9. Entry of September 20, 1962; Mori, *Babiron*, 223–37.

10. Kimura Tadashi, (1889). *Mori Sensei-den* [A biography of Mr. Mori Arimasa] (Tokyo: Kinkōdō Shoseki, 1889).

11. Mori, *Sabaku*, 172–73, quoted in Kimura, *Mori Sensei*, 7.

12. John van Sant, ed., *Mori Arinori's Life and Resources in America*. (Lanham, MD: Lexington Books, 2004), xviii–xix.

13. van Sant, *Mori Arinori's Life*, xxii.

14. van Sant, *Mori Arinori's Life*, xxx.

15. Sekiya, *Ippon no kashi no ki*.

16. Hagiya Yukiko *Wīn ni Rokudan no shirabe—Toda Kiwako to Burāmusu* [The vibrating tune of "Rokudan" in Vienna—Toda Kiwako and Brahms] (Tokyo: Chūōkōron-shinsha, 2021), 164–72.

17. Sekiya, *Ippon no kashi no ki*, 19.

18. Entry of September 28, 1959; Mori, *Sabaku*, 377.

19. Mori, *Babiron*.

20. Mori Arimasa, *Ikiru koto to kangaeru koto* [To live and to think] (Tokyo: Kōdansha, 1970b), 25.

21. See their website: https://kyojokai.com/about.

22. Sekiya, *Ippon no kashi no ki*, 168–69.

23. Mori Arimasa, *Furui mono to atarashii mono* [Things old and new] (Tokyo: Nihon Kirisutokyōdan Shuppankyoku, 1975), 193.

24. Sekiya, *Ippon no kashi no ki*, 148–49.

25. Entry of February 16, 1954; Mori, *Babiron*, 74–75.

26. Sekiya, *Ippon no kashi no ki*, 151–53.

27. Entry of October 2, 1959; Mori, *Babiron*, 380–87.

28. Sekiya, *Ippon no kashi no ki*, 179.

29. See the Rimer essay in this volume.

30. See Takahashi Hiroshi, "Mori Arimasa chosaku mokuroku" [Comprehensive list of writings by Mori Arimasa], *Hokusei Gakuen Joshi Tanki Daigaku Kiyō* 22 (1983): 67–82.

31. Mori Arimasa, (1967). *Harukana Nōtoru Damu* [Notre Dame in the distance]. (Tokyo: Chikuma Shobō, 1967), 155–56.

32. Sekiya, *Ippon no kashi no ki*, 230–33.

33. Mori Arimasa, (1969). *Tabi no sora no shita de* [Under the traveler's sky] (Tokyo: Chikuma Shobō, 1969), 194–95. This volume contains several essays (e.g., "Bunka no ne to iu mono ni tsuite" [The "roots" of culture] (Dec. 1955), 149–73, and "Kotoba ni tsuite" [Reflections on language] (1968 October 11, 133–148.

34. Mori, *Sabaku,* 255.

35. Entry of January 12, 1966; Mori, *Sabaku*, 96.

36. W. C. Hackett, *Outside the Gates.* (Brooklyn, NY: Angelico Press, 2021).

37. Emmanuel Levinas, *Ethics and Infinity: Conversations with Philippe Nemo* (Pittsburgh: Duquesne University Press, 1985), 55.

38. Jean Wahl, "On Reading the Four Quartets," *Poetry* 73, no. 6 (March 1949): 317.

39. Mori, *Ikiru koto,* 44.

40. Mori Arimasa, *Tōzakaru Nōtoru Damu* [The Notre Dame becoming more distant] (Tokyo: Chikuma Shobō, 1976), 125.

41. Mori Arimasa, *Kigi wa hikari o abite* [Trees busking in the sun] (Tokyo: Chikuma Shobō, 1972), 13.

42. Entry of December 26, 1953, in London; Mori, *Babiron*, 57–58.

43. Mori, *Ikiru koto,* 44; and Mori, *Tōzakaru Nōtoru Damu*, 16.

44. Mori, *Harukana Nōtoru Damu*, 154; and Mori, *Sabaku*, 88.

45. Mori, *Sabaku*, 142.

46. October, 1966; Mori, *Harukana Nōtoru Damu*, 143.

47. Entry of September 22, 1957; Mori, *Babiron*, 239.

48. Entry of December 5, 1965; Mori, *Sabaku*, 80.

49. Mori, *Tabi no sora*, 133.

50. Mori, *MAZ* 13: 447.

51. Mori, *MAZ*, 13: 449

52. Mori, *MAZ*, 13: 55.

53. See Michiko Yusa, *Zen and Philosophy: An Intellectual Biography of Nishida Kitarō* (Honolulu: University of Hawai'i Press, 2002), 87–88.

54. See entries of March 14 and May 5, 1958; Mori, *Babiron*, 282, 296.

55. Mori Arimasa, "Cheminement et direction de la pensée au Japon dans sa nouvelle génération d'après-guerre" [The direction of thought in Japan among the new postwar generation]," *L'Age Nouveau*, nos. 101–102 (April-May): 83; Mori, *MAZ*, 15: 89-90. Original French text and translation into Japanese by Ninomiya Masayuki are compiled in Mori, *MAZ*, 15: 63-84.

56. Entry of October 16, 1965; Mori, *MAZ*, 13: 272–73.

57. Mori Arimasa, *Keiken to shisō* [Experience and Thought] (Tokyo: Iwanami Shoten, 1977), 18–19.

58. Ralf Barton Perry, *The Thought and Character of William James (Briefer Version)* (New York and Evanston, IL: Harper & Row, 1935), 341–42.

59. Perry, *Thought and Character of William James*, 343. Emphasis in the original.

60. Nakamura Yūjirō, "Mori Arimasa ga nokoshita mono—sono messēji o dō uketomeru ka" [Unpublished writings left behind by Mori Arimasa: How do we receive their message?], *Tenbō* 236 (August 1978): 132–33.

61. Nakamura Yūjirō, *Nishida tetsugaku no datsukōchiku* (Deconstructionist elements present in Nishida's philosophy), (Tokyo: Iwanami Shoten), 153-54.

62. Yusa, *Zen and Philosophy*, 17–18.

63. Yusa, *Zen and Philosophy*, 35.

64. Nishida Kitarō, Nishida Kitarō zenshū [Collected Works of Nishida Kitarō] vol. 17 (Tokyo: Iwanami Shoten 1980), 13 (Hereafter, NKZ); and Yusa, Zen and Philosophy, 84, 106–7.

65. Nishida Kitarō, 1980. Diary, December 29, 1909, *NKZ* 17.233.

66. Sugimoto Haruo, 1982, 4; also see Takahashi Hiroshi, 2010.

67. Mori, *Kigi wa hikari*, 52.

68. Mori, *Babiron*, 130.

69. Entry of July 14, 1956; Mori, *Sabaku*, 32.

70. December 25, 1786; Johann Wolfgang von Goethe, *Goethe's Travels in Italy together with his Second Residence in Rome and Fragments on Italy*, trans. A. J. W. Morrison and C. Nisber (London: George Bell & Sons, 1885).

71. Mori, *Sabaku*, 288–89.

72. Mori, *Tabi no sora*, 210, 217–18, et passim.

73. Entries of June 16 and June 18, 1967; Mori, *Sabaku*, 225, 238.

74. Mori, *Tōzakaru Nōtoru Damu*, 31–32.

75. Mori, *Tōzakaru Nōtoru Damu*, 68–69.

76. Mori, *Kigi wa hikari*, 196–205.

77. Mori, *Kigi wa hikari*; Mori, *Tōzakaru Nōtoru Damu*; and Mori, *Keiken to shisō*.

78. Mori, *Tabi no sora*, 147.

79. Entry of November 3, 1967; Mori, *Sabaku*, 282.

80. Mori, *Kigi wa hikari*, 50–53.

81. Entry of October 8, 1953; Mori, *Babiron*, 3.

82. Personal communication with the author, February 10, 2023.

83. See David Chandler, "Paul Mus (1902)-1969): A Biographical Sketch," *Journal of Vietnamese Studies*, Vol. 4, No. 1 (Winter 2009) 149-191. Online: jstor. org/stable/10.1525/vs. 2009.4.1.149.

84. Paul Mus, "Paysans et paysages: Ense et aratro" [Peasants and landscapes: With service both in war and in peace], *Esprit* 353, no. 3 (March 1967): 461–67.

85. Mori, *Sabaku*, 153, 159, and 259-60, et passim.

References

Abbreviations

MAZ (1978–1982). *Mori Arimasa zenshū* [Collected works of Mori Arimasa] 15 vols. (Tokyo: Chikuma Shobō). Volume number is followed by the page number(s).

NKZ (1979–1980). *Nishida Kitarō zenshū* [Collected works of Nishida Kitarō] 19 vols. (Tokyo: Iwanami Shoten).

TDH. *Tokyo Daigaku hyakunenshi-shi* [One hundred years of the University of Tokyo], edited by Tokyo Daigaku Hyakunenshi Henshū Iinkai. Tokyo: Tokyō Daigaku Shuppan, 1986.

Chandler, David. "Paul Mus (1902)-1969): A Biographical Sketch," *Journal of Vietnamese Studies*, Vol. 4, No. 1 (Winter 2009) 149-191. Online: jstore.org/stable/10.1525/vs. 2009.4.1.149.

Goethe, Johann Wolfgang von. *Goethe's Travels in Italy together with his Second Residence in Rome and Fragments on Italy*, translated by A. J. W. Morrison and C. Nisber. London: George Bell & Sons, 1885.

Hackett, W. C. *Outside the Gates*. Brooklyn, NY: Angelico Press, 2021.

Hagiya Yukiko. *Wīn ni Rokudan no shirabe—Toda Kiwako to Burāmusu* [The vibrating tune of "Rokudan" in Vienna—Toda Kiwako and Brahms] Tokyo: Chūōkōron-shinha, 2021.

Kimura Tadashi. *Mori Sensei-den* [A biography of Mr. Mori Arimasa] Tokyo: Kinkōdō Shoseki, 1889.

Levinas, Emmanuel. *Ethics and Infinity: Conversations with Philippe Nemo*. Pittsburgh: Duquesne University Press, 1985.

Mori Arimasa. *Babiron no nagare no hotori ni te* [On the shore of the river flowing through the region of Babylonia]. Tokyo: Chikuma Shobō, 1968.

Mori Arimasa. "Cheminement et direction de la pensée au Japon dans sa nouvelle génération d'apprès-guerre" [The direction of thought in Japan among the new postwar generation]. *L'Age Nouveau*, nos. 101–102 (April-May 1958): 80–95.

Mori Arimasa. *Furui mono to atarashii mono* [Things old and new]. Tokyo: Nihon Kirisutokyōdan Shuppankyoku, 1975.

Mori Arimasa. *Harukana Nōtoru Damu* [Notre Dame in the distance]. Tokyo: Chikuma Shobō, 1967.

Mori Arimasa. *Ikiru koto to kangaeru koto* [To live and to think]. Tokyo: Kōdansha, 1970b.

Mori Arimasa. *Keiken to shisō* [Experience and Thought]. Tokyo: Iwanami Shoten, 1977.

Mori Arimasa. *Kigi wa hikari o abite* [Trees busking in the sun]. Tokyo: Chikuma Shobō, 1972.

Mori Arimasa. *Mori Arimasa zenshū* [Collected works of Mori Arimasa]. Vol. 13. Tokyo: Chikuma Shobō, 1982.

Mori Arimasa. *Mori Arimasa zenshū* [Collected works of Mori Arimasa]. Vol. 15. Tokyo: Chikuma Shobō, 1982.

Mori Arimasa. *Sabaku ni mukatte* [Heading into the desert]. Tokyo: Chikuma Shobō, 1970a.

Mori Arimasa. *Tabi no sora no shita de* [Under the traveler's sky]. Tokyo: Chikuma Shobō, 1969.

Mori Arimasa. *Tōzakaru Nōtoru Damu* [The Notre Dame becoming more distant]. Tokyo: Chikuma Shobō, 1976.

Mus, Paul. "Paysans et paysages: Ense et aratro" [Peasants and landscapes: With service both in war and in peace]. *Esprit* 353, no. 3 (March 1967): 461–67.

Nakamura Yūjirō. "Mori Arimasa ga nokoshita mono—sono messēji o dō uketomeru ka" [Unpublished writings left behind by Mori Arimasa: How do we receive their message?]. *Tenbō* 236 (August 1978): 129–46.

Nakamura Yūjirō. *Nishida tetsugaku no datsukōchiku* [Deconstructionist elements present in Nishida Philosophy], (Tokyo: Iwanami Shoten), 1987.

Nishida Kitarō, *Nishida Kitarō zenshū* [Collected Works of Nishida Kitarō]. Vol. 17. Tokyo: Iwanami Shoten, 1980.

Pascal, Blaise. *Pensées*, translated with an introduction by A. J. Krailsheiner. Harmondsworth, UK: Penguin Books, 1966.

Pascal, Blaise. *Pensées*, established by Léon Brunschvicg, edited by Dominique Descotes. Paris: Garnier-Flammarion, 1976.

Perry, Ralf Barton. *The Thought and Character of William James (Briefer Version)*. New York and Evanston, IL: Harper & Row, 1935.

Sekiya Ayako. *Ippon no kashi no ki—Yodobashi no ie no hitobito* [The lone oak tree—People associated with the house in Yodobashi]. Tokyo: Nihon Kirisutokyōdan Shuppankyoku, 1981.

Sugimoto Haruo. "Mori-san no shinkō" [Mr. Mori's Christian faith]. In *Furoku* [Leaflet]. Vol. 4. Tokyo: Chikuma Shobō, 1978, 2-9.

Takahashi Hiroshi. "Mori Arimasa chosaku mokuroku" [Comprehensive list of writings by Mori Arimasa]. *Hokusei Gakuen Joshi Tanki Daigaku Kiyō* 22 (1983): 67–82.

Takahashi Hisashi. "Mori Arimasa ryakunen'pu" [Abridged chronology of Mori Arimasa], 2010, 8. http://bon.mond.jp/files/arimasa_nenpu100411.pdf.

van Sant, John, ed. *Mori Arinori's Life and Resources in America*. Lanham, MD: Lexington Books, 2004.

Wahl, Jean. "On Reading the Four Quartets." *Poetry* 73, no. 6 (March 1949): 317.

Yusa, Michiko. *Zen and Philosophy: An Intellectual Biography of Nishida Kitarō*. Honolulu: University of Hawai'i Press, 2002.

Japan, France, and Mori Arimasa

1

> "Aah, the West"—what a sound of wonder that phrase holds.
>
> —Nagai Kafū

With the coming of the Meiji period in 1868, Japan opened her doors to the West, and since that moment in time, Japanese writers, artists, and intellectuals have continued to visit Europe in ever increasing numbers, held back only during the years just before and during the Pacific War.

In the early years, unlike the politicians, engineers, and others who made their way to England, Germany, and France to learn specific Western methods and techniques, intellectuals and writers in particular were soon to begin seeking to grasp the import and significance of the cultures and civilizations of Europe that they were virtually encountering for the first time. Several of Japan's greatest modern writers visited Europe in the early decades of the twentieth century, and their discoveries, disappointments, and self-discoveries helped reshape, expand, and define the nature of modern Japanese literature and thought.

In the early years, the concept of the "West" remained somewhat undifferentiated, with each nation in Europe seen as a sort of individual subset of the whole of Europe itself. English was the prominent choice of foreign languages in the Meiji period and after, so that even those writers discovering German and French thought and literature were in earlier phases of this continuum only able to acquaint themselves with those texts through English translations. Through the efforts of a series of highly gifted Japanese visitors, however, the outlines of the diverse cultures of Europe gradually became increasingly clear.

The earliest of these important writers and intellectuals was doubtless Mori Ōgai (1892–1922), who lived in Germany from 1884 to 1888 while studying Western medicine, and whose enthusiasm for German poetry and prose alike led him not only to introduce German and other European writers to Japanese readers through his own essays and translations but also to write several of his own trenchant stories concerning life in Germany, and, after his return, about both contemporary and historical Japan.

If Ōgai's visit to Germany found him enthusiastic, another celebrated figure to visit Europe was Natsume Sōseki (1867–1916), arguably Japan's greatest modern novelist, whose time in London found him troubled with doubts and fears, which after his return began to be reflected in his increasingly darker novels. Like Mori Arimasa, half a century later, who before his departure for France, was already highly respected in Japan for his scholarly essays on Blaise Pascal and René Descartes, Sōseki was already well-known as a scholar, in this case of British literature. For both of them, their difficulties abroad, as each came to ruefully acknowledge, came from their struggles in making a transition from something they believed they had grasped intellectually while still living in Japan to the actual challenges of facing on a daily basis the realities of the foreign cultures they had heretofore been able to observe only in the abstract, and from afar.

Eventually it was to be France, more than any other European country, which was to attract significant numbers of gifted Japanese poets, writers, and painters. Two writers who in the early years doubtless made the most significant efforts to grasp the nature of French society and civilization were Nagai Kafū (1879–1959) and Shimazaki Tōson (1892–1943). Kafū had long admired aspects of French civilization, but his opportunity to work there briefly in 1906 opened him up to even wider influences, which in turn led him to develop his own talents as a writer. The novelist Shimazaki Tōson (1892–1943), who lived in self-imposed exile in France from 1913 to 1915, set out to examine the realities of daily life in Paris, writing accounts for Japanese newspapers and magazines, as well as essays and an important novel, all dealing in a thoughtful fashion with questions concerning the complexities and nuances of comparative cultures, identifying the issues that, several generations later, were to become as well the focus of many of Mori's own speculations.

Tōson remained convinced that the most efficacious way to grasp the significance of European civilization was through the arts. "As a traveler in a foreign land," he wrote in 1915, "I have come to realize again and again the supreme value of the arts. I am deeply convinced that if two disparate peoples wish to understand each other, really wish to grasp each other's point of view, there is no straighter, no surer road than through the arts."[1] In the early postwar years, similar convictions would come to be articulated by a number of Japanese writers such as Mori, Endō Shūsaku, and many others.

In prewar Japan, the essays and novels of such writers, and those of many other literary travelers as well, helped create a whole climate for a new Japanese literature.

Their work and significance have been widely studied and written about by Japanese and Western scholars alike, who have pointed out how the aggregate of their fresh views and attitudes helped create a culture of curiosity and acceptance in Japan for a whole range of Western cultural values. By the 1930s, however, this enthusiasm was to be sharply curbed by the rise of militarism. The attempts to suppress Western cultural ideas and ideals would continue until the war ended in 1945.

In this shifting continuum, the early postwar period was, for Japan, a particularly troubling time. In the case of Mori, the Japan of his generation living in the early postwar period still remained, both in terms of economic hardship and its spiritual state, in a state of shock; Japan's burgeoning attempts to again seek a secure and more positive footing with other nations, particularly with those who had been former adversaries, still appeared to remain a difficult and tiring road.

Among many intellectuals of this early postwar period there remained a conviction that it had been the failure by their countrymen to perceive the true nature and status of the West and Western culture that had contributed so much to those miscalculations that brought about the war in the first place. Now it seemed clear to them that a still deeper understanding was required. And there was also a conviction that to achieve this would be a far more difficult task than had been assumed by many of those who addressed these same questions in the prewar period. In the view of some early postwar intellectuals, those in the prewar generation who undertook to understand such matters had not made sufficient attempts to raise the level of their own self-consciousness as they had observed the significance and power of European culture.

2

> Generally speaking, the intellectual is more sensitive than the average citizen to foreign culture and more readily influenced by it . . .. This is a phenomenon common whenever one country comes in contact with the culture of another more advanced country and is not peculiar to Japan.
>
> —Katō Shūichi[2]

During the war years, Katō Shūichi (1916–2008), who would later become one of the most significant cultural critics of postwar Japan, was pursuing his medical studies in Tokyo when he first met Mori, then still a teaching assistant. "In those days," Katō remembered, "Mori was living in a room at the Hongō YMCA where he buried himself among books, cigarette stubs, dust, and unlaundered underwear and socks." At the time, Katō was highly impressed with Mori's already advanced level of knowledge concerning European culture. "In between reading Pascal in French or Calvin in Latin and playing Bach's organ pieces, he would converse eloquently."[3] It was at this time that Katō also met Mori's friend Kinoshita Junji (1914–2008), who later became one of the most admired playwrights of the postwar period.[4] By 1948, Mori was teaching at the University of Tokyo and would soon become a much-respected writer of academic works on Pascal and Descartes, among many other accomplishments. His life would change, however, when in 1950 he received a scholarship from the French government to study in France, where he would work, among others, with Jean Wahl, much admired for his writings on Hegel and Kierkegaard. Katō would follow Mori to Paris a year later. Both their lives were to alter substantially. Katō would return to Tokyo four years later, soon afterward giving up his medical career to become an important cultural critic. Mori remained in France.

Endō Shūsaku (1923–1996), the renowned novelist, later a close friend of Mori and perhaps the most famous Japanese Catholic intellectual in the postwar period, also made the decision to further his own studies of modern French literature in Lyon at roughly the same time that Mori went to Paris. Like Katō, Endō only remained in France for a few years.

In Endō's trenchant novel *Foreign Studies* (*Ryūgaku*), published in 1965, he explicates with considerable poignancy, during the course of the three fictional accounts he provides, a range of problems he identifies that the Japanese have in learning how to grasp the genuine significance of the many layers of French civilization. His observations are presented in fictional form, but they are closely based on his own personal reactions to his attempts to make a life abroad.

In one striking incident in the third and longest narrative, Tanaka, the protagonist, newly arrived in Paris, is urgently warned by his new acquaintance, the aspiring architect Sakisaka, about some of the difficulties he will face.

> as I told you once before, there are three types of Japanese who come to this country. There are those who ignore the weight of history embodied in these stones, those who cleverly seek to imitate the weight of that history, and those who, like me, lack that ability and end up going under.[5]

Later, the pair visits a museum of history in Paris, where Sakisaka continues his analysis.

> Tanaka-san, we may be only foreign students, yet just by entering an insignificant little museum, we can stand in the great flow of European history spanning all those centuries. . . . I felt that, unless I as a Japanese could confront the actuality of that great flow, then my whole motivation for coming here would have been made meaningless. What are you going to do? Are you going to ignore the flow and return home unaffected by the experience?"[6]

Endō's paradigm can serve as a useful way to frame for the reader of Mori some of that writer's own concerns, as well as his attempts to come to terms with them.

Although there are obvious difficulties in comparing a memoir with a novel, there are a number of points in common shared by these two writers that can be easily identified. First of all, of course, is the fact that the two men were contemporaries. Both were in France at roughly the same time, observing the same situations at that moment in the evolution of French postwar intellectual and cultural life. Secondly, Mori and Endō shared many of the same convictions and later continued to maintain a certain level of contact, as evidenced by their friendly and thoughtful exchanges in a number of roundtable discussions dating from the 1970s and later, made available in the collection *Entretiens* published by Chikuma Shobō in 1982.

Both writers had strong connections with Christianity, Endō through his Catholic faith, and Mori through his experiences as the son of a Protestant pastor and his early education in a Catholic private academy. For both, these experiences led them to privilege in their own minds a search for the deeper significance of French and European civilization, which they both identified as arising from the stream of Christian history. Both were men of letters, yet in *Foreign Studies* and *The Waters of Babylon*, both concentrate many of their observations and comments on the visual arts—sculpture, painting, and architecture. Neither were trained as art historians; their respective comments seem rather to have been made in an attempt to seek out for themselves from visual evidence in broader terms the nature and significance of the civilization that had created them, rather than commenting on the details of the individual works they observed in the fashion that an art historian might have done. Endō's references to art, while numerous, are brief, while Mori's records his reactions more often, and in considerable detail. These are often highly personal, even idiosyncratic.

In that regard, a comparison may clarify the somewhat unusual nature and personal significance of Mori's commentaries. Both Mori and Endō showed great enthusiasm in looking at actual works of art, since the museums in Japan at that time still contained very little in the way of important examples of European painting and sculpture. Mori was particularly anxious to see works of sculpture. In that regard, such trips to Europe were crucial for both men.

Anesaki Masaharu (1873–1949), a renowned Japanese scholar of comparative literature, still read and well-respected today for his 1930 *A History of Japanese Religion*, wrote an account of his trip to Italy in 1909, *Hanatsumi nikki*, now available in a felicitous translation as *Flowers of Italy* by Susanna Fessler. Both he and Mori visited a number of the same sites in Florence and elsewhere. The differences in the character of their particular responses are striking. Both visited the convent of San Marco to see the numerous works found there created by Fra Angelico (circa 1395–1455), the renowned Italian painter whom both much admired.

In summing his responses to his *Resurrection of Christ* and other of the artist's works, Anesaki characterized his impressions as follows.

Angelico's ability to express people's personalities, their thoughts, and their feelings through one brush is truly shown . . . in a most satisfactory way. He is able not draw just a person's countenance but also his entire body and thus his spirit. He concentrates on the attitude of the person and his expression (especially the look in his eyes), and is able to capture in his painting the inside of a person's spirit through his outside appearance. This is an ability that has remained unmatched throughout time. There have been many masters to appear on the scene in recent times, but none of them has the power of Angelico.[7]

Anesaki's comments seem apt and thoughtful, basically constituting an objective and historical response. He views each work of art with a calm sense of himself, observing each work of art he examines with knowledge and enthusiasm.

Half a century later, Mori pays the same visit to Florence, but the tonality of his remarks is quite different. Studying with great care *Christ and Mary Magdalene*, he writes:

> what astonishes the viewer as well is the fact that the figure of Christ is that of a real man, and Mary Magdalene is represented as a real woman. . . . In the end, I am startled at this superb work of art, which shows the rise of a Renaissance spirit of paganism in the Renaissance art of Florence. . . . There are no traces whatsoever of any decadence in his work. And in this beautiful luminescence he witnessed the universal sway of God's love. Standing before *Christ and Mary Magdalene* I found myself deeply moved. At the same time, I realized all too painfully that such a world of harmony does not belong to me. I examine myself with an uneasy glance [p. 29–31].

Here, Mori as spectator turns almost relentlessly subjective and inward. Throughout his travels, in his comments about works of art, Mori most often seems quite unafraid insert himself, to record his own personal and emotional responses, eschewing the kind of objective analysis that would be expected from an art historian. Mori's responses move quickly to the interior. His strategies perhaps seem closest to those found in André Malraux's 1951 *Les voix du silence* (*The Voices of Silence*), where a wide range of the author's personal psychological responses to individual works of art he examines provide an important element in the French writer's aesthetic.

The purposes of the two writers, in this light, can be seen as strikingly different. Anesaki, seemingly confident in his own cultural identity, remains a more typical foreign observer; Mori, however, is endlessly troubled and often uncertain.

Both writers stress the importance of religion and the arts that help explicate the centrality of Christianity in the development of European culture. In this effort, Anesaki is explicit when he writes that "the most visible and tangible product in which a religion manifests its actual influence upon human mind and civilization is art. The one thing which strikes most the mind of an Asiatic in Europe is the grandeur of religious architecture".[8] And although Mori seldom makes any such general statements, his focus on churches and cathedrals throughout his memoir makes clear a similar conviction.

Mori's knowledge of modern French and European literature was wide and deep, yet in *Babylon* he mentions only a few writers, such as Alain, Paul Valéry, Samuel Beckett, and privileging in particular Rainer Maria Rilke. Indeed, one of Mori's favorite texts, Rilke's only novel, *The Notebooks of Malte Laurids Brigge*, reveals quite a similar inwardness and capacity for an almost morbid self-reflection. Elsewhere, Mori wrote on Jean-Paul Sartre and other postwar figures in French intellectual life, but their names seldom appear in *Babylon*. Of French modern art, and French music, past or present, there is virtually no mention at all.

Nor are there any references in *Babylon* to the complex political situation at the time. When Mori arrived, the costly war of the French in Indochina was just ending, and the war with Algeria was starting up, yet, other than a passing reference to Algerian workers in the early pages, these crucial events that were bringing such changes to French life go unremarked upon.

Mori's focus on European and French culture is also virtually absolute. There are a few passing references to some classic Japanese literary texts, but little more concerning his own culture. Yet during his actual lengthy stay in Paris, Mori consistently turned back to his prior knowledge of his own country, sustaining himself through his teaching Japanese at the National Institute of Oriental Languages and Civilizations and at the University of Paris, facts barely mentioned in *Babylon*. His translations of a selection of stories by the renowned modern Japanese author Akutagawa Ryūnoske, *Rashōmon et autres contes* (*Rashōmon and Other Stories*) was published by Gallimard in 1965.

In his commentary to the Japanese edition of Mori's text that I made use of in preparing this translation, Ninomiya Masayuki, the highly respected scholar and translator, speaks of the "character" of *boku* (an informal term for I") used by Mori in *Babylon* as the "narrator." I was at first puzzled by the use of this particular characterization, as the text is written in the first person in an epistolary style (although none of the commentaries presently available to me indicate precisely to whom, if anyone, these letters may actually have been addressed). On the surface, the text is simply Mori expressing his thoughts and reflections. However, in reading through the various roundtable discussions contained in *Entretiens* and other secondary sources, it becomes exceedingly clear that Mori's "narrator" in *Babylon* presents a presence considerably more restricted in his experiences than the one actually reflected in the life in Paris led by Mori himself. In these various recorded chats and interviews, Mori often discusses his daily life and mentions various people he has encountered, events attended, amusing incidents involved in living abroad, and so on. In sum, Mori can be observed as living a relatively busy and largely conventional life working and living both in Paris and elsewhere on his travels. The narrator of *Babylon*, however, is most often alone, sometimes harboring a certain level of distress, and a relentless self-probing. Indeed, his ruminations often move toward the realm of Kierkegaard's "fear and trembling." Mori's narrator in *Babylon*, it would seem, is at least a partial literary construction, a projected persona suitable to serve as a conduit for the framing certain of the author's particular and intimate emotional and intellectual responses to what he considered as the central intellectual and spiritual aspects of his life in France. His sense of unease and dislocation seems to subside only in the final pages of *Babylon*, where, staying in a friend's home in Provence, and surrounded by books, he feels at peace.

In fact, there is a rhythm to the text that is closer to the spirit of poetry than to prose, a constant circular movement from Mori's sharp and often poetic observations concerning the outside world he is observing, then moving toward his relentless self-exploration of his innermost thoughts and feelings, followed by a movement back to the world again.

Then too, the structure of the text might be described as the verbal equivalent of a musical theme and variations. In his case, there are two themes or motifs involved. These constitute his main concerns, which are expressed in the opening pages of the book. The first is his conviction that the deepest realities of one's life are nascent from the very beginning, soon to be made manifest with personal growth and the passing of time. The second is that, within the human psyche, there is a constant movement from desolation to consolation and then back again, a fluctuation that constitutes the deepest rhythm of one's inner life. These two themes are constantly at play, often in subtle variations, throughout the book.

Professor Ninomiya, in his commentary, defines *Babylon* as a "literature of exile," stressing among other things the difficulties faced by Japanese intellectuals coming to terms with the realities of the early postwar period. And the title of the memoir itself reinforces the ideal of exile. But exile from what? One's own culture? The period in which one lives? The slippage between one's ideas and one's emotions? It is well to bear in mind the final words of Mori's epilogue to the text:

> My title has been taken from a section in the *Pensées* of Pascal. The reader may attach any meaning to this that is deemed suitable.

3

There is a considerable amount of testimony that during those years of Mori's long stay in France, Japanese younger writers and members of what might be termed the intelligentsia read with great enthusiasm his commentaries concerning his experiences there. For them, he provided a connection, living as they did during that period in what they took to be a still parochial Japan, with what they perceived to be a larger literary, philosophical, and artistic world of France and Europe. Yet Japan's more superior status, which they implicitly hoped for, was not to arrive until well after Mori's death in 1976.

Although the circumstances surrounding Japan's standing in the world have certainly changed since Mori's era, the bulk of his work remains well worth examining, fascinating to read and to ponder over.[9] Of course, his thoughts and observations provide an important marker for his generation in terms of the history of thought in postwar Japan, and, read in that context, provide eloquent witness to the struggle of Mori's generation to look both backward, in order to try to understand how Japan had failed, and forward, to see what strategies Japan might employ to reach a more positive potential.[10]

But beyond this historical context, Mori's *Babylon* can be examined with the same interest that we find in reading travel memoirs of any historical period by any number of writers from many countries and backgrounds, since we can enjoy vicariously experiencing the way in which a writer's sensibilities and convictions reveal themselves, often in surprising ways, when actually brought face to face with a culture other than their own. Mori's encounters with the cultural and literary monuments of Europe, and his ardent desire to grasp their deeper significance, mirrors a long list of writers and artists in our own country and elsewhere who tried, and continue to try, to accomplish the same goal during their visits to Europe. As we read Mori's comments, his discoveries, disappointments, and pleasures can become ours as well. And in fact, in Mori's case, most of the monuments of art and architecture to which he responds so strongly still remain in place to be seen and wondered over by every subsequent generation, including our own. On one level, his quest is a pilgrimage we will always be making.

Notes

1. Shimazaki Tōson, *Tōson zenshū*, vol. 6, *Paris dayori* [News from Paris] (Tokyo: Chikuma Shobō, 1967), 246.

2. Katō Shūichi, *Form, Style, Tradition* (Berkeley: University of California Press, 1971), 20.

3. Katō Shūchi, *A Sheep's Song* (Berkeley and Los Angeles: University of California Press, 1999), 173.

4. Mori was the first to introduce Kinoshita and his work to Western readers in an eloquent essay included in *Les théâtres d'Asie* (*The Theatres of Asia*), published by the Centre Nationale de la Recherche Scientifique in Paris in 1961.

5. Endō Shūsaku, *Foreign Studies*, trans. Mark Williams (London and Chester Springs, PA: Peter Owen, 1989), 114.

6. Endō, *Foreign Studies*, 119–20.

7. Masaharu Anesaki, *Hanatsumi nikki: Flowers of Italy: A Japanese Intellectual's Journey to Europe*, trans. Susanna Fessler (Fukuoka: Kurodahan Press, 2009), 61.

8. Anesaki, *Hanatsumi nikki*, xxi-xxii.

9. For Mori's Japanese readers, his works can be divided into several categories. Works such as *Babylon*, which shows such distinctive literary qualities, quickly found a wide readership, but his extensive work as a philosopher, as Professor Michiko Yusa has suggested in her essay, also helped to sustain his reputation. James Heisig has characterized Mori's work as concentrating on "the distinctive quality of the Japanese language and its reflection of human relationships in Japanese social structures and modes of thought." See James Heisig, Thomas P. Kasulis, and John C. Maraldo, eds., *Japanese Philosophy: A Sourcebook* (Honolulu: University of Hawai'i Press, 2011), 1047.

10. Concerning the significance of Mori's work in this sphere, I would like to mention here the eloquent 2014 thesis from the University of Strasbourg by the gifted young French scholar Laurent Rauber, which I very much hope can be published in an English version. Professor Rauber, trained in the field of philosophy, undertakes here a meticulous analysis of Mori's concepts and ideas, as well as his relationship to French thought in various periods. He and I have enjoyed a stimulating exchange of views on Mori and his significance. See Laurent Rauber, "Mori Arimasa: le Japon et l'Europe au travers de sa philosophie de l' «experience»" [Mori Arimasa: Japan and Europe seen through his philosophy of "experience"], (PhD diss., Université de Strasbourg, École des Humanités, 2014).